BE All YOU CAN BE!

HUOAH !

A Global Warrior

Hugo Strand

MG US ARMY (RET)

signature, SSG, U.S. Army

ISBN 978-1-957262-03-1 (Paperback)
A Global Warrior

Yorkshire Publishing
4613 E. 91st St,
Tulsa, OK 74137
www.YorkshirePublishing.com
918.394.2665

Printed in the USA

Contents

Acknowledgements

Endeavors of this sort generally represent a host of individuals who have contributed in some fashion, whether it be providing photographs, documents or personal reflections. First, this project would never have come to fruition absent the countless hours that Hank and Linda Stratman invested with me, responding to my scores of detailed questions during our dozens of interviews while also digging through boxes of photos and military documents spanning several decades of history. It was a long journey from that first interview with Hank and Linda, when we began mapping the direction the biography would take, to our arrival at the final product that you now have before you. I am thankful for the friendship we have developed in the process and look forward to sharing many of Major General Stratman's military experiences and keen observations with the world. I am also indebted to my friend, Coast Guard veteran Dennis Hall, who lent several hours to edit the manuscript and identify those pesky grammatical or structural errors that may have escaped my notice.

Dedication

Hank Stratman: To my wife, Linda, for standing by her man throughout the journey; and all my soldiers who did the heavy lifting.

The author: To my wife, Tina, who has always been there for me in my writing endeavors and serves as my number one cheerleader. Thank you, my love.

Preface

The life of Hank Stratman seems to be defined by overcoming challenges— whether pushing to victory during high school basketball games or crossing into enemy territory during the Persian Gulf War, the military officer never backed down from a challenge and always found a way "to make things happen."

My initial introduction to Hank came in 2014, at which time he was long retired from the U.S. Army and was, with the assistance of his wife, working to restore and develop a historic property on the east side of Jefferson City. Someone in my veterans' social circle advised me that he was a retired two-star general with a storied career and that I should consider interviewing him for one of my newspaper articles. I was soon able to conduct my first interview with him, penning a summary story of his military service for the *Jefferson City News Tribune*.

One characteristic that I observed about Hank, having myself served in the military, was that his demeanor appeared rather stoic and reserved, but I recognized he was a focused individual who had carried great levels of responsibility upon his shoulders during his thirty-three-year career as an Army officer. Many times, especially during combat deployments, he had been placed in positions where his decisions impacted the health and safety of those under his command, resulting in a no-nonsense determination to accomplish the mission while looking out for his subordinates. "Train hard, fight easy" became his mantra.

Our personalities are quite different, but we developed a mutual respect and quickly became friends in the subsequent years, often attending an assortment of veteran's events together throughout

Mid-Missouri. On several occasions, I had the opportunity to listen to Hank speak to audiences, emanating a profound passion when speaking to youth groups and encouraging them to consider service in the military. When I was in the process of coordinating a program for Helias Catholic High School in 2018 in recognition of the career of the late Air Force Major General Don D. Pittman, I asked Major General (retired) Stratman to say a few words at the event. He was able to connect to the students, inspiring them to be proud of the accomplishments of General Pittman and encouraging them to aspire to be all they can be in their own lives. Following the event, I was pleasantly surprised when Hank asked me if I might someday consider writing his biography. Since I was involved with another writing project at the time, I noted that I would be happy to do so, but it would be a little while before I completed a previous writing commitment.

In the summer of 2020, I was able to wrap up this project and we almost immediately began the process of building Hank's biography by conducting interviews at his home near Holts Summit. Soon, we were also busy sifting through countless military records and photographs from his career spanning more than three decades. The focus from the beginning, he maintained, was not simply a biography that bragged about his accomplishments, but rather to serve as an inspiration to younger generations looking for direction in their lives and who might someday consider a career in the armed forces of the United States. As he noted, he had risen from inconspicuous beginnings in a small Missouri town, attended a historically-Black university and then rose to the rank of general officer in his U.S. Army career.

With great humility, the focus of the dozens of stories shared with me were framed in a manner to inspire and encourage youth to be all that they could be, striving to be good citizens and never ceasing to improve themselves. As he explained in many of his speeches to youth groups, there will always be challenges one encounters, but what elevates one to success is persistence, never giving up, and always maintaining the drive to pursue excellence while also inspiring those around them.

For more than three decades, Hank has helped mold young soldiers, mentoring them in their careers and emboldening them to always give one-hundred percent of themselves to every mission. In his personal life, he embraces the same mantra and has gone on to be successful in property development because of this resolve.

Hank and Linda are true patriots whom I am blessed to now call friends. Having the opportunity to pen his story has not only been insightful from a historical perspective, but has been an experience of encouragement in my own life, ensuring that I will continue to strive to become the best that I can be as a husband, parent and writer of the stories of our nation's veterans.

God bless you, Hank and Linda, for your service to our country and our friendship. Your love of country is infectious and it has been a treat to have been able to share some of your impressive service. And as we ol' soldiers love to exclaim, "Hooah!" and God bless the U.S.A.

Jeremy P. Ämick
Russellville, Missouri
December 2021

CHAPTER 1

A Budding Leader

An 18-year-old Henry "Hank" Stratman is pictured in one of his graduation photographs from high school in Vienna, Missouri, in the spring of 1968. He excelled at a number of sports, aspiring to become a high school coach. His participation in athletics throughout high school years provided him with the motivation to strive for excellence and helped promote a sense of teamwork that eventually prepared him for a successful career in the U.S. Army.

Emerging from the meagerness of the Great Depression and the financial insecurities experienced by many families in the years following the end of World War II, Henry "Hank" W. Stratman was welcomed into the world by his family at a small hospital in the community of Waynesville, Missouri, on July 21, 1950. The sixth of ten children born to Leo Frank Stratman and the former Mary Catherine Wieberg, Hank Stratman spent his formative years in the small Maries County town of Vienna, Missouri, where he was instilled with a deep-rooted work ethic.[1] From the earliest of his days, the young boy began to acquire what would become the building blocks of a lifelong interest in physcial fitness, athletics, teamwork and leadership—a collection of traits that would eventually lead him on the path to an extensive and impressive career as a flag officer in the United States Army.

"While growing up, there were ten of us children altogether," Stratman paused, lowering his head, "but one of my sisters died shortly after birth. Of the nine who lived into adulthood, their were five boys and four girls." With a slight chuckle, he added, "I had two older brothers, two older sisters and two younger brothers and two younger sisters—so I grew up suffering from the middle child syndrome and it seemed like I had to work hard for attention at home."

His great-grandfather, Francis "Frank" Stratmann (the last "n" was later dropped from the surname), was born in the Prussian province of Westphalia in 1813, but later immigrated to Missouri with his family. He eventually set down roots in the area of Osage County, where many former Germans had already begun to build new homes and establish their farms. Within his family circles, it is believed that his departure from Germany and journey to the United States was motivated by the potato famine that impacted a large swath of the European population, resulting in the loss of one of the main staples

---

[1] Leo Frank Stratman was born July 4, 1910, to Henry Joseph Stratman and the former Pauline Antoninette Richter. He was seventy-seven years old when he passed away on February 17, 1988, and lies at rest in Visitation Cemetery in Vienna, Missouri. His wife, the former Mary Catherine Wieberg, was eighty-four years old when she passed away on May 8, 2001, and is buried next to her husband. FindAGrave, *Leo Frank Stratman*, www.findagrave.com.

of their diet. Research also demonstrates that another factor in such immigrations was that many of these former German citizens had been dependent tenants and worked small plots of land. Additionally, they often "relied on supplementary income from such sources as linen weaving and migratory labor in Holland, which were slowly but surely drying up as the nineteenth century progressed." When the sordid realities of bad harvests were shadowed by the promise of "cheap farmland and better opportunities in America," the tipping point for many families pondering immigration had been reached.[2]

Stratman's paternal grandfather and namesake, Henry J. Stratman, became a first-generation U.S. citizen when he was born in Osage County in 1856. Following the Stratman family's relocation to the United States, the family's legacy of farming continued while the German language remained one of their enduring connections to their homeland, passed down through the generations but essentially reaching its end with the children of Leo Stratman.

A young Henry "Hank" Stratman, left, is pictured during the summer of 1954 swinging a piece of wood while two of his sisters, Kathleen (center) and Marian, play on the family's small farm in Vienna, Missouri.

"There were times I can recall both my mother and father speaking German and that's the language they would use if they wanted to discuss something at home that they didn't want us kids to know about," he humorously recalled, reflecting on pleasant moments from his childhood. "They never spent any time teaching us German, though, because

---

2   Kamphoefner, *The Wesfalians: From Germany to Missouri*, 4.

after both world wars, it really wasn't a very poplular language to be speaking."

In addition to being a successful farmer through sweat, dedication and hard work, his grandfather also became a rather influential individual in Maries County politics, serving in a capacity similar to what is now known as the recorder of deeds. Throughout his agrarian career, he was able to purchase substantial tracts of productive and fertile property that ran along the Maries River, a beautiful tributary that reminded many of the former Germans of those that crisscrossed their homeland. Sadly, he passed in 1951, before his grandson Hank was even a year old, and was buried in Visitation Cemetery in Vienna.

Stratman's father, Leo, was inducted into the United States Army during World War II but was not retained because of a disqualifying medical condition. In the years prior to the war, Leo was employed on his father's farm near the town of Argyle but in the years following World War II, he was able to purchase the home of a local grocer in Vienna, Missouri, named Cecil Hutchinson. The property was sold along with thirty-two acres of land, affording Leo the means to expand into a fruitful business endeavor that helped provide for his family's welfare in the coming years.

"This was back before the time of all of the corporate poultry operations you now see with companies like Tyson and Cargill, but it was very similar in structure," said Hank Stratman. "My dad was not a big farmer, by any means, but he decided to raise chickens for people to barbecue and cook for other purposes. I remember that he had one building on our property that he used for hatching the eggs and two or three other buildings that were erected for finishing out the chickens in their growth cycle and, when they were ready, they would be shipped out late at night to slaughter."

Despite any limitations that may have been associated with the possession of only a fourth-grade education, Hank's father experienced an impressive level of success in his poultry-raising endeavors partially attributable to his engineering skills and ingenuity. He was able to devise a gravity-feed system that carried water from a pond to all of the poultry buildings, which provided the water for the chickens being raised. Additionally, one building had a basement erected under the area where the chickens were held that featured rows of slots in the floor that allowed the chicken feces to be shoveled into the beds of truck pulled into the basement area. The manure whas then used as fertilizer for their agricultural growing endeavors throughout the farm. Additionally, like many rural familes of the era, they raised cattle and hogs and worked together to butcher their own meat to help provide for the full range of their nutritional needs.

"We were a very self-sufficient family and also very typical of many of the German Catholics who had immigrated to the states during the mid-1800s," he maintained.

Several years later, while Stratman was attending college, his father would experience some unexpected success on the farm in his efforts to raise sheep. In 1970, the newspaper in Jefferson City reported on some of Leo Stratman's achievements, explaining that "(d)uring the past 16 months, one of his ewes has given birth to seven lambs." The newspaper added, "Stratman said all of the lambs did fine and with the exception of the last twins, all were marketed."[3]

A large portion of their time in the spring and summer months also involved the additional responsibility of assisting their mother with a two-acre garden patch that she chose to plant and cultivate every year. Their father had the initial obligation of plowing up soil for the garden but their mother, with some assistance from the children, took on the duties of planting, pulling weeds and harvesting a variety of vegetables that tended to include corn, potatoes, beans, cabbage and lettuce. The large family also toiled to maintain a five-acre strawberry patch and would often pick as much as one hundred gallons a day at the height of the harvest to sell to their neighbors in the surrounding community, earning them the nickname of "Strawberry Stratmans."

He humbly remarked, "We weren't financially rich by an means, but we weren't poor either and we got by as a family by working our asses off. Everyone contributed to the family farming business— work was an expectation. It was not a rich county where we lived

---

[3]   June 5, 1970 edition of the *Daily Capital News*.

and there was very little employment other than farming, but I can assure you that we never went hungry. Also," he grinned, "my mother happened to be a great cook!"

The Stratman children not only invested countless hours assisting their parents in their assorted agricultural endeavors and other household chores, but managed to earn a modest income through a paper route that was passed down through the family. A young Hank Stratman and his siblings pedaled their bicycles in and around the Vienna community delivering the Jefferson City newspaper to local residents. He explained, "I did that through most of my elementary years and into the early part of high school. And it wasn't like nowadays where you chuck it from a moving car into a yard … back then we got off our bikes, walked up to the house and placed it behind the screen door."

Their traditional "German" raising consisted not only of his parents instilling an unyielding work ethic supplemented by a strong focus on their Catholic faith. His parents ensured they never missed mass or religious holidays. There may have existed little to no disposable income during his childhood, yet all of the Stratman children were able to receive a quality Catholic education through the eighth grade at the nearby Visitation Parochial School in Vienna. His parents' emphasis on a Catholic upbringing resulted in one of Stratman's brothers nearly becoming a priest followed by a sister who also considered becoming a nun, and also inspired young Hank to consider enrolling in seminary to pursue a career in the ministry.

"The priest and sisters at the church and school were grooming me to become a priest, but …" he trailed off, "let's just say I became more interested in girls. But at one point," he continued, "they trusted me to the extent that they placed me in charge of conducting the training for all of the altar boys. One moment that I still clearly recall was when President Kennedy was killed, the nun took four or five of us eighth-grade students over to the convent to watch the television coverage because his assassination was a big deal since he was the first Catholic president." [4]

Athleticism was also weaved into his daily activities and remained a resolute interest while he refined many of his performance skills on a simple dirt bastketball court that consisted of a hoop attached to the side of a shed adjacent to their home. On one occasion, he recalls that the coach at Vienna High School hosted a basketball tournament while young Stratman was still in the eighth grade. Their parochial school put together a team for the event with Stratman being chosen as captain. Embracing their speed and agility, the young Catholic players went on to easily win the tournament.

"A lot of my skills that I developed were learned while playing against my older brothers," he maintained. "After seeing me at the tournament, Coach Parker, the public school coach, was happy to know that I would be coming to play for him the next school year." [5]

During the four years that followed while he attended Vienna High School, Stratman maintained his focus on athletics. Whether it was basketball, baseball or track, he often served as his team's captain and remained spirited in the competition of the moment. The concepts of teamwork in addition to the fundamentals that he refined through these athletic experiences, he affirmed, would later be applied when leading troops in various military capacities.

"Years later, I discovered that there is a profound link between being an athlete in high school and college and being in the military," he remarked. "The Army is looking for physically fit recruits with athletic and leadership ability while the young people are looking for someone to coach them in their early lives."

---

[4] A forty-six-year-old President John F. Kennedy was assassinated on November 22, 1963, while he rode in a motorcade through Dealey Plaza in downtown Dallas, Texas.

[5] Coach Bill Parker was a native of Vienna, Missouri and graduated from Vienna High School in 1955. Four years later, he graduated from Central Missouri State College in Warrensburg and went on to enjoy a lengthy career as a physical education teacher and coach at schools in Vienna, Linn and Warrensburg. He was seventy-four years old when he died in 2012 and is interred in the Vienna Public Cemetery.

Through the fog of numerous recollections of moments in his high school sports history, one memory that emerges, and which seems to have instilled some early leadership qualities, took place during his sophomore year. As the former basketball player explained, the upperclassmen who played basketball at Vienna High School chose to rebel against the coach and refused to play basketball for him. Stratman, as well as many of the student athletes in his class that were on the "B-Team," were unexpectedly introduced to the intensity of basketball competition at the high school level.

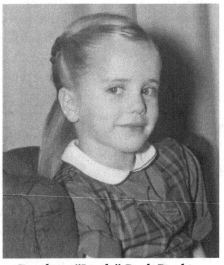

Eucolona "Linda" Ruth Deakins, who would later become the love of Stratman's life, is pictured in an adoption photograph from November 1955, at which time she was 5-1/2 years old.

"All of a sudden, with all of the older players now out of the picture, we became the A-team!" Stratman excitedly recalled. "We had to learn quickly and by the time our team reached our senior year, we were ready to play, had developed the skills to compete and won the OMMC (Osage, Maries, Miller and Cole County) conference." He continued, "We weren't really a team with a bunch of tall players—I think that tallest guy we had playing for us was six foot one. But we were a fast break team where all members scored ten to fifteen points, which is what helped us win our games and resulted in us winning our conference." He added, "We didn't have one superstar player on the court but rather five team players. I was more proud of the number of rebounds and assists I had rather than the points I scored."

His studies and participation in a number of sports activities notwithstanding, Stratman developed an enduring romantic interest in a young lady in his class, Linda Ruth Deakins. She had been a German orphan who was adopted by a military family that was stationed in Germany in the early part of the Cold War. In 1960, at the age of ten, she became a naturalized U.S. citizen in Lawton, Oklahoma. Her adoptive parents later made the decision to retire to central Missouri, where she spent many of her teenage years.

"My parents did not allow me to date while I was in high school," recalled Linda. "It was during the sports activities at school that Hank and I got to see each other—he was an athlete and I was a cheerleader."

Linda went on to humorously recount that the young man who would later become her husband was not at first smitten by her, expressing his wishes to date other women from the area. Regardless, the couple eventually developed an intimate and committed connection that would fully blossom during his time in college.

Linda Deakins is pictured in her senior photograph from Vienna High School in 1968, where she was crowned homecoming queen in her senior year. She and Stratman would marry three years later.

Stratman noted that his athletic abilities, which he worked hard to build upon and refine during his time in high school, inculcated him with the initial motiviation to become a high school coach. The athletic drive he demonstrated in pursuing this goal revealed he had the ability to compete at the collegiate level and helped shape the direction of his post-high school educational experiences.

"My grades remained rather well in high school—I would guess that I was an A- student and always seemed to achieve my best grades in math and algebra," he said. "I lettered in baseball, basketball and track, which were the only sports that were offered at our small school, and I was president of the student council my senior year."

Their high school team continued to demonstrate their prowess on the court during their basketball games and earned Stratman a spot on the all-district team in the spring of 1968. Frequently, he further explained, Vienna High School won their track meets as well, even when possessing only a fraction of the athletes other schools could manage to place on the field. Since there were so few athletes on their team due to the small student population at Vienna High School, each person participated in four or five events at the track meets— and performed quite well in each. The *Daily Capital News,* which Stratman had at one time delivered to residents in Vienna, reported in the spring of 1968 that

During an assembly at Vienna High School in 1968, Stratman and a school cheerleader show a trophy won by the basketball team. At the time, Stratman was the captain of the varsity team. His future wife, Linda, is seated in the front row, far right.

Stratman, who was finishing up his senior year, was amongst the top finishers in a local meet. During this event, he competed with little rest in the one-mile run, 880-yard run, 440-yard intermediate hurdles, the mile relay and the broad jump, while other schools had athletes specifically designated for each of these individual events.[6]

Another complexity that unfolded during his senior year was the Vietnam War. With both the draft and war in full swing, Stratman, who would soon be graduating, did not have military service in his sights but rather intended to embark upon the path to achieving his dream of becoming a high school coach. He realized that their were generally only a few means to a deferment from military service—enroll in college or get married and have children. Fortunately, his success in high school athletics and academics appeared to lay out the direction that he should now choose.

He explained: "I was able to earn a partial scholarship for baseball and track through Lincoln University in Jefferson City, so the best option for me at the time seemed to be pursuing my college education. After I graduated from Vienna High School (in the spring of 1968), I began college in the fall and was able to become a walk-in for the basketball team, but I only did that for two or three months because of all the other educational, sports, work and commitments I was contending with during that time."

---

[6] The May 24, 1968 edition of the *Daily Capital News.*

While in high school at Vienna, the school's mascot was an eagle, as reflected on this pencil sketch of their 1968 class ring that was included in the school yearbook. As Stratman noted, this eagle has remained a representation of his career throughout the years, considering the its symbology to both the U.S. Army and the country.

There was little freetime throughout this period in his life since, in the moments he was not involved in college-related sports activities or studying, he was working part-time for a cousin who owned Stratman Construction Company. One of the fortunate aspects of this employment situation was not only earning an income to help pay his bills, he explained, but that his relative was willing to work around his schedule of classes and sports commitments. Much of their constuction business consisted of pouring concrete structures such as curbing and guttering for various sub-divisions throughout Jefferson City. In addition to the torrential collegiate schedule he maintained, Stratman jokingly remarked that he was able to increase his stamina by "spending a lot of time on the end of a long-handled shovel moving concrete."

Rather than remain living with his parents and making the daily drive of more than one hour each direction into Jefferson City for work and to attend classes, Stratman partnered with several of his former classmates from Vienna, and young men from neighboring communities who were also attending Lincoln University. They pooled their money to rent a house a short distance from the campus and for the first year, he mirthfully explained, his life consisted of activities enjoyed by young men now on their own and evolved into a cycle of sleeping, playing pitch, drinking beer, working and studying.

Soon his thoughts returned to his former classmate, Linda, and through asking around, he discovered that she was attending classes at Florissant Valley College in St. Louis. After locating her telephone number, the two began communicating and after a semester at Florissant, Linda moved to Jefferson City and worked full-time as a bank teller at Central Trust

Hank and Linda Stratman enjoy the time-honored tradition of cutting the first piece of their wedding cake following their marriage ceremony on March 21, 1970.

Motor Bank. This arrangement afforded opportunities for her and the basketball player she admired in high school to begin seeing one another on a regular basis.

In reflection, Linda explained, "I don't think my parents cared for him very much at first because he was Catholic. While my father was in the service, we attended Protestant services wherever he happened to be stationed at the time." She added, "But my parents really grew to like him a lot over the years."

The part-time work with Stratman Construction Company, in addition to his pursuit of a post-secondary education, neither paused nor delayed another major life event for the young man; he and Linda made the decision to get married during his sophomore year of college on March 21, 1970. Their nuptials took place at Visitation Catholic Church in their native communtiy of Vienna. As Stratman explained, his older brother Butch, who had been Hank's role model after becoming the first of his family to graduate from college at the Missouri School of Mines in Rolla, was preparing to deploy to Okinawa (accompanied by his wife and child) as an engineer and second lieutenant with the U.S. Army in April 1970. Stratman and his fiancee moved their wedding date forward to ensure Butch and his family would be able to attend.

"Linda's father, John Deakins, was a person whom I became very impressed with because of all his distinguished experiences in the military and the knowledge he possessed," Stratman said of his late father-in-law. "In addition to Linda, they had three sons and the primary reason that they moved to Missouri in the first place was they were interested in raising quarterhorses. Back many years ago, Missouri was vying to be considered one of the quarterhorse capitals of the United States ... if not the world," he added.

Deakins achieved the rank of major during his twenty-two years of service in the Army Medical Service

Linda's father, John Deakins, served twenty-two years in the Army Medical Service during both World War II and the Korean War, achieving the rank of major.

Corps.[7] He was a veteran of both World War II and the Korean War, having commanded mobile assault surgical hospitals (MASH) during both conflicts. He earned an impressive collection of awards to include the Bronze Star with Oak Leaf Cluster. As Stratman maintained, the retired U.S. Army officer was one of the motivating forces behind his own decision to later make a career in the U.S. Army.

"Here I was, someone who had grown up in a small town that fortunately ends up meeting someone who'd been around the world and experienced events I could only read about!" Stratman exclaimed. Grinning, he added, "And here I was in the middle of college, in ROTC, married and the Vietnam War was going on—it was certainly a challenging period in our lives."

An expected component of the educational experience for young males who were attending classes at Lincoln University during this time-frame was the requirement to participate in the Reserve Officer Training Corps program for the first two years of their college experience. It was during the early part of his sophomore year, in December 1969, that the Vietnam War Draft Lottery began and redefined compulsory military service. "As the war in Vietnam dragged on, draft deferments and exemptions generated increasing public outcry,"

Stratman is pictured while serving in the role of cadet major for the Reserve Officer Training Corps program at Lincoln University in 1972.

---

[7] John Arthur Deakins was seventy-five years old when he passed away on January 12, 1997. He was laid to rest in Dripping Springs Cemetery in Columbia, Missouri. His wife, the former Phyllis Sailor, passed on July 1, 2005, and now lies at rest next to her husband. FindAGrave, *John Arthur Deakins*, https://findagrave.com.

which inspired reform of the draft system and the implentation of the lottery.[8] This was the first draft lottery held since 1942 and determined the order in which men of draft age could be called into military service. The lottery, along with the realization that he was approaching the end of his schooling during a time of war, resulted in a critical decision point for young Stratman. He recognized the likelihood of being drafted, especially since he possessed the low lottery number of seventeen.

"With the way everything was unfolding back then, I made the reasonable assumption that I would eventually be drafted for Vietnam once I was finished with school," he recalled. "That is the reason I chose to remain in the ROTC program since it would help me become an officer and, at a minimum, provide me with a little control over my destiny if I were to become a member of the military and sent to Vietnam."

It was during his junior year of college that he made the decision to sign a contract with the ROTC program, receiving a meager scholarship that helped cover some of the remaining costs associated with his education.

Another major milestone occurred when he and his wife welcomed their first child, Jodie, on January 19, 1971. The remaining months of his college experience were all the more hectic since he now had to continue to focus on his studies while working a part-time job, in addition to his responsibilities to both the ROTC program and his growing family.

In the summer of 1971, when his daughter was still in her infant stages, Stratman traveled to Fort Riley, Kansas, for the ROTC Advanced Camp. For the next six weeks, he and several of his fellow cadets were put through the paces as the instructors strived to instill the level of discipline and training necessary to ensure their success as leaders in both a garrision and tactical enviroment. During this training, they competed in obstacle courses, learned rapelling, trained with a number of weapons and were assessed on their ability to apply first-aid while developing a number of other important mil-

---

[8]   Kriner & Shen, *The Casualty Gap*, 76.

itary skill sets. The sweltering heat of eastern Kansas and the swiftness of activities may have proved a profound challenge for many of his compatriots undergoing the training, but as Stratman recalls, it was just another trial among many in his military experiences. Fortunately, this became a challenge for which he was prepared and resulted in an unexpected accolade that carried with it an unanticipated opportunity.

"Since I had been involved in sports and working construction in oftentimes unfavorable conditions like hot and humid summer days, I happened to be in excellent shape and physically prepared for the training," he said.

Several weeks later, Stratman, who had been appointed the cadet major (the equivalent of battalion commander) for the ROTC, spoke of the leadership qualities he developed during the training in a short statement that was printed in the *Lincoln Clarion*—the former student newspaper of the university. He remarked, "I personally found summer camp both physically and mentally challenging. It gave me an excellent chance to find out what the Army is like, and also it taught me the problems of leading men."[9]

One of the highlights of the camp was the opportunity to earn the coveted RECONDO Badge, which was awarded to cadets who demonstrated high levels of proficiency that included such military-focused training regimens as physical fitness, land navigation, the confidence (obstacle) course, marksmanship, first-aid and road marches. Due to his studies and physical condition, Stratman was one of the few cadets who earned the badge and because of his demonstrated proficiencies, was extended the opportunity to select the officer branch in which he wished to serve once he received his commission as an officer.

Throughout the entirety of his ROTC training in college, he was exposed to exceptional leadership from diverse backgrounds. Two of the captains in the program, he explained, were associated with field artillery and encouraged the future Army officer to consider pursuing such a direction in his own military career. They explained that it

---

[9] The October 1, 1971 edition of the *Lincoln Clarion*.

was a fascinating branch that offered many opportunities, especially during the period of the Cold War that they were at that time living within.

"They were quality people ... and I had nothing but the highest admiration and respect for them," Stratman clearly recollected. "One was a Black officer, Captain Julian Johnson. He had been a company commander for the 3rd Infantry Division Honor Guard in Washington, D.C., and I became very impressed with his general presence and leadership abilities. It was an eye-opening experience for me because having been raised in a small town in Mid-Missouri, college and ROTC were my first exposures to minorities. Lincoln University," he added, "was where I learned to measure a person by their character and performance, not the color of their skin."

This experience, Stratman went on to explain, served as a key component in his approaching military career and any successes he would experience in his development as an officer. Often, more than half of the soldiers he would come to lead in his later duty assignments were minorities.

Upon graduating with his bachelor's degree in physical education in December 1972, Stratman, so inspired by the leadership and example of the professional soldiers that had guided him in the ROTC program, made the decision to fulfill his military commitment by going on active duty with the United States Army instead of pursuing a National Guard or Reserve commission. Initially, he recalled, it was not his intent to remain in the military as a career; instead, he viewed it as a springboard to acquire some full-time military experience before moving on to fulfill his long-held dream of becoming a high school coach.

Reflecting on the momentous decision, he said, "I had been given a great job offer to remain in construction but Linda and I had another child on the way. I knew what was waiting for me if I stayed in Missouri; instead, I wanted to know what other opportunities were awaiting me out in the world. If I'm going to do this," he said of his decision to go on active duty, "I told myself that I am going to make a full commitment to it. Thankfully, my wife supported me the entire time even though it wasn't always easy." He added, "Also, the economy wasn't doing so great during that period, so the decision really seemed to make good sense."

The *Daily Capital News* reported in a brief article printed on December 19, 1972, "Henry William Stratman, son of Mr. and Mrs. Leo Stratman of Vienna, will receive a regular army commission in the field artillery. The regular army commission is offered only to those ROTC graduates who have demonstrated exceptional potential and continuous outstanding performance. Less than 10 percent of all ROTC graduates can qualify for the regular army commission."[10]

Within less than a month, he was saying his temporary goodbyes to his family so that he could board a bus bound for Fort Benning, Georgia, where he was scheduled to complete airborne training. The young soldier from smalltown Missouri mirthfully remarked that he quickly came to discover that the U.S. Army was going to place him in many uncomfortable situations, most of which would help shape him as a leader and solidify his desire to continue his military career.

"Let's just say that my training at Fort Benning was the first time in my life that I had ever flown on an airplane … and what does the Army do to help memorialize that experience for this smalltown boy? Well, they give me a parachute and expect me to jump out of it five times," he remarked with a hearty laugh.

---

[10] December 19, 1972 edition of the *Daily Capital News*.

The Journey Begins

The newlywed Hank and Linda Stratman are pictured in their marriage photograph taken at Visitation Catholic Church in Vienna on March 21, 1970. From left: Linda's parents, John and Phyllis Deakins; Linda and Hank Stratman; and, Hank's parents, Leo and Mary Stratman. The marriage received the blessing of Hank's uncle, Father Ambrose Stratman, a Catholic priest who also served as the officiant for their ceremony.

A second lieutenant in the U.S. Army begins their climb from the lowest rung of the career ladder, receiving a salary and associated benefits that tend to reflect their fledgling military status. With finances being rather tight for the newly married couple with added concern of raising a young child and another on the way, the Stratman family was living paycheck to paycheck and could only afford to own and maintain one vehicle. Since his wife was to remain in Jefferson City, Missouri during the early days of his military training, Stratman left their only vehicle with Linda so that she could travel to doctor appointments, the grocery store, and other associated errands. It would best suit their family cirumstances for him to purchase a bus ticket to travel to Fort Benning, Georgia, to begin the first official school of his active duty military career. The initial commitment he selected was three years with the U.S. Army since it might afford him the opportunity to see the world and then return to his construction job, or perhaps a career as a physical education teacher if the military was not a good fit for him.

"The officers in charge of the ROTC at Lincoln University encouraged new officers to complete both Ranger School and Airborne School for leadership development," recalled Stratman. "But in 1973, times were different since they were pulling troops out of Vietnam and drawing down the military. Because of these budget constraints, they soon began to encourage one school or the other." He added, "I didn't need to prove myself in Ranger School because I grew up on a farm and could live off the land ... and also, I had done quite well in my advanced school in ROTC. Instead, I chose Airborne because something about it just sounded like fun."

The Airborne School at Fort Bragg remains an intense regimen of advanced instruction beginning with "Ground Week," which is structured to inculcate the trainees with basic parachute landing and aircraft exiting skills. From there, they transition to more realitic landing training in "Tower Week," where they begin to master "the mass exit procedures from the ... tower, gain canopy confidence and learn how to manipulate the parachute from the 250-foot tower." In the third week, they progress to "Jump Week" and "successfully complete five jumps at 1,250 feet from a C-130 or C-17 aircraft." Through this intense regimen of military training by dedicated and experienced instructors, the soldiers are instilled with an understanding of the proper "use of the parachute as a means of combat deployment and to develop leadership, self-confidence, and an aggressive spirit through mental and physical conditioning." Upon successful completion, they earn the coveted "Silver Airborne Wings" that is worn on their uniform.[11]

Looking back on his time in the brief airborne training program, Stratman noted with a wry grin, "The entire experience was thrilling and all seemed to go fine until Jump Week. The first jump is what I would have called perfect but the chance for malfunctions increased with each subsequent jump. During the final jump, after exiting the aircraft near the C-17's jet engine, my profile was ugly, resulting in a line twist in the risers that almost choked me, but I relied on my training and was able to correct it before I landed." In humble reflection, he concluded, "I realized Airborne wasn't for me because even though I wasn't afraid of heights or landing, voluntarily exiting a perfectly good aircraft played with my mind. I realized that I had a wife, daughter and another child on the way who I was now responsible for and that I should not be taking these risks."

During the early days of February 1973, he returned to central Missouri, to pick up his wife and daughter, Jodie, and then made the journey to Fort Sill, Oklahoma, for the next step in his military training regimen. Throughout the next several weeks, he underwent further specialized indoctrination in the Field Artillery Officer Basic Course (OBC) while his family lived off post in a small duplex. Stratman admits that he struggled during the next three months of the artillery training since everything he had experienced in ROTC was focused on physical fitness and infantry skill sets. Additionally, he recalled, there was a substantial amount of mathematics associated with ballistic calculations. The training was also mixed with the complications of learning cannon artillery systems and munitions along with the various intricacies of fire direction.

"When I was encouraged to consider Field Artillery as my branch while still in ROTC at Lincoln University, they failed to tell

---

[11] United States Army, *Airborne School*, goarmy.com.

me one important detail that I didn't learn until later—the life expectancy of a second lieutenant field artilleryman in Vietnam was only three months," he explained. "Because they had the wherewithal to employ field artillery fire, the North Vietnamese targeted them first, then the company commander."

OBC also served as the new officer's abrupt introduction to a computer system designated the Field Artillery Digital Automatic Computer (FADAC). Rudimentary in design and monstrous in size when viewed through the lens of current systems, the artillery computer could be programmed to compute firing data for different projectiles while also factoring in meteorologic specifics such as humidity and windspeed. The FADAC—which had already been in use for a number of years when Stratman began working with it—measured a substantial 24 x 14 x 34 inches and weighed nearly 200 pounds. The solid-state computer system was designed with the capability "of operating under field conditions, without a major overhaul, for at least 2,500 hours" and could "provide firing data for mortars, howitzers, guns, and free-flight rocket systems, firing any ammunition these weapons will use."[12]

Artillery may have initially appeared to be a rather foreign concept to the young second lieutenant, especially when combined with the challenges of learning to operate a computer system in a new field of military learning. Regardless, he applied himself both academically and in his quest to become an effective leader, and received the recommendation from his leadership as a potential future instructor for the course. The *Academic Report* he received upon completion of the training notes the young officer was viewed as "a natural leader with almost unlimited potential."[13]

It was in the latter days of his Field Artillery Officer Basic Course when Stratman was approached by Captain Robert Shadburn, his training battery commander, who posed an interesting question. Captain Shadburn inquired of Stratman whether he might have an

---

[12] History of Computing Information, *Electronic Computers Within the Ordnance Corps*, https://ftp.arl.army.mil.

[13] DA Form 1059, *Academic Report* covering the Field Artillery OBC training period of February 16, 1973 to May 11, 1973.

interest in becoming a platoon leader with the new Lance missile system in Europe (Shadburn remained in military and retired years later at the rank of colonel). It was during the height of the Cold War when the United States and Allied forces maintained a presence in Europe that was auspiciously supplemented by a mixture of missiles and armament intended to serve as a deterrent against potential Soviet aggression. The U.S. Army Aviation and Missile Life Cycle Management Command (AMCOM) noted the Lance "was a mobile field artillery tactical missile system used to provide both nuclear and non-nuclear general fire support to the Army Corps" and possessed the

In 1973, Stratman completed the Lance Cadre Training Course at Fort Sill, Oklahoma, in preparation for his assignment as a platoon leader with a Lance missile battalion in Germany. Pictured is a Lance missile in flight that was fired by Stratman's battery in during a training exercise in 1974.

capability "to attack key enemy targets beyond the range of cannon artillery ..." The AMCOM further explained that the LANCE system's primary targets included troop concentrations, airfields, transportation centers, missile firing sites and command and logistic installations.[14]

---

[14] U.S. Army Aviation and Mission Life Cycle Management Command, *LANCE*, https://history.redstone.army.mil.

During the captain's discussion with Lieutenant Stratman, it was explained that the U.S. Army had plans to field four new Lance missile battalions in Germany, and if Stratman were interested, he would receive an endorsement to become part of the 2nd Lance Battalion stationed in the German city of Giessen. As Stratman went on to explain, the proposal sounded like an ideal opportunity for several reasons—first, to experience Germany, Linda's birthplace; secondly, for the excitement; and, finally, to progress in his military career field.

Following discussions with his wife, the decision was made that he would accept the offer and move to Germany.

For several weeks following completion of his initial field artillery training, Stratman remained at Fort Sill and served as the executive officer for the training battery, assisting with the administrative processing of classes and ensuring that battery administration was properly maintained. In late July 1973, he began several weeks of specialized training as a student in the Lance Cadre Training Course, which was designed to familiarize him with the new Lance missiles being fielded and his specialized duties as a platoon leader within one of the newly-formed batteries. Within his training group were several captains slated to receive an appointment as battery commanders in the coming weeks. Stratman recalled that as the officers worked diligently to familiarize themselves with the new missile systems and their responsibilities in the emerging artillery structure, there were scores of non-commissioned officers (NCOs) and enlisted personnel handpicked for Lance assignments, who were also undergoing a parallel regimen of training. The training course culminated in a field training exericise during which enlisted personnel, NCOs and officers worked together to demonstrate their abilities to effectively employ the Lance missile system while also helping them bond into a cohesive unit.

"Linda gave birth to our second child, Jon, on August 1, 1973," he recalled of the transitional period in his life. "When I finished the Lance training course in the fall of 1973, Linda remained at Fort Sill with the children while I flew to Germany, unaccompanied, because

I first had to locate off-post housing before the Army would allow my family to come and join me there."

The artillery officer was immediately immersed in uncovering the intricacies of his new duty assignment. The days passed quickly while he worked at the U.S. Army cantonement in Giessen, which was home to battalions of the 42nd Field Artillery Brigade in addition to the new Lance missile battalions. It was there that the young officer received assignment to his first unit as a platoon leader with A Battery, 3rd Battalion of the 79th Field Artillery Regiment. As intended, his wife and children were able to join him four months into his new assignment, after he located housing in a small German community outside of Giessen. For approximately six months, they lived in the accomodations that were very tight for his growing family but he was soon able to secure housing on post in a large, four-story building that had years earlier been used by the German military during World War II. Each floor had sixteen apartments with stairwells on each end of the building. Although the layout of the military facility at Giessen was not as expansive as many of the ones they had experienced back in the states, it was large enough to provide housing, a post office and a hospital. Initially, Linda remained at home with the children while her husband drove their only vehicle, an Opel (a small car manufactured by the Germans), to his battery offices to perform his daily routine of assorted duties and training; however, once they moved to the facility on post, she was able to secure employment at the base post office.

Stratman remarked of the developmental stages of his new regiment: "We got the cream of the crop with regard to new soldiers coming into the two Lance battlalions that were stationed in Germany because of the nuclear capabilities of our mission. At the time," he continued, "it did not seem to us to be a Cold War but rather, a direct standoff against the Soviet Union. Because of this, the Lance battalions had the grave responsibility of using our weapons to break up any potential Soviet forces attack invading Germany through the infamous Fulda Gap should the already tense situation in the region escalate into a full-scale war."

***Hank Stratman, back row, left, is pictured while serving as a
platoon leader for A Battery, 3ʳᵈ Battalion, 79ᵗʰ Field Artillery
in 1974. His platoon was participating in live-fire certification
exercises on the Greek island of Crete. Stratman explained
the certification exercise ensured their ability to accurately
deploy a tactical nuclear weapon by firing dummy warheads
into established target areas in the Mediterranean Sea.***

"NATO planners have pinpointed the Fulda Gap—several
open passes running through the hills about 60 miles northeast of
Frankfurt—as a likely invasion route into Western Europe for Soviet
Bloc forces," reported the *Los Angeles Times* in their March 1, 1987
edition. The newspaper hauntingly added, "The Fulda Gap is the
only area in the world where large numbers of U.S. and Soviet soldiers are lined up so close to one another. Backing them on both sides
is the savage power of hundreds of medium-range nuclear missiles."[15]

---

[15] Los Angeles Times, *Fulda Gap is a Key Point in NATO Defense Against Soviet
Forces*, March 1, 1987.

Stratman added that the gap was widely considered to be the traditional high-speed avenue of approach in the region.

This stressful responsibility placed on the shoulders of the units in Europe, who were on the frontline of a potential powderkeg, afforded military leaders within the new Lance battalions to be much more selective in the personnel assigned to their units because of the high-profile nuclear mission. The high standards associated with their nuclear capabilities later evolved to include a regular and thorough review of medical records of all battery personnel. This helped to ensure there were no identifiable physical or psychological conditions that might lead a soldier to compromise their highly secretive mission. The thorough review process was supplemented by oversight of some of the personal affairs of the soldiers that might reveal a potential for alcohol and drug abuse, financial problems or divorce, which might place them in a high risk situation resulting in a susceptibility for receiving bribes in exchange for classified information.

In his role as a firing platoon leader, Stratman remained focused on taking care of the enlisted soldiers under his command while concurrently striving to ensure everyone in the platoon understood their specific role in accomplishing the mission. Not only did the young lieutenant have the ulitimate responsibility of supervising the training for A Battery, but he was also given the additional duty of serving as the battery's supply officer. Both his company commander and battalion commander quickly came to recognize the fledgling officer's potential, writing in Stratman's first *Officer Evaluation Report* (covering his assignment as firing platoon leader) that he possessed a "technical proficiency [that] is worthy of emulation," asserting that the junior officer tends to perform his best work under stressful conditions. The report also also documented that Stratman went above and beyond his responsibilities as platoon leader by using the carpentry skills he had developed when working construction in college to assist the enlisted personnel in the battery to improve the appearance of several battery dayrooms and section areas. His technical knowledge, demonstrated leadership abilities and overall performance resulted in his being rated in the top five percent of his contemporaries.

*During a change-of-command ceremony held in June 1975
in Giessen, Germany, Lt. Hank Stratman takes command
of A Battery, 3rd Battalion, 79th Field Artillery. Stratman
is pictured on the right accepting the battery guidon
from Lt. Col. Shoffner, the battalion commander.*

His designation as firing platoon leader would undergo a transition to the title of Lance Assembly and Transport Platoon Leader, which was followed by his promotion to first lieutenant in January 1974. During this early point in his career, he was singled out as part of a technical proficiency inspection conducted by the Inspector General's office of the Department of the Army for his tactical competence and broad understanding of the overall artillery and missile defense mission in Europe. In addition to training personnel in the deployment of the Lance battery in a wartime environment, he dedicated a portion of his off-duty time to morale-building improvements that oftentimes consisted of an array of athletic competitions and adventure training on whitewater rapids.

A year following his promotion to first lieutenant, in January 1975, the upward arc of military career continued with his appointment as the executive officer for the battery. His role shifted slightly in that he was now responsible for planning, organizing and conducting all training for the battery in a manner that complied with the V Corps General Defense Plan. (V Corps, during the Cold War, became an important fixture in Europe with a structure that provided combat and support troops that could quickly be deployed throughout the region.)[16] In this capacity, Stratman's commanding officer, Captain David Zacchetti, wrote a glowing appraisal of Stratman's abilities, noting he "is the most outstanding officer with whom I have served." Zacchetti lavished futher praise upon his junior officer by adding, "He is well out in front of his contemporaries because of his competence, versatility, and hard work. He has developed imaginative, tough, comprehensive training programs for all sections in the battery and continuously seeks additional responsiblities."

Shortly after his promotion to first lieutenant, Stratman engaged in a brief conversation with the battalion commander, Lieutenant Colonel Wilson "Dutch" Shoffner. During their exchange, the enthusiastic lieutenant requested that he be considered for command of A Battery in the near future, despite it being such an early point in his career. He was informed by his superior officer that he might as well receive some command credit since he had essentially been running the battery in his position as executive officer.

Stratman said, "He allowed me to take command for three months—just long enough for me to receive a command OER (Officer Evaluation Report) for the period of June to September 1975. That was the longest I could be in command because I was only a lieutenant ... and I believe that I was the only lieutenant commanding a battery or company in the entire USAREUR."[17]

---

[16] V Corps General Defense Plan presented "NATO with an unfavorable situation for the opening stages of a war. In this scenario, Warsaw Pact forces commence conventional offensive operations on short notice and NATO has only hours warning time to occupy and prepare defensive areas." The plan helped lay the groundwork for the deployment of V Corps and defensive measures under a framework endorsed by NATO should there be a war with the Soviet Union in the region. Woodrow Wilson International Center for Scholars, *Military Planning of the USA and NATO*, https://wilsoncenter.org.

[17] Stratman is referring to the *United States Army, Europe*—the Army Service Component Command responsible for directing U.S. Army operations throughout the European command area.

The evaluation report he received for this brief command period reflected the faith Lieutenant Colonel Shoffner placed in Stratman's potential for higher level command responsibilities when he affirmed that the lieutenant's "performance of duty is better than most captains" and that "(h)e should be promoted now."

When pausing to reflect upon his early moment of command experience, Stratman stressed that Lietuenant Colonel Shoffner was a very intelligent and demanding leader who expected nothing but the best performance from his junior officers. Shoffner became very influential in his own budding career and was the first of many important role models in his many years of military experience. Additionally, Stratman affirmed that his superior officer's leadership style and competence easily became one of the primary inspirations for his own decision to make a career in the U.S. Army and strengthened his personnel file. (Stratman explained that a strong personnel file would be of utmost importance when the military began to undergo significant budget and personnel cuts in the coming months and years.)

While stationed in Germany in the mid-1970s, Lt. Stratman received a commendation for his battery's performance during technical and tactical evaluations.

"Lt. Colonel Shoffner allowing me to take command for that brief period of time was very important because it was a transitional time in the Army," Stratman explained. "The Vietnam War was behind us and our forces were being drawn down, resulting in overstrengths and excesses at virtually every level of the military structure." He continued, "If a soldier didn't have a strong personnel file—had a history of drug or alcohol abuse, was invovled in any kind of racial unrest or other such things—the battalion commanders were granted the authority to eliminate them from the units. They also increased our physical fitness standards and tightened the weight standards as well, which hurt some people in the process. I lost a lot of good non-commissioned officers who just couldn't meet these heightened standards."

When his command time came to an end on September 21, 1975, Stratman was moved to the Headquarters and Headquarters Battery in the battalion to serve as the Fire Direction Officer. Although this change of duty would only last 102 days, he again managed to earn high marks and ratings from his superiors by demonstrating his expertise in developing and leading technical fire direction training for the battalion. His competency in this capacity helped ensure the battery's accuracy during strategic nuclear attack firing exercises; additionally, he was afforded opportunities to advise the battalion commander on matters related to special weapons as part of his additional duty assignment in the capacity of Special Weapons Officer.

Lieutenant Colonel Shoffner, in carrying out his responsibilities of battalion commander, not only impressed Stratman with his demonstrated leadership characteristics, but with his broad understanding of the Lance mission and the manner in which it dovetailed into overarching European defense plans. Since the mission was new and undergoing development, Shoffner helped guide his subordinates in the development of the doctrine that would later serve as the foundation of their operational guidelines.[18]

"It was a new system—the Lance—and there was no established doctrine on how it was to be effectively deployed; it all had to be developed," Stratman said. The Pershing missiles had a greater range and were intended to take on the Russian hordes in Eastern Europe

---

[18] Wilson "Dutch" Shoffner Sr. would later serve as the Commandant of the United States Army Command and General Staff College, achieving the rank of lieutenant general. The esteemed military officer was seventy-five years old when he passed away in Texas in 2014.

if war occured, but as I mentioned before, with our range and capablities, the Fulda Gap was our focus." He continued, "Lieutenant Colonel Shoffner was a very intuitive and insightful leader, and the doctrine he helped create later evolved into the Army Tactical Missile System and MLRS Tactics, Techniques and Procedures."[19] A number of the officers with whom Stratman served happened to be graduates of Ivy League schools, anxious to finish their initial terms of service before departing for more lucrative opportunities in the private sector. This, mixed with the reductions in force ravaging Army personnel levels, opened up many opportunities for the farm boy from smalltown Mid-Missouri who chose to become a U.S. Army officer.

The Stratman family posed for this family photograph in August 1976 while living on the small military base in Giessen, Germany. From left: Jon, Jodie, Linda and Hank.

The battalion S-2 officer (who was responsible for intelligence operations and security) became a victim of these force reductions, which soon resulted in Stratman's reassignment to fill the vacancy. As Stratman affirmed, the battalion was subject to the Technical Proficiency Inspections of their nuclear weapons to include storage, training and deployment, all of which was considered a "ZERO" deficiency mission. Many officers in varous levels of responsibility within the overall Lance structure had fallen complacent in their duties, often leading to defi-

---

[19] The Army Tactical Missile System (ATACMS) is a conventional surface-to-surface artillery weapon system capable of striking targets well beyond the range of existing Army cannons, rockets and other missiles" and had demonstrated success during Operation Desert Storm. The MLRS represents the weapons platform used to fire the ATACMS missiles. Lockheed Martin, *Army Tactical Missile System*, https://lockheedmartin.com.

ciencies or negative efficiency reports that soon ended their careers. During his tenure; however, Stratman remained diligent in maintaining high levels of dedication to the battery mission and learning multiple aspects of the duties and responsibilities of higher level officers within the battalion. His unyielding drive, performance and thirst for knowledge assisted the battalion in earning recognition as the best battalion in all the United States Army, Europe.

"The Lance battalions just weren't very forgiving—if you didn't meet the standards, you were likely reassigned to a cannon artillery unit," he remarked. (This, he later realized, would be a welcome reassignment considering future opportunities for promotion.)

Stratman's personal efficiency reports shone brightly upon his abilities, noting that the lieutenant "completely reorganized the battalion system for processing emergency action messages and nuclear control orders, and developed an innovative training and evaluation program for all personnel." Furthermore, his attention to detail and unwavering commitment to the mission resulted in the development of "efficient fire direction procedures to accommodate new and demanding Lance tactics."[20]

As a lower-grade officer, Stratman explained that a major component of his drive to maintain high performance standards was a result of the influence wielded by the battalion commander, Lieutenant Colonel Shoffner. The battalion commander would go on to finish an impressive military career punctuated by his achievement of the rank of lieutenant general (three-star). Shoffner was of the mindset that he would not settle for excuses but rather found ways to inspire those under his command to be innovative in their thinking and exceptional in their performance ... or else move on to another assignment, whether in or out of the military.

"I greatly respected him and learned a lot from his exemplary leadership style and intellect, all of which served me well throughout my career," Stratman affirmed.

---

[20] U.S. Army Officer Evaluation Report for Lt. Hank Stratman covering the period of January 7, 1976 to August 25, 1976.

One of the challenges that the battalion commander placed upon Stratman and the other officers of the battalion was improvement of their launch schedules. Hitherto, the standard had been for the battalion to launch one Lance missile per hour in an operational environment, while also maintaining the ability to self-destruct the warheads in case the deadly weapons were at risk of capture by enemy forces. Though challenging, Shoffner wanted the personnel of the battalion to begin training toward the goal of launching three missiles per hour. It took a year of dedication and focused exercises and maneuvers, but, Stratman explained, hard work and determination prevailed and allowed his soldiers to achieve the grand vision set forth by their battalion commander.

"The goal we attained was to be able to shoot, move, reload, shoot again, move, reload and then fire the third missile," he said.

Stratman's tenure as the battalion's S-2 came to a close in December 1976, and was highlighted by receipt of an *Officer Evaluation Report* bestowing the lieutenant with superlative ratings by his superiors. His supervisor, Major Lawrence Karjala, glowlingly reported that Stratman should, "without reservation, …be selected for early promotion to captain."[21] His promotion to captain did arrive weeks later followed by orders to depart his assignment in Germany and return to Fort Sill, Oklahoma, to attend the Field Artillery Advanced Course. Captain Stratman was soon joined by his family back in the states while he spent the next seven months struggling with acquiring a more detailed understanding of cannon gunnery. Upon completion of the training, he was informed that he was slated for assignment to the Weapons Department at the U.S. Army Field Artillery School as a Lance missile instructor.

"If I had to describe myself during this period of training, I would say that I was an average student and certainly didn't distinguish myself, graduating somewhere in the middle of my class," he bluntly recalled. "One of the best moments of that difficult training cycle was making friends with some West Point graduates who had

---

[21] U.S. Army Officer Evaluation Report for Lt. Hank Stratman covering the period of August 26, 1976 to December 3, 1976.

spent time in divisional cannon artillery units, and had the knowledge to help me with my own gunnery classes."

The assistance he received from classmates, when combined with his own dedication to learning all aspects of cannon artillery, resulted in Captain Stratman completing the course with overall superior ratings. The senior faculty advisor for the course noted on his *Service School Academic Evaluation Report* that the captain "maintained a superior overall average in the required writing assignments during the course, an accomplishment achieved by few of his peers."

Captain Hank Stratman is pictured in 1977 while serving as an instructor (and later senior instructor) for the Basic and Advanced Courses at the Field Artillery School at Fort Sill, Oklahoma. Months earlier, he completed the rigorous requirements of the Gunnery Instructor Training and Evaluation Program, demonstrating his mastery of cannon artillery.

With an eye toward the future and a focus on career progression, Stratman recognized the writing on the wall with regard to the limitations of his current assignment. His experience as a "missileman," though providing him with much valuable training, was such a narrow career field within the artillery structure that it did not possess the long-term competitive potential. This, he remarked, was because of high standards tied to the nuclear mission of the Lance battalions and the low number of officers assigned to the units. Additionally, the Lance personnel were not perceived as "mainstream" by his fellow officers within the field artillery culture. Ruminating on what path lay ahead, Stratman recognized he had arrived at another dynamic decision point in his career and soon resolved that if he were going to make a career of the United States Army, he would need to master field artillery cannon gunnery.

Since he had already been advised that he had been selected to serve within the Weapons Department at Fort Sill after completion of his advanced course, Stratman instead requested placement in the Gunnery Department. This department was focused on improving all aspects of field artillery to include equipment, mobility and fire support operations. Fortunately, for the captain's long-term career outlook, his request was granted and he immediately committed himself to mastering cannon artillery by completing the intense Gunnery Instructor Training and Evaluation Program. The training was administered by his instructors from the Officer Advanced Course he had only recently completed.

"The gunnery instructors didn't cut me any slack and many were surprised that I succeeded," recalled Stratman. "At the time, no one from the Lance or Pershing battalions had been able to accomplish this. And to make a long story shorter, I was able to commit myself and mastered the material, and became an instructor of the "SLUG" section of the Field Artillery Basic and Advanced Courses," he added. (The SLUG section consisted of students who encountered difficulties in mastering the course material. Stratman maintained that because of his own past difficulties in grasping the many intricacies of cannon artillery, he was able to mentor the students to help ensure their successful completion of the courses.)

The evaluations from his tenure as an instructor, which followed him through 1977 and 1978, revealed that his rating officials perceived his technical competence as often far exceeding that of his contemporaries. As noted within both of the *Officer Evaluation Reports* that he received during this timeframe, he was awarded scores of "70." Based upon the weighted criteria used to assess his performance, this reflected the highest score attainable on the evaluations. On Feburary 1, 1979, Stratman underwent the next change in his duty assignment from "Instructor" to "Senior Instructor," the latter of which he held for the next three months.

Stratman explained, "Colonel Jim Wurman assigned me to the Gunnery Department, Research and Development Branch at Fort

Sill, where I held the duty title of Computer Systems Officer and assisted in the development of doctrine for how we employed tactical computers in the field artillery fire directions centers. Me, a first-generation computer geek … who would have thought it!"

It was in this capacity that he and a Department of the Army civilian worked together to develop cannon gunnery software for the Texas Instruments (TI-59) Handheld Computer. By doing so, they were able to replace the two-hundred-pound Field Artillery Digital Automatic Computer System that had been in use for decades.

The handheld device was widely embraced by a number of government agencies seeking to utilize its calculating capablities for their own specialized purposes. The United States Department of Agricutlure purchased the TI-59 for the Forestry Service, finding that it provided a quick, easy and handy means for calculating fire behavior predictions in the field and in the office. Furthermore, the specialized programming of the calculator for the Forestry Service was not only able to "process calculations too complex for manual methods," but afforded the user the ability to supplement fire prediction programs through the use of formatted cards, otherwise referered to as solid state software modules.[22] The calculator quickly became a device with a potential recognized by those in the upper levels of field artillery leadership in addition to Stratman and his civilian contemporary.

"This became the first handheld, off-the-shelf computer for cannon gunnery," he explained. "During our collaboration, I told the civilian who I worked with what type of solution I wanted and needed the calculator to perform, and then he developed the software for it accordingly."

Colonel James Wurman was appointed commander of the 212th Field Artillery Brigade, and, in May 1980, chose to bring Captain Stratman aboard as the commander for the Headquarters and Headquarters Battery (HHB) for the brigade.[23] It was disappointing

---

[22] Andrews, *Methods for Predicting Fire Behavior*, 7.

[23] James Wade Wurman was born in 1933 and was a graduate of Oklahoma State University. His career in the U.S. Army spanned forty years in the field artillery and included service during Vietnam and the Persian Gulf War. He retired at

for the young officer since he maintained an overwhelming desire to command a cannon artillery firing battery rather than have to deal with much of the administrative drudgery often associated with a headquarters battery. Regardless, when given the order to command the HHB, he snapped a sharp salute to Colonel Wurman, accepted the fate he had been dealt and immediately set forth to effectively lead and train the soldiers under this command.

For the next nine months, he demonstrated his drive to succeed while successfully commanding nearly 150 soldiers and having overall responsibility for thirty-six vehicles and a property book exceeding four million dollars. During this command period, Captain Stratman continued to achieve the highest degree of competency ratings in the fourteen measured areas that were evaluated by Colonel Wurman, including his performance under physical and mental stress and his capacity to acquire knowledge and grasp concepts.

It was only a few years earlier that the Women's Army Corps was disestablished, thus opening up many additional opportunities for the women who were then integrated into the regular U.S. Army. It was during Stratman's command tour that the field artillery brigades began the process of assigning female soldiers to the HHB to serve in such support occupational specialties as drivers, communications specialists and mechanics. Since it was a relatively new concept to incorporate female soldiers within the once male-dominated combat units such as the field artillery, there were some new and unique challenges encountered.

With the economy in decline and the job market tanking, a greater number of women chose to explore the military as a means to make a living during the late 1970s and early 1980s. The difficulties that arose, Stratman discovered, was that there were new soldiers entering the ranks who did not appear to possess the motivation necessary to thrive in the fast-paced field artillery environment. Additionally, there were challenges with regard to physical limita-

---

the rank of major general and died in 2001 following a lengthy battle with cancer. Maj. Gen. Wurman is interred in Barrancas National Cemetery in Pensacola, Florida. FindAGrave, *James Wade Wurman*, https://findagrave.com.

tions that included two female soldiers often being necessary to carry a toolbox normally carried by one male soldier. The field artillery jobs were labor intensive and the influx of a new set of soldiers within a paradigm where Stratman had worked with his leadership to weed out substandard performers, made it even more difficult to maintain the high standards and timetables that still existed in their mission structure. Regardless, just as he did not perceive any color or other potentially differing characteristics in the those placed under his authority, he remained committed to treating all soldiers in a consistment fashion despite their gender.

"Although we had been in the process of clearing out overstrength from the Vietnam War, there was a strong political movement to begin accepting more females into the units. There was no preferential treatment for any female soldiers under my command—everyone had the same performance standards and received the same level of support and opportunities to succeed because none of our readiness standards had been lowered and the mission still had to be accomplished," he recalled. "While commanding the HHB, the brigade commander informed me that he needed a new driver, so I assigned him a female PFC (private first class) who was available." He added, "She lasted about a week before the brigade commander sent her back to me because, unfortunately, she—like some male soldiers before her—didn't meet with high standards for that duty assignment." Reflecting on the transformative period in his U.S. Army experience, he concluded, "Fortunately, the Army recruited more qualified females who truly wanted to be part of the mission once the "All Volunteer Army" concept was established in the early 1980s."

There were difficulties encountered during his HHB command period but nothing that was perceived as insurmountable for the young captain. Many successes were attibruted to his leadership that included achievement of the reenlistment objectives set forth by the Department of the Army, his rewarding efforts to increase the efficiency of the unit's maintenance program (which improved the unit's overall combat readiness posture), and his continuance in leveraging his love of athletics by working with those under his command to field some highly successful teams in an intramural sports program.

His triumphs and proficiencies resulted in Colonel Wurman noting that Stratman be selected for Command and General Staff College (CGSC) prior to his contemporaries, but it would be a little more than a year before this recommendation would come to fruition.[24]

Stratman explained, "It was an interesting period because in the late 1970s and into the early 1980s, a large number of the West Point graduates that I had worked with decided to leave the Army for more lucrative job opportunities in the private sector by leveraging the education they had received at West Point. I had graduated from a historically black college and didn't have an Ivy League education; also, I had a wife and two kids whom I was responsible for." Pausing, he added, "There was an economic recession going on in the early '80s and I did seriously consider getting out of the Army ... especially after I was issued orders for duty in South Korea, unaccompanied (meaning he could not take his family with him)."

Struggling with uncertainties as to the next step in his career, Stratman spoke with the Department of Army assignment officer about finding an alternative to the tour in Korea, but was callously informed, "Accept the assignment to Korea or get out of the military." The Army continued in the process of paring down troops that had been built up during the Vietnam War and the young captain had reached the stage in his military tour where he was now on the list for completion of an unaccompanied tour. Following a brief period of reflection and discussions with his wife, Stratman recognized that he enjoyed the excitements offered by military life along with all of its associated opportunities to train and lead soldiers.

Resolving to make the best of the pending overseas assignment, Stratman asked Colonel Wurman if he would request of his contemporary, Colonel Thomas J.P. Jones—artillery commander for the 2nd Infantry Division—that he might consider recommending the junior officer for a cannon artillery command in Korea. Colonel Jones agreed to the request and although Stratman's wife, Linda, was not thrilled by the pending separation from her husband while she

---

[24] CGSC is a full-credited, collegiate-structured program led by the military chain-of-command that educates and develops future military leaders.

raised their children alone, she fully understood his decision to pursue his career in the Army and remained supportive of his military endeavors.

"At the time, we were all just doing what we had to do, but looking back on it all, it was an amazing experience," he said. "I managed to excel regardless of the assignment, but it was not an individual achievement ... because of Linda I was able to do so. She faithfully soldiered on and remained a very supportive spouse throughout my entire career."

CHAPTER 3

Defending the Korean DMZ

In late February 1981, Captain Hank Stratman (second from right, hands folded behind his back) assumed command of A Battery, 1/38th Field Artillery Battalion at Camp Stanley, South Korea. Located about an hour north of Seoul, the battalion had the responsibility of deploying along the demilitarized zone within two hours of receiving an alert and being ready to fire their 105mm Howitzers.

A thirty-year-old Captain Stratman reported for his new duty assignment in South Korea in late February 1981, ready to embark upon his one-year unaccompanied tour as commander of A Battery,

1/38th Field Artillery Battalion stationed at Camp Stanley near the city of Uijeongbu. A Battery, he explained, averaged a troop strength of approximately one hundred and twenty soldiers whose primary mission was the operation of six howitzers in the event hostilities reignited along the demilitarized zone (DMZ) between North and South Korean forces. This new assignment represented the third command of his career, but it was the first time that he commanded a cannon artillery firing battery.

"I had the three-month command in a Lance unit and later commanded the brigade headquarters battery, but this command of a cannon artillery battery is what I aspired for," he said. "We were located about an hour north of Seoul and in the event that we received an alert, we had to be at our designated firing position along the DMZ within two hours and be ready to fire." He continued, "This was accomplished by keeping the ammunition uploaded on the 2-1/2-ton trucks in our motor pool, being trained to quickly issue every soldier's individual weapon and ready to roll with full battle gear—that was the critical task."

While completing his command time in Korea, his wife and children remained living in the home they had purchased in a sub-division near Fort Sill in the community of Lawton, Oklahoma. Stratman explained that this arrangement afforded their children the opportunity to continue residing in the home and school environment familiar to them while providing him the comfort of knowing that his wife had available support resources in the community and at Fort Sill if needed. It was also while living near Fort Sill that Linda committed herself to returning to college and earned her bachelor's degree from the University of Cameron through their satellite campus in the Lawton area. She not only pursued her undergraduate education and raised her children during this timeframe, but remained engaged in the local workforce as a substitute teacher at schools both on and off the nearby military base.

For the next three months, Captain Stratman provided leadership to his unit while participating in live-fire exercises and combat maneuvers near the DMZ, responding to alerts and supporting an infantry brigade under the overarching Eighth Army structure should there be an escalation of hostilities. His rating officer and battalion commander, Lieutenant Colonel Ronald Steinig, vividly reported that Captain Stratman "is the best battery commander of the five that I rate" and that the officer's "innovative approach to training and his field artillery expertise have led to a dramatic improvement in fire direction techniques and howitzer crew drills in the battery."[25] Steinig would go on to achieve the rank of colonel, retiring in July 1990 as the range deputy commander at National Range Operations Directorate, White Sands Missile Range, New Mexico.

The assorted duties Stratman was given placed him in charge of providing a salute battery for a ceremony to honor a South Korean four-star general. Stratman led his troops in rehearsals in the morning hours, preparing for the event scheduled a few hours later.

"Our practice firing seemed to be riddled with problems, whether it be firing the wrong number of rounds or everything just being out of sequence," he said.

"All I know is that it all seemed to go wrong. So, I pulled my NCOs and platoon leaders aside and provided encouragement, stressing that we can do better."

The battery continued their practice firing through the lunch hour and, when it came time for the ceremony attended by local high-ranking military officers from both the U.S. and South Korea, the salute was fired perfectly.

"Maybe there was an element of luck or divine intervention involved," he grinned.

Stratman continued, "One day I was informed by my battalion commander that the 2nd Infantry Division Artillery Commander, Colonel Thomas J.P. Jones, told him that I didn't need to be wasting my abilities in a firing battery when he could use my talents within the division artillery headquarters," said Stratman. "2nd Infantry Division was fielding the M198 nuclear capable, 155mm howitzers into three battalions under his command. I had a nuclear weapons background with Lance units and a gunnery background from my time as an instructor at Fort Sill, and he believed that this expertise

---

[25] *U.S. Army Evaluation Report for the period of February 27, 1981* to May 5, 1981.

and knowledge were needed in the Counterfire Duty Officer slot in the division artillery headquarters."

After making the unsolicited move to the division artillery headquarters also located on Camp Stanley, Captain Stratman spent the next several months assisting with the process of transitioning the battalions from light to heavy artillery along with coordinating the addition of their nuclear capabilities. A large part of his responsibilities during this period of evolution in artillery was teaching the staff of the three individual battalions how to establish and administer a personnel reliability program. Some of the focused training he provided often consisted of more hands-on tasks such as assembling and securing nuclear rounds while also demonstrating how to destroy the rounds in case of imminent capture by enemy forces. Stratman's guidance helped in introducing the M198 howitzers to the personnel of the battalion, who then succeeded in passing their certification test through the Army Training Test/Technical Proficiency Inspection.[26]

He explained, "By introducing the M198s to the theater, the military not only increased lethality of indirect fire capabilities but gave our battalions the resources to fire many different types of projectiles at a much greater range. This was a much more lethal option against North Korea and became a big deterrent measure for our forces during the Cold War."

Embracing the array of experiences that he collected and refined during the intense regimen of previous duty assignments, Stratman again earned the praise of his leadership and was cited for his outstanding level of performance. It was noted that he effectively planned, coordinated and implemented a battalion-level Army Training and Evaluation Program (ARTEP) for three field artillery battalions that was realistic in design and helped prepare the artillery soldiers for real-world battlefield missions. His demonstrated knowledge and expertise in a range of competencies to include gunnery, ammuni-

---

[26] The Defense Technical Information Center reports that the Army Training Test/Technical Proficiency Inspection was implemented in October 1972 and was "a combining of what was formerly a separate test and an inspection for 155 mm howitzer field artillery battalions." *DTIC, The Army Training Test,* https://apps.dtic.mil.

tion allocations, range oversight and S-3 operations resulted in his commanding officer's assertion that the junior officer was deserving of the recommendation that he be considered for promotion ahead of his contemporaries.[27]

The next change in duty assignment of his military career arrived on October 16, 1981, with his appointment as the Operations Duty Officer for the headquarters section of the 2nd Infantry Division at Camp Stanley. Though only spanning a period of four months, in this position Stratman continued to assist in the development and execution of training programs in support of division level operations. One of the highlights of this brief period was the glowing acknowledgment he was given for improving the "quality of the tactical and technical fire direction procedures and safety practices of the Division Artillery by conducting quality classroom instruction and by developing a thoroughly professional safety exam and cannon firing SOP (standard operating procedure).[28] It was also during this timeframe that he approached the scheduled conclusion of his one-year hardship tour, at which point he began to develop a modicum of concern after he did not receive orders for his return back to the states and the opportunity to reunite with his family.

"When my orders didn't come in, I did some checking and discovered that I had been selected for CGSC (Command and General Staff College) next summer, but that was still six months away," he recalled. "It was an interesting moment in the Army because they were working to identify high-performing senior captains for CSGC when in the past they only sent majors and lieutenant colonels to the course. The Army wanted to identify talented officers for promotion and created what they referred to as below-the-zone promotions, meaning if you had demonstrated consistent and outstanding performance, you could be promoted to major without the time-in-grade required as a captain."

---

27 *U.S. Army Evaluation Report for the period of May 6, 1981* to October 15, 1981.
28 *U.S. Army Evaluation Report for the period of October 16 1981* to February 12, 1982.

As flattering as the selection for CSGC may have been, Stratman was now anxious to see his wife and children while struggling to identify some means that would also afford him the opportunity to attend CGSC and boost his career potential. Approaching the assignment personnel, he requested that they consider releasing him from his duty in Korea so that he could relocate to Fort Leavenworth, Kansas, (where the CGSC course is administered) to begin working toward his master's degree. A graduate degree, he affirmed, was becoming required for an officer's competitiveness especially when the military continued its trend toward personnel reductions, and those officers with an impressive educational background were more likely to be promoted or retained. His request was granted and he soon received orders for return to the states, departing Korea in February 1982.

The first several months following his arrival at Fort Leavenworth were a flurry of activity that included the purchase of a new home off-post and then waiting several months for his family to join him. The delay in the arrival of his family, he explained, was to ensure that his children had the opportunity to finish their schooling in Lawton, Oklahoma. Additionally, he was required to take the SAT ("Scholastic Aptitude Test" is a national college admission exam) to determine his knowledge in a range of subjects in order to be approved for enrollment in a master's level course. Since he had not been in a college-level course for nearly a decade, he did not qualify on his first attempt; however, with a little patience and practice, he was soon able to retake the test and received a qualifying score.

In early summer of 1982, the promotion-eligible captain began the Command and General Staff College course while concurrently pursuing his master's program through a satellite campus of the University of Southern California located on Fort Leavenworth. This was an academically demanding period for the officer since the CGSC immersed him in college-level studies "of leadership, the conduct of joint and combined land warfare, and the synchronization of Joint, Interagency, Intergovernmental, and Multinational organizations to achieve national objectives."[29] In addition to being the senior tactical

---

[29] U.S. Army Command & General Staff College, *CGSC Circular 350-1*, 1-2.

school for the U.S. Army, in 1983, the year that Stratman attended the CGSC, it was reported that the course "had students from 50 allied countries and each service of the U.S. military."[30] Pursuing a systems management degree at the graduate level during his off-duty hours, this dual military/civilian educational path did not negate his duties as a husband and parent, requiring that he carve out time to spend with his family as well. With all the activities of this period, it represented a very involved moment of his career that would later yield big dividends in his preparation for increasingly progressive responsibilities and career assignments.

"I happened to be in the middle of the pack academically at CGSC and generally with all of my military schools," Stratman maintained. "The course was preparing us to be staff officers and I wanted to be a commander, but you had to be able to tolerate staff assignments and do well in them to be considered for promotions. As I said, it was a very competitive environment in the U.S. Army at that time. Staff analysis and other similar responsibilities ... let's just say that all that paperwork and administrative drudgery wasn't my greatest interest; just give me my mission and get out of the way became my motto."

When CGSC came to an end with his graduation on June 3, 1983, Stratman earned superior ratings from his instructor for his written and oral communication skills, leadership abilities, contributions to group work and his research expertise, but still finished sixty-ninth out of a student body of one hundred forty-nine. His academic counselor and evaluator noted, "Captain Stratman has demonstrated a potential for success in demanding and responsible positions. He should be assigned to high level staff positions and selected for battalion command at the earliest possible time."[31]

---

[30] June 22, 1983 edition of the *Rocky Mount Telegraph* (Rocky Mount, North Carolina).
[31] DA Form 1059, *Service School Academic Evaluation Report* for Henry W. Stratman, June 3, 1983.

Built in 2007, the Lewis and Clark Center on Fort Leavenworth, Kansas, became the new home to the Command and General Staff College. The state-of-the-art, 413,000 square foot instruction facility and the J. Franklin Bell Hall were used by Stratman during his training on the post, and is where the class of 1983 graduation plaque is installed. **U.S. Army photograph.**

Days following his graduation from the course, Stratman returned to Fort Sill, Oklahoma, and was assigned as the Chief, Modern Battlefield Techniques Committee with the Combat Development Directorate. He and his family again packed up their belongings after purchasing another home in a subdivision located off post. Now a promotable captain, Stratman worked for the former 2nd Infantry Division Artillery Commander under whom he had been assigned while stationed in Korea approximately three years earlier—the recently promoted Brigadier General Thomas J.P. Jones.

General Jones was now serving as assistant commandant for the U.S. Army Field Artillery School and wanted Stratman's expertise, advice and competencies in developing new and emerging field artillery capabilities. In this new duty assignment, Stratman was essentially a free agent, working directly for Brigadier General Jones, who advised Field Artillery School directors in the Weapons Department, Gunnery Department, Communications Department and the Signal

Department in coordinating the creation of a professional school system that effectively integrated separate and critical battlefield components.

"Artillery provides fire support to infantry and armor—and it's a complicated task," he said. "It's something that we've struggled with in the past and our task was to provide for a successful integration of all these components." He continued, "Me and a couple of junior officers and non-commissioned officers reviewed certain problem areas where we had not met standards and then provided our recommendations on how to correct it and improve communications at a number of levels."

In his position as a senior captain who possessed a detailed comprehension of many facets of the effective use of artillery, Stratman was selected for a special trip to the Middle East in September 1983. Approximately 1,800 U.S. Marines had been sent to Beirut, Lebanon, the previous year by President Ronald Reagan as part of a peacekeeping mission during the Lebanese Civil War. President Reagan's "administration feared that conflict between Lebanese factions backed by Syria and Israel, along with clashes between Israel and the Palestine Liberation Organization (PLO) could escalate into an Arab-Israeli War," explained the Department of State's Office of the Historian.[32] Frequently, the Marines had become targets by Syrian artillery and were outranged and outgunned in their response capabilities. In an effort to identify a solution for dealing with the attacks, the Department of Defense sent the Chief of the Field Artillery, Major General John S. Crosby, to the region along with a team comprised of target-acquisition experts, a State Department representative, the Weapons Department Chief along with Captain Stratman, who fulfilled the role of aide-de-camp to Major General Crosby during the temporary assignment.[33]

---

[32] Department of State, *The Reagan Administration and Lebanon*, https://history. state.gov.

[33] Commissioned through the ROTC program at North Carolina University, John S. Crosby achieved the esteemed rank of lieutenant general and, at the time of his trip to Lebanon, was also the commandant of the Field Artillery School at Fort Sill.

On a visit to Beirut, Lebanon in September 1983, Capt. Stratman, second from right, served as aide-de-camp to Maj. Gen. John Crosby, center, the Chief of the Field Artillery. The group is pictured aboard the USS New Jersey off the coast of Beirut, which had fired sixteen-inch shells against Syrian targets the previous night.

"The Navy was in charge of the theater and they flew us in through Germany," Stratman noted. "The target-acquisition folks stayed in Germany and the Navy brought us into the area aboard the USS *Guam*—their command ship. It was very hot in Lebanon at that time." He further explained, "General Crosby went ashore along with the Weapons Department Chief and the State Department representative, and I remained on the *Guam*."

The *Guam*—a helicopter landing ship—was no stranger to military action and was temporarily redirected in October 1983 to serve as the flagship during *Operation Urgent Fury*, the invasion of the Caribbean Island of Grenada. The invasion resulted in the loss of three of the ship's helicopter pilots who were killed in the initial assault.[34]

One of the goals of the team's trip off the Lebanese Coast, Stratman added, was to effectively deploy the AN/TPQ-36 and AN/TPQ-37 Firefinder radar systems to assist U.S. forces in addressing recurring threats in Lebanon. These systems are a "lightweight, small, highly mobile radar set capable of detecting weapon projectiles launched at any angle within selected 90-degree azimuth sectors over 360 degrees of coverage. The AN/TPQ-36 can locate simultaneous and volley-fire weapons. It can also be used to register and adjust friendly fire. Upon projectile detection, the weapon location is computed and is used to direct counter-battery fires (timely return fire)."[35]

Stratman said, "When the general returned from his visit to shore, the Navy received approval later that night to fire on Syrian targets. I was still on the USS *Guam* about a mile away from the USS *New Jersey,* watching as it used its mighty sixteen-inch guns on targets off the coast of Lebanon. Being an artilleryman," he added, "it was fascinating to watch a battleship open up on targets because that is the epitome of firepower."

After returning to the states, a plan was quickly devised to deploy the radar systems and supporting artillery equipment to U.S. forces in Beirut. Sadly, less than thirty days following Stratman's departure from the coast of Lebanon, 241 U.S. military personnel were killed on October 23, 1983, when suicide bombers with ties to Hezbollah drove two truck bombs into barracks facilities at the airport in Beirut where U.S. and French military personnel were housed. The attack was soon followed by President Reagan's signing of National Security Decision Directive 11, which called for "broadening strategic cooperation with Israel and Arab opponents of Syria, reducing Syrian influence ... and expanded rules of engagement regarding naval and air support for the Lebanese Army."[36] A few months later, when bat-

---

[34] December 24, 1983 edition of the *Wisconsin State Journal.*

[35] Military Analysis Network, *AN/TPQ-36 Firefinder Radar,* https://fas.org.

[36] Department of State, *The Reagan Administration and Lebanon,* https://history. state.gov.

tered by increasing congressional criticism, Reagan made the decision to withdraw U.S. troops from Lebanon.

In the months following his return to Fort Sill, Stratman received his early, below-the-zone promotion to the rank of major on March 1, 1984.

"If you were in the year group before the primary zone—no matter how strong your file was or whether you had completed your key development assignments—you were automatically considered for below the zone consideration …whether you wanted it or not," explained Maj. Lucas Rand in a 2020 article discussing changes to the U.S. Army officer promotion process during the timeframe of Stratman's promotion.[37]

Stratman's promotion was followed by the transfer of Gen. Thomas J.P. Jones, who, within three years, would become the major general in command of White Sands Missile Range in New Mexico.[38] When Jones' replacement, Brigadier General Dennis Reimer, reported to the assistant commandant's position, Major Stratman became his transition officer and assisted the incoming flag officer in settling into his new duties and responsibilities. Reimer's career would experience a meteoric rise since he would eventually receive promotion to the rank of four-star general and serve as the Chief of Staff of the U.S. Army under the presidencies of both George H.W. Bush and Bill Clinton. However, on June 4, 1984, Stratman's own career continued its unerring climb with his assignment to a battalion executive officer slot that would provide him the means to subsequently qualify for his very own battalion command.

Remaining in the familiar background of Fort Sill, Stratman integrated into the S-3 training officer duty with Headquarters and Headquarters Battery(P) of III Corps Artillery. The corps artillery reinforced the divisional artillery units and the new major had the substantial peacetime charge of managing and coordinating all the artillery fire for the school on the fort. Furthermore, under war con-

---

[37] Suits, *Changes to Promotion Process Provide Officers More Career Flexibility*, https://army.mil.

[38] March 21, 2013 edition of the *Albuquerque Journal*.

ditions, he then became responsible for managing and coordinating the artillery fire of divisional assets anywhere in the world.

Maj. Stratman became the transition officer for Brig. Gen. Dennis Reimer when he became assistant commandant of the Field Artillery Center and School at Fort Sill in 1983. The Reimers became good friends and mentors to the Stratmans. Reimer was promoted to four-star general in 1991 and served as the Chief of Staff of the U.S. Army from 1993 to 1995.

"It was a privilege to work for good quality people and we all highly respected each other," Stratman maintained. "Many of them went on to have great careers like Lieutenant Colonel Randall Rigby and Lieutenant Colonel John Pickler, who became three-star generals."

Similar to what he had previously experienced, this particular assignment was also brief in tenure, lasting only about eight months. Stratman excelled in his performance and earned accolades for a host of achievements related to combat readiness and the effective implementation of training programs and policies. But as he would soon discover, the moving from one job to another was intentional to acquire new skill sets and further develop his leadership potential. This, he would soon learn, was all part of an overall plan to help provide for his upward mobility in the ever-changing leadership paradigm of the U.S. Army and ensure he had an overarching comprehension of various levels of command staff responsibilities.

A major step in his progression came in March 1985, when he received appointment as the executive officer for Headquarters, 1st

Battalion, 17th Field Artillery also stationed on Fort Sill. Throughout the next year-and-a-half, he managed and coordinated training for the units within the battalion, assisted with the implementation of varied programs and logistical support while also helping to coordinate the professional development of the soldiers of the battalion. Successful outcomes were many in this assignment, highlighted by his commanding officer's declaration that Statman "supervised the complete revision of the deployment plan based on the change of the battalion's primary mission." His senior officer also noted that Stratman was able to maintain "an operational readiness rate above 90%" in his additional duty appointment as the material readiness officer during a timeframe in the military supply system when budgets were hacked and the funds to purchase repair and maintenance parts were extremely limited in availability.[39]

The executive officer, Stratman said, had a responsibility to ensure maintenance preparedness and logistical readiness of the battalion's subordinate units and batteries. Oftentimes, it was a grand struggle to maintain the wartime readiness of his artillery units when they often were not provided the necessary funds for repair parts needed to replace engines on the howitzers in addition to other critical components.

"When I was the executive officer for the battalion," he recalled, "that's the point I began working with the TACFIRE—a huge digital computer system that allowed artillery components to communicate on many different levels. It was housed within a container in the back of a five-ton military truck and allowed us to communicate with battalion, brigade, division artillery and at the corps level as well." He added, "It gave us the capability to send down and receive information transfers like fire plans during our exercises." Pausing, he continued, "But it took us a long time to get the programming to work. Since it was our first digital system, we struggled with it for years."

Many of the automated computer systems Stratman trained and employed in his various artillery assignments had been a long

---

[39] U.S. Army Evaluation Report for the period of December 14, 1984 to March 14, 1985.

time in both development and implementation. According to a report by the National Defense University Research Directorate, the development of the TACFIRE officially began in December 1967, when the prime contract was awarded to Litton Industries. The emergence of the system soon grew to be defined as the following: "TACFIRE is a system which applies automatic data processing techniques to the seven field artillery functions of technical fire control, tactical fire control, fire planning, artillery target intelligence, artillery survey, meteorological data, and ammunition and fire unit status. It also provides a capability for preliminary target analysis, nuclear target analysis, nuclear fire planning, chemical target analysis, and fallout prediction."[40]

The larger strategic purpose of the TACFIRE, Stratman reiterated, was its integration within the greater defense plan to ensure artillery units could effectively map their fire in response to the threat of Soviet armor and troop invasions in Western Europe. As he explained, despite the initial difficulties he and others encountered with regard to the implementation of the TACFIRE, it helped to bequeath the artillery with top-down command and control.

A soldier is pictured working with a component of the TACFIRE, which was a huge digital system that allowed the field artillery to communicate on several different levels. Stratman's introduction to this system came while serving as a battalion executive officer. U.S. Army photograph

One of the greatest lessons of his tenure as executive officer came in April 1986, when the battalion prepared for a mission to assist with the annual training and evaluation of a National Guard

---

[40] Salisbury, *The Making of a Weapon System*, 4.

artillery battalion. Stratman was appointed as the commander of the battalion convoy that would travel from Fort Sill to the training site of Camp Shelby, Mississippi. He soon discovered that the battalion commander, rather than participating in the convoy of jeeps and other military vehicles, coordinated an air-conditioned bus aboard which he and his five battery commanders would make the lengthy journey.

"Many times, I observed my battalion commander being too friendly with his subordinate battery commanders," he explained. "My job as battalion executive officer was to mentor and train these battery commanders so that they had the tools to deal with any challenges that may arise at their command level." He added, "The leadership style that my battalion commander displayed was totally foreign to my leadership principles."

The battalion and its subsidiary commands soon embarked upon their highway journey to meet up with the National Guard unit in Mississippi. Although Major Stratman did not hear any negative comments whispered by soldiers regarding their leadership traveling by air-conditioned bus while they had to drive rudimentary military vehicles lacking amenities such air-conditioning or AM-FM radios, Stratman affirmed that he would always remain among his soldiers and lead from the front.

During the highway journey, Stratman's' battalion was traveling through Dallas in rush hour traffic on April 15, 1986, when dozens of passersby began honking their horns at the convoy of soldiers. At first, he believed it was because of the slow movement of their bulky vehicles during a busy period of the day and the fact that it was the post-Vietnam era when support for the troops was waning; however, they soon realized that the honks were followed by shouts of spirited support and not middle-finger gestures. It was not until later that evening when they realized all of the commotion on the Dallas interstate was connected to a historic military event.

Upon arriving at the National Guard armory in south Texas where they would spend the night before embarking upon the last leg of their journey to Camp Shelby, Mississippi, the battalion was informed that the United States, under orders from President Ronald

Reagan, had launched air strikes against military and terrorist targets in Libya. These strikes were in retaliation for Libya's sanctioning of terroristic activities against U.S. troops and citizens such as the bombing of a West Berlin dance hall frequented by U.S. servicemembers. The U.S. air strikes included an attack on the headquarters of Libyan leader Muhammad al-Qaddafi and resulted in the death of his fifteen-month-old adopted daughter and the injury of two of his young sons.

Once arriving at Camp Shelby, Mississippi, Stratman and the battalion staff worked to train and conduct an operational readiness test for their National Guard artillery counterparts. Fortunately, Stratman never heard any rumblings of dissatisfaction from soldiers who were not granted the same privileges as those embraced by their leadership, who had traveled in relative comfort. However, the event had all the appearances of a selfish gesture that always remained engrained in Stratman's reflections and steeled his resolve to make sure he never put his soldiers through circumstances he was himself unwilling to endure.

Following the battalion's return to Fort Sill, Stratman continued his tenure as executive officer, which, he remarked, had been slated to conclude after approximately twelve months. This became delayed when the battalion commander moved on to another assignment and Stratman was retained in the position for several additional months to assist with the transition of the new battalion commander.

Reflecting on the total of sixteen months he remained in the executive officer position at the battalion level, Stratman maintained, "I never had the discussion with my former battalion commander about his over-friendliness with his subordinate officers because it wouldn't have yielded any results. I had a job to do and that's what I was committed to accomplishing."

He added, "One of the greatest lessons that I learned from that entire experience came from having to do all the little things that the battalion commander did not want to do. For instance, this included attending the funeral of a Samoan soldier killed during training at Fort Sill. It was the noble thing to do and I graciously represented the command and the U.S. Army.

CHAPTER 4

Building a Career

"I believe that Linda was ready for the change ... for a new environment, and knew that a battalion command was very important to me. After we arrived in Germany, she was very busy because she worked as an accountant for the Baumholder Community Club, was substitute teacher at both the elementary and high school level, volunteered for the Red Cross and also volunteered at the base hospital recording medical tests for aviation candidates." –Stratman discussing the active life of his wife while they were stationed in Baumholder, Germany.

The late 1980s brought with it new and unique circumstances when the U.S. Army began assigning secondary specialties to career-minded officers. With the primary consideration focused on placing combat and field experienced officers within staff positions of various sorts, it was an effort on behalf of the Army to ensure they could identify good, quality officers for training positions that had previously been viewed as mundane and career-ending. Stratman explained that many of these staff assignments were at locations within TRADOC (United States Army Training and Doctrine Command) and often pulled officers out of the mainstream since it was through field and command assignments that they could best demonstrate their abilities and competencies. Efficiency reports and Officer Evaluation Reports were being reviewed for promotion purposes and generally officers who had been serving in one of these field units received a higher level of consideration for promotion.

"That's why I was transferred to the headquarters for TRADOC at Fort Monroe, Virginia, in December 1986," Stratman affirmed. (TRADOC is now located at Fort Eustis, Virginia.) "I had the field experience but they needed some of that experience in staff positions as well. The position that I was placed in was defined as a Combat Developments Staff Officer and it provided me with a significant level of insight in the development of weapons systems within the larger defense structure," he added.

Created in 1973, TRADOC has evolved into a command consisting of four major functions—the recruitment and training of soldiers, the development of adaptive leaders, guiding the Army through doctrine, and shaping the Army "by building and integrating formations, capabilities, and materiel."[41] The latter of these functions—the building of capabilities—became one of the primary tasks for Stratman during the time he was stationed at the Virginia military base.

Saying goodbye to their temporary home of Fort Sill, the entire Stratman family made the moved to the East Coast, and were initially

---

[41] U.S. Army Training and Doctrine Command, *About TRADOC*, https://tradoc.army.mil.

placed in a low income, small housing complex on Fort Monroe that had frontage to Chesapeake Bay. Despite the stunning view of the Virginia coastline, there initial accommodations essentially provided just enough living space for the family to sleep and eat. His daughter was a junior in high school and their son a freshman at the time, but the family appeared amenable to the move since there were more activities and points of interest than had been available to them in Oklahoma. Six months following their arrival in Virginia, their wait yielded longed-for results when better housing opened up and the family moved into a large duplex that was a short walking distance to Stratman's office.

"Linda was able to use her business degree right away when we moved to Fort Monroe because she got a job as the director of operations for a restaurant and hotel—the old Chamberlin Hotel," said Stratman. "My son and daughter worked waiting tables at the restaurant in their free time, which was a really upscale place," he added.

Now known simply as the Chamberlin, the former restaurant and elegant nine-story hotel complex has since made the transition to one of the largest retirement communities in Hampton, Virginia. It was situated on the site of Fort Monroe, which closed in 2011 as a result of the recommendation of the 2005 Base Realignment and Closure Commission (BRAC). Despite the loss of the military base, the state of Virginia still managed to gain 5,250 defense jobs under the BRAC. The portion of the original site of Fort Monroe has been preserved as a national monument under the National Park Service and is known as the Fort Monroe National Monument.[42]

Stratman's daily work routine provided a new and engaging level of responsibility he had never before witnessed. In his new capacity as Combat Developments Staff Officer, he helped ascertain and develop future weapons requirements for the U.S Army Field Artillery. If it were determined that the Army needed a new bullet, missile or other types of weapons components or systems, it was the major and the personnel in his office who would validate the Field Artillery School's requirements documents before coordination with

---

[42] February 11, 2015 edition of the *Daily Press* (Newport News, Virginia).

the U.S. Army and Department of Defense for approval. One of the most dynamic activities of his time in this assignment was linked to the modernization of all field artillery systems within the U.S. Army.

While stationed at Fort Monroe, Virginia, in the late 1980s, Linda Stratman became the director of operations for the historic Chamberlin Hotel, which is pictured on this vintage linen postcard. Fort Monroe closed as a military base in 2011 and the Chamberlin has since become a senior living community.

A focus of much of their development efforts was the Army Tactical Missile System (ATACMS). The long-range, guided missile system "gives commanders the immediate firepower to shape the battlespace ... [and are] packaged in a Multiple Launch Rocket System look-alike launch pod...."[43] As part of this project, Stratman and his contemporaries helped establish a state-of-the-art system with two missiles that possessed a much greater range than was previously available to soldiers in the field. Stratman and his counterparts served as the link between the defense industry and the end user, coordi-

---

[43] Lockheed Martin, *ATACMS*, https://lockheedmartin.com.

nating the development of capabilities the users wanted to see in a specific weapons system in addition to locating funding and securing Department of the Army approval for the projects. There were many meetings with senior-level officials throughout all development phases, affording Stratman opportunities to witness the integration of new and exciting technologies within the field artillery system.

Off-duty hours offered the family a number of unique and interesting activities while at Fort Monroe. One memorable occasion Stratman recalled was being able to visit the Naval Station Newport (Newport News, Virginia) and watch as the USS *Iowa* came into dock after suffering an explosion of the Number 2 turret during gunnery exercises off the coast of Puerto Rico, which sadly claimed the lives of forty-seven sailors.

"The *Iowa* was all charred up," he recalled. "On other weekends, I would go to the Navy base with Linda and the kids, and there was always a submarine or a carrier having an open house or family day, so we'd go on a tour of the ship," he added.

There was a moment of sadness that struck the family on February 17, 1988, when Stratman was contacted by one of his sisters to inform him that their father had passed away at seventy-seven years of age. For some time prior to his death, their father had resided in an assisted living facility and suffered from a number of health problems brought on by years of smoking and breathing in noxious fumes and particles during his work around the farm. Taking leave of his military duties, the Stratman family returned briefly to Missouri as the family patriarch, Leo Frank Stratman, was laid to rest alongside his parents and many of his relatives in the cemetery of Visitation Catholic Church in Vienna.

After returning to Fort Monroe, many of the projects Stratman continued to work on were related to tactical missile systems development under what was labeled as "black programs." These top-secret assignments were used to design a specialized warhead that could effectively deploy between eight-to-ten smart, laser-guided munitions; however, this weapon system was never fully developed or integrated into the military arsenal.

"It was an interesting assignment and I learned a lot," Stratman explained. Everything we were working on was geared toward preparing for a major Soviet attack in Western Europe. Much of it focused on addressing the perceived Soviet armor threat that was possibly unfolding in that region."

His work with one of the secretive black programs soon landed him in the office of a two-star general and later served as an experience that provided some benefit in one of his overseas assignments. On one occasion, Stratman and a Department of the Army civilian with whom he worked on several projects were ordered to report to the office of a two-star general who was scheduled to report on the status of on one of the black projects in development to a four-star general in his chain of command.

"It wasn't long after we reported to the general's office that he proceeded to chew our asses over something to do with the program," said Stratman. "After listening to that for a little while, I said, 'General, if you will go into receive mode, I will tell you everythingyou need to know to report on.' He calmed down and said, 'O.K.'"

During his second tour in Germany in the late 1980s and early 1990s, Stratman was stationed at the U.S. Army base in Baumholder, which was at the time the headquarters for the 8th Infantry Division. U.S. Army photograph

This, Stratman later discovered, would not be the last time he had an encounter with this particular general.

Weeks later, the lieutenant colonel who had been serving as his immediate supervisor retired from the U.S. Army, thereby resulting in Major Stratman being moved up to the position of Chief, Field Artillery Division. In this specific role, he had now inherited the responsibility for the management of fire support combat developments and integration of field artillery capabilities. The colonel for whom he worked possessed an air-defense artillery background, so between the two officers they had a significant amount of insight regarding combined fire support operations. When it came time for his *U.S. Army Officer Evaluation Report,* after fulfilling nine months in this position, Colonel John B. Rogers noted of Major Stratman's performance: "Without peer—most tactically and technically capable officer in fire support I've known in 24 years of service."[44]

The next step toward a battalion level command began to unfold in May 1989, when Stratman received orders to return to the United States Army Europe, this time in Baumholder, Germany, to serve as the Division Artillery S-3 (Operations and Training Officer) with HHB, 8th Infantry Division Artillery. His daughter, Jodie, was in the process of graduating from high school, so Stratman took seventeen days of leave combined with three days of permanent change of station travel to set his daughter up at the dorms of Southwest Missouri State University in Springfield to begin college classes. It was a good university in a safe community, Stratman explained, and also placed her in proximity to family should she need something while her parents were living in Germany. Their son, Jon, was sixteen years old at the time and accompanied his parents on their new adventure overseas.

"I believe that Linda was ready for the change ... for a new environment, and knew that a battalion command was very important to me," he said, praising his wife's support. "After we arrived in Germany, she was very busy because she worked as an accountant for

---

[44] *U.S. Army Officer Evaluation Report* for the period of August 6, 1988 to May 12, 1989.

the Baumholder Community Club, was a substitute teacher at both the elementary and high school level, volunteered for the Red Cross and also volunteered at the base hospital recording medical tests for aviation candidates. Oh," he continued, "she also taught adult citizenship and naturalization classes in her spare time," he chuckled.

Jon, much like his mother, was also very engaged in a slate of activities during the time he lived in Germany. Not only was he busy from an educational perspective by attending classes at the base high school, he was also employed part-time at the NCO and enlisted clubs while also delivering newspapers in the early morning hours. Faith also became a focal point in his life and he was dedicated and instrumental as a leader in support of a non-denominational ministry at Baumholder.

Linda affirmed, "Not only was he an incredible support to his ministry group, he was an inspirational support to me and my efforts in working on behalf of our military families."

The U.S. Army Garrison at Baumholder was at the time the largest concentration of U.S. troops outside of the United States. Located in western Germany, the base is referred to as the "Rock" and was taken over by French forces after World War II, until being transferred to the United States in 1951. The base continues to host American units; however, is frequently taken over by NATO troops who conduct assorted training exercises and maneuvers.[45]

"When we first arrived at Baumholder, we lived in temporary housing for about three months," Stratman recalled. "We were then able to secure housing in a small commander's home near the officer's club."

As the Division Artillery S3, he had substantial responsibility for the development and implementation of fire support tactics, techniques and procedures utilized in support of the mission of the 8th Infantry Division. Much of this planning regimen included the scheduling of resources and training assessments as an assurance that the General Defense Plan remained executable should a flare-up occur with Soviet forces in the region. (The General Defense Plan

---

[45] Military Bases.com, *USAG Baumholder*, https://militarybases.com.

was organized by NATO during the Cold War and defined command authorities and defense responsibilities in the event of an attack by Soviet or Warsaw Pact forces.) During this timeframe, Stratman also helped plan and oversee major aspects of a training and certification exercise held in Grafenwöhr, Germany, named Operation REFORGER, which helped test the General Defense Plan. (REFORGER "stands for Return of Forces to Germany and is held to demonstrate that thousands of active duty and reserve troops from the United States can be deployed to Europe as quickly and smoothly as possible.)[46]

While stationed in Baumholder, Germany, Stratman was promoted to lieutenant colonel and became the Division Artillery S-3 (Operations and Training Officer) for the 8th Infantry Division.

This exercise represented a large-scale movement of troops, "simulating the type of reinforcement operation that would be needed to sustain Western forces in the event of a Warsaw Pact attack." The Warsaw Pact was a defense agreement established by the former Soviet Union and seven other Soviet satellite states including Albania, Bulgaria, Czechoslovakia, East Germany, Hungary, Poland and Romania. However, Albania made the decision to leave the Pact in 1968. In 1988, a year prior to Stratman's arrival at Baumholder, REFORGER "involved the deployment of about 17,000 soldiers to Europe. Once they arrived,

---

[46] November 14, 1989 edition of the *Bangor Daily News* (Bangor, Maine).

ground and aerial maneuvers were conducted in West Germany with a total of 97,700 American and allied troops."[47]

Shortly after his arrival at Baumholder, Major General David Maddox was assigned as the commanding general of the 8th Infantry Division.[48] Initially, Stratman was marginally concerned with the new change in leadership since Maddox happened to be the same general officer he had bluntly suggested go into "receive mode" at Fort Monroe several months earlier. As a common practice, the general held an in-brief to gain familiarity with his new assignment and subordinate personnel—a gathering that was attended by Major Stratman given his position as the division artillery operations and training officer.

"When he walked in the room, you'd have thought we were old drinking buddies," Stratman laughed. "He came up and shook my hand because I guess I was the only guy in the room that he recognized. After that, I had no problems getting what I needed from the division staff."

Several momentous and historic occurrences came to pass while the major was serving at Baumholder, one of the most impressive of which was the collapse of the Berlin Wall. "The barbed wire beginnings of the Berlin Wall on 13 August 1961 divided, overnight and with savage finality, families, friends, neighborhoods in what had until 1945 been the thriving, populous capital of Germany," wrote Frederick Taylor in *The Berlin Wall: A World Divided, 1961-1989*. "The wall represented a squalid, violent—and, as we now know, ultimately futile— episode in the post-war world" and led to an environment "that seemed if it could escalate at any time to a terrifying nuclear confrontation between the US and the Soviet Union."[49]

As noted in the *Proclamation on World Freedom Day, 2020* issued by former President Donald Trump, "For almost 30 years, the

[47] February 2, 1918 edition of the *Des Moines Register* (Des Moines, Iowa).

[48] David M. Maddox retired at the rank of four-star general and was the twenty-eighth commander of U.S. Army, Europe from July 9, 1992 to December 19, 1994. U.S. Army Europe and Africa, *General David M. Maddox*, https://europeafrica.army.mil.

[49] Taylor, *The Berlin Wall: A World Divided, 1961-1989*, XVII.

Berlin Wall symbolized the divide between the free world and communism. On its eastern side, the rights that democratic societies hold dear — the fundamental freedoms of religion, speech, the press, association, and petition — were replaced by forced secularism, oppressive censorship, monolithic propaganda, and inhumane division," all of which was under the influence of the Soviet Union. [50] This great cultural and political symbol of division and stalwart emblem of the Cold War came to an abrupt end on November 9, 1989. It was on this date that the Berlin Wall began to come down through the hammers and picks of a joyous crowd after an announcement was made by the East German Communist Party that citizens of the German Democratic Republic (East Germany) were now extended the freedom to cross the border that separated East and West Germany whenever they wished. Stratman quickly discovered that the military posturing that had taken place in the face of the Cold War threat posed by the Soviet Union would soon result in many changes in the U.S. military structure in the region.

Shortly after Stratman reported to Baumholder, Germany as the Division S-3 for the 8th Infantry Division, Major General David Maddox, pictured, assumed command of the division. Maddox would later retire at the rank of four-star general.
U.S. Army photograph

"At the time the wall came down, I was performing my duties as Division Artillery S-3 by conducting an evaluation of our artillery battalions in the 5K Zone (designation for an area of no man's land

---

[50] The White House, *Proclamation on World Freedom Day*, 2020, https://whitehouse.gov.

separating East and West Germany) in the vicinity of Grafenwoehr," said Stratman. "Our howitzers were right on the border when all of the East Germans began driving across the border on the Autobahn. They appeared shocked to see artillery right on the border and I can remember the Trabant cars made in East Germany packed full of sightseers."[51] Recalling the surprise of the moment, he added, "We knew the Berlin Wall event happened but were caught by surprise that the border was simply thrown wide open like it had been. It was a good thing we were conducting our training in a dryfire mode with no ammunition."

On March 1, 1990, several months before his fortieth birthday, another momentous moment came to fruition with his promotion to the rank of lieutenant colonel. In the ensuing months, as military tensions in the region began to subside with the beginnings of "a slow process of democratization that eventually destabilized Communist control and contributed to the collapse of the Soviet Union," plans began to emerge to stand down the 8th Infantry Division.[52] Many of the battalions under the division, Stratman explained, were going to be inactivated while others were slated to be "re-flagged" under different designations. The administration of President George H.W. Bush proposed in early January 1990 a number of major troop reductions in Europe, and leading to widespread speculation that this would include the 8th Infantry Division. "The Bush Administration proposed the cutbacks in response to the political changes that have swept Eastern Europe in recent months," reported the *Sacramento Bee* on April 1, 1990. The newspaper further reported that these proposals could negatively impact the local economy since "U.S. forces employ about 33,000 civilians, the vast majority of them German" and that an estimated 1,000 of these civilians were employed at the headquarters of the 8th Infantry Division in Bad Kreuznach, Germany.[53]

---

[51] Trabant cars were produced by East German manufacturer VEB Sachsenring from 1957-1990.

[52] Department of State, *The Collapse of the Soviet Union*, https://history.state.gov.

[53] April 1, 1990 edition of the *Sacramento Bee*.

Before making the leap into the next step of his progressing career, Stratman took thirty days of leave so that he could spend some time with his family before reporting for his new command assignment. His daughter, Jodi, flew to Germany from Springfield in early summer of 1990 to accompany her parents and brother during their vacation in Europe. Only months following the historic fall of the Berlin Wall and yet still several months away from the date of the official reunification of East and West Germany, the Stratman family had a very memorable visit to the still-divided German capital city of Berlin.

"Linda, Jodi, Jon and I toured West Berlin and crossed through Checkpoint Charlie," he recalled.[54] "The day we went through the checkpoint, they were taking it down to place it in a museum. We traveled into East Berlin and much of it was like it was after World War II—bullet-ridden buildings and windows blown out." He added, "A lot of the storefronts were outdated as well, appearing as though they were from the 1950s."

Their travel into the eastern sector was aboard an austere passenger rail system. During one of their stops in East Berlin, Stratman explained, the family was able witness the East German equivalent of guards on duty at the Tomb of the Unknown Soldier.[55] Again, boarding the train at one of stops to continue their tour of the east, the family watched as several of the train stations they passed were blocked off and no longer in active use. Several hours into their journey, they boarded a train during rush hour to return to West Berlin; however, they soon discovered they were heading in the wrong direction.

"It didn't take me long to figure out that we had boarded the wrong train and were heading deeper into East Germany when we

---

[54] Checkpoint Charlie was a high-profile crossing that existed between East and West Berlin and became a popular symbol of the division in Germany during the Cold War.

[55] The "Neue Wache," or "New Guardhouse" in English, was established in 1960 by the East German government as the "Memorial to Victims of Fascism and Militarism." Following reunification of the divided Germany, the memorial was redesignated the "Central Memorial of the Federal Republic of Germany for the Victims of War and Dictatorship."

started passing more and more of the boarded up and closed rail stations," Stratman said. "I was wearing my Class B's (military uniform) and everyone was looking at us, but I told my family not to panic and we got off the next stop and then boarded a train headed in the right direction."

It was also during this exciting vacation adventure that Stratman and his wife were advised by their daughter that she had made the decision to leave college in Springfield, Missouri, to transfer to the University of Michigan in Dearborn to continue her education.

In the midst of the uncertainty surrounding the future of the 8th Division and the historic changes unfolding in Europe, the next major milestone in Stratman's career arrived when he accepted command of 2nd Battalion, 29th Field Artillery on June 12, 1990. There came with this assignment an even greater level of obligation since he had now been given the responsibility for the training and maintenance preparedness of 675 personnel in addition to 115 wheeled and tracked vehicles. Furthermore, there was the added stress of maintaining performance standards related to the performance of all aspects of conventional and nuclear operation, training and fire support planning. The years of increasing command background experience he acquired at the platoon and battery level in both Lance and traditional field artillery battalions, supplemented by the proficiencies he accrued in weapons and support device development at Fort Sill and Fort Monroe, provided him with the range of competencies to ensure he would be successful at this new level of command.

Remarking on the progression of his command experiences, Stratman affirmed, "My time in division artillery was one of many positions during my career that had prepared me for this moment. Each duty assignment was a building block that introduced me to the skills, doctrine and troop leadership methods that I would need to be successful in a battalion level command. In conclusion, he affirmed, "The Army was focused on developing qualified and competent battalion commanders because in the grand scheme of things, they are a key link in the combat chain."

CHAPTER 5

Battle Ready Command

2-29
FA

DESERT SHIELD
FAMILY SUPPORT PLAN

DEPLOYMENT BRIEFING 26 NOV 90
LTC HANK STRATMAN

"I know that world events and our deployment make this a stressful time for all families associated with the 2nd Battalion, 29th Field Artillery. I hope you feel pride in your son's demonstrated professionalism and his commitment to peacekeeping anywhere in the world. It is dedicated soldiers like your son who make the difference." – Lieutenant Colonel Stratman in a letter he wrote to the families of the battalion's soldiers preparing for deployment during the Persian Gulf War.

74

Within thirty days of his June 12, 1990, assumption of command of 2nd Battalion, 29th Field Artillery stationed at Baumholder, Germany, Lieutenant Colonel Stratman and his soldiers deployed to the Combat Maneuver Training Center in Hohenfels, Germany. The battalion, he explained, had previously been under good leadership and was fundamentally sound; his mission became to take his soldiers to the next level of efficiency and capability. The arduous training scenarios they confronted had helped the soldiers to boost their combat abilities in a fashion that would be of significant benefit within the coming months.

The Combat Maneuver and Training Center has roots dating back to 1938, when the German military used the area to practice the combat maneuvers in preparation for breaching the Maginot Line and invading France during World War II. Additionally, a section of the expansive site was used to house thousands of British prisoners of war. In the years after war's end, "U.S. forces claimed the area for military training purposes" and an agreement was reached with the German government that would "extend the training area to its current size of about 40,017 acres." The site hosted training exercises such as REFORGER and contained number of weapons ranges and ample space for a firing and maneuver area. In 1987, the Combat Maneuver and Training Center was officially formed and, three years later, added the additional training simulation of OPFOR ("Opposing Force," which generally describes a military unit that represents an enemy force during training exercises or war games).[56]

"The brigade was going through maneuver training—a war game exercise where he had a live opponent," said Stratman. "The center was structured for tank battles, infantry tactics along with artillery providing the fire support. These maneuvers were very important in the development of my understanding of divisional fire support and how different brigades maneuver and interact in a combat environment. We, as the artillery, practiced forward and rearward passage of lines because we had to be able to create lanes through friendly forces to move forward, shoot our mission and then

---

[56] 7th Army Training Command, *100 Years of History*, https://7atc.army.mil.

withdraw back without being attacked by the friendlies." He added, "Our batteries quickly learned how to coordinate on the local level as they went through these passages to ensure we could safely perform the mission we were given."

One of the greatest benefits yielded from these training exercises were the regular after-action reviews (AARs) that afforded an opportunity for the participants and those serving in leadership capacities to openly share their opinions and views on what went right, what went wrong and how to improve upon outcomes in the future. The AARs, Stratman explained, were "non-attribution," meaning those participating could freely discuss errors that occurred in decision-making or planning with the intent of improving overall combat performance and thus saving lives in the process.

"It was alright to make a mistake in these training situations, but the expectation was that you would learn from that mistake and not make the same one again," said Stratman.

Weeks later, on August 2, 1990, a major event that reverberated on newsreels worldwide revealed to Stratman the importance of the maneuvers he and the soldiers of his battalion had only recently completed. It was on this date that television airwaves exploded with early descriptions of the invasion of Kuwait—an oil-rich country in the Middle East—by the military forces of the neighboring country of Iraq. At the time possessing the world's fourth-largest military, Iraq's "overwhelming invading force consisted of "more than 100,000 Iraqi troops (who) moved tanks, helicopters and trucks across the border into Kuwait.[57] Iraq's mechanized and armored divisions soon moved along the border of Saudi Arabia, resulting in a request for military assistance from the United States. Within days, the 82nd Airborne, two F-15 Squadrons in addition to two carrier battle groups were deployed to the region and, shortly thereafter, the President authorized the activation of 200,000 Selected Reserve members. Almost overnight, the name of Iraqi dictator Saddam Hussein becoming a household name throughout the United States as the country was

---

[57] Johns, *The Crimes of Saddam Hussein*, https://pbs.org.

embroiled in what was soon designated "Operation Desert Shield/ Storm."

"Our artillery battalions had for so long been in Europe to defend against Soviet aggression and now the U.S. was going on the offensive in the Middle East," recalled Stratman. "The plans in the works meant that V Corps would stay in Germany while a master plan was in in development to deactivate VII Corps, which our brigade was under. However, the Gulf War would delay some of what had been planned."

Another significant event that helped increase their level of combat readiness occurred in late October 1990. The battalion underwent the Army Training and Evaluation Program (ARTEP) at the Grafenwoehr Training Area. Utilizing a Mission Essential Task List ("METL"—a written requirement of a wartime mission), the battalion practiced safe crew procedures and ably demonstrated they were able to meet clearly defined standards in accuracy and timeliness of artillery delivery while participating live-fire missions in support of a maneuver brigade combat team. By the conclusion of the evaluation period, the battalion fired 1,500 rounds and had lived in a tactical training environment for seventeen out of a total of twenty-one days.

An article printed in *Army* magazine in recognition of the twenty-fifth anniversary of the First Gulf War, noted that "VII Corps was ordered to the Middle East on Nov. 8 (1990) with what, for the most part, was a no-notice announcement to units and families because planning had been restricted to a small group."[58] Stratman's notice of pending action in the war came in an unexpected fashion a couple of days later. The true benefit of all of their recent training and evaluation began to come into focus on the afternoon of November 10, 1990, when Stratman was attending a cross country competition for his son at Heidelberg, Germany. At the conclusion of the race, Brigadier General John P. Otjen, the assistant division commander for the 8th Infantry Division, approached Stratman since his son was also there competing in the same event.

---

[58] Franks & Fontenot, *The First Gulf War*, 40.

"General Otjen advised me that he had selected my battalion, out of the three artillery battalions in the division, to deploy to Kuwait," noted Stratman. "We had in our battalion inventory what was at that time the most modern M109A1 self-propelled 155mm howitzers and we were detached from the 8th Infantry Division and moved to the 42nd Field Artillery Brigade." Lowering his head in reflection, he added, "Linda and I owned a nice Mercedes at that time that had once been used for a pace car for some race. After that meeting with the general, we must have driven ninety miles an hour all the way back to Baumholder." He added, "I was excited because this was a big deal and it was an honor to have the battalion selected for such a critical mission."

The aforementioned article explained that rapid expansion was a large part of the reason Stratman's artillery battalion was caught in the net of combat deployment. The "U.S. VII Corps rapidly expanded, going from a Germany-stationed peacetime strength of 76,000 soldiers to 146,000 American and British soldiers deployed in Desert Storm." The authors, retired U.S. Army General Fred Franks and Colonel Gregory Fontenot, explained that the units comprising VII Corps "were drawn from forward-deployed corps, U.S. Army Europe, U.S. Forces Command, the Army National Guard and the Army Reserve, the British Army, and two Return of Forces to Germany units...."[59]

Stratman further explained that he and Linda worked diligently during the next several weeks to make sure all of the families of soldiers in the battalion had their affairs together in preparation for the pending deployment to the Middle East. While he was meeting with his battery commanders and senior staff to discuss the various nuances of their mission, Linda worked with the spouses of the commanders and senior staff to assist with the development of a family support plan. Lacking any type of template with regard to care and support resources for the families of those deployed, Stratman noted that he and his wife labored to build one from scratch. Since more than half of the soldiers in the battalion were married, he realized

---

[59] Franks & Fontenot, *The First Gulf War*, 41.

that those left behind would need to know how to perform such simple tasks as paying the bills and where they could find medical care should an emergency arise for themselves or their dependents.

"Shortly after I received initial notice that our battalion had been selected for deployment, I held a meeting at Wagon Wheel Theater on Baumholder because rumors were already beginning to circulate about what was going on. The meeting was intended to inform every soldier of our operational mission and was also tailored toward all of the families in attendance. We also held a pre-deployment briefing and I invited representatives from the Red Cross, finance, the medical clinic and school personnel to attend. It was our intent to ensure everyone had an identified network of support and while there, we also took care of such things as next-of-kin and drawing up wills."

In the final days of 1990, while the military base at Baumholder, Germany, took on the stunning appearance of a winter wonderland often pictured on scenic vintage postcards, Lieutenant Colonel Stratman and the soldiers of 2nd Battalion, 29th Field Artillery, scrambled to prepare for their pending deployment to the deserts of the Middle East.

A battalion *Desert Shield Family Support Plan* had been drafted and was distributed to members of the battalion and their families during the pre-deployment briefing. The plan contained a survival checklist for the spouses with the telephone numbers and contact information for military staff who would serve as part of the Family Support Team during the deployment. One of the highlighted features of the plan was a training calendar denoting many of the training and preparatory activities the battalion would be engaged in while preparing for combat deployment. Additionally, the plan shared an extensive listing of deployment tips, information on military pay and taxes, and a questionnaire. The questionnaire, he explained, was designed to help determine any specific areas of need among the family members who were remaining in Baumholder while their loved ones traveled to the Middle East.

Following this important meeting, Stratman had the battalion break out into individual batteries so that the commanders and leadership staff could work to identify and address the specific needs of every soldier serving under their command. During one of the pre-deployment briefings for the entire battalion and the dependents of the soldiers, Stratman strongly encouraged the families to remain in Baumholder during the deployment because of the support structure that had been established. For the next few weeks, Linda focused much of her time in making arrangements for the families that would be left behind while her husband ensured the battalion was superbly trained and prepared to perform the mission on the horizon.

Pictured on much of the pre-deployment material given to families of the soldiers and t-shirts produced to raise funds for the family support group was the symbolic image of the heroine nicknamed Molly Pitcher. Mary Ludwig Hay McCauley was born in 1754 as the daughter of dairy farmer from New Jersey. She later married a barber who enlisted in the Philadelphia Artillery and served as a gunner during the Revolutionary War. Although legend and stories passed down through generations have blurred the lines between truth and fiction, it is reputed that during the Battle of Monmouth in 1778, Mary's husband was wounded while manning his gun. Mary had been carrying water jugs to parched troops during the battle and after observing her husband's injury, began loading the artillery in his stead.[60]

"The t-shirts we made read 'Desert Shield, Stand by Your Man,' and had a picture of Molly Pitcher loading her husband's cannon," said Stratman. "We chose Molly as our mascot because it represented the support provided by the spouses and families during our deployment."

These briefings and meetings held at Baumholder, Stratman noted, were not only an opportunity for leadership to disseminate information on available resources, but to allay many unwarranted fears that had the potential to spread like wildfire. As with any war or major conflict, propaganda often runs rampant, and, as Stratman maintained, the Persian Gulf War certainly was no exception.

Linda Stratman wears a special t-shirt reading "Desert Shield, Stand by Your Man," which was designed for sale prior to the battalion's deployment in the Gulf War. Profits from these sales were used to support family emergencies that arose during the deployment.

---

[60] Both Molly Pitcher and her husband survived the Battle of Monmouth and the Revolutionary War. The couple later settled in Pennsylvania but her husband passed away in 1786. She later remarried and was eventually awarded a pension for her service by the state legislature. Sadly, the eighty-seventy-year-old Revolutionary War icon passed away in 1832 and is interred in Old Graveyard in Carlisle, Pennsylvania. U.S. History, *Molly Pitcher*, https://ushistory.org.

"There was a lot of hysteria about Saddam's capabilities, but we did the best we could to explain that they were largely unfounded. It was a new and challenging experience because we had six weeks to prepare for the deployment and we had never done this before," he remarked. "We had been trained to deploy in Europe and this was an entirely different set of circumstances for all of us. I relied a lot upon my executive officer, S-3 (operations officer) and battery commanders to do their jobs."

While Linda was busy making preparations with the spouses of leaders of the different batteries, Stratman had begun to oversee the transportation of their equipment to the combat zone in the Middle East. The battalion had to load their ammunition, in addition to howitzers and support equipment, onto rail cars. Their wheeled vehicles were transported to Mannheim and loaded on barges. Once their equipment reached Bremerhaven, Germany, it was turned over to European Command for final delivery overseas. Each battery in the battalion was also provided with a forty-foot shipping container to load with ancillary supplies to included rifle racks, spare parts, toilet paper and, as Stratman depressingly recalled, body bags.

The *Desert Jayhawk Magazine* described in an article about the VII Corps that "[w]hile waiting for their turn to deploy, the heavy divisions that gave the corps its striking power continued training while getting their equipment and themselves ready for war." The article went on to note there was a method behind the madness that many units experienced while they "trained with chemical equipment, rifles and other weapons. They learned about the hazards of a new land. Doctors poked and prodded them, lawyers wrote their wills and leaders drove them around the clock."[61]

In a Thanksgiving Day letter that Stratman wrote to his family in Missouri, he explained, "My 18 years of troop leading/training experience has prepared me (and Linda) well for this mission. My troops are excited as I am. Kinda like the 'HIGH' football players get prior to the Superbowl. I am their coach and quarterback." He continued, "Not only am I responsible for winning the game (battles),

---

[61] Jayhawk Magazine, *VII Corps in Action*, 3.

my decisions directly influence their survivability. By the way, I'm only (a single) unit commander of the hundreds who primarily feel the same way I do."

Stratman repeatedly stressed the investment of time and sweat made by Linda since she was not only left to cope with the absence of her husband during the deployment, but also scurrying to take care of those family members who were remaining in Baumholder. In the letter to members of his family, Stratman wrote, "Linda has her hands full taking care of the three hundred wives and kids of my soldiers. I think she has a harder job than I do, and she doesn't even get paid for it." He added, "Those of you who were planning on visiting Germany next spring should still do so. Linda welcomes the company and I know you will enjoy the visit. Who knows, I may even be back by then."

Prior the deployment of the 29th Field Artillery in Operation Desert Storm, Stratman was among a group of commanders who visited Saudi Arabia in early December 1990, to get an overview of the terrain on which they would have to maneuver their troops and equipment under combat conditions.

The November 22, 1990 edition of the *Champion Times*, the official newspaper of the military base on Baumholder, reported, "Stratman said he will be relying heavily on the battalion's combined wives' club to provide support to the families remaining in Germany, both during and after the unit's deployment." The article quoted Stratman, "We have good, cohesive wives' clubs at the battery and battalion level. This will be a test of their mettle as they start to meet the demands connected with our deployment."

Reflecting on the assortment of pre-deployment preparations, Stratman added, "I wanted to make sure everything was in good hands and that we had a good structure of support in place because once I left, I no longer had any influence over things at Baumholder. I had a new captain in the battalion that I left back in the rear to work with any problems that came up"

An overview of the terrain on which they would have to maneuver in the Middle East was provided in early December 1990, when Stratman joined other U.S. Army officers for a commander's reconnaissance. The small group flew to Saudi Arabia and then boarded Blackhawk helicopters, which carried them to the camp where they would soon assemble their battalions. In Germany, their equipment was road bound: however, this brief trip to the Middle East revealed to Stratman the openness of the desert landscape and the battalion's ability to maneuver without significant limitations.

"We could travel cross-country and would be able to quickly move, orient and setup to provide timely fire support," he said.

He maintained the highest confidence in his battalion's ability to meet the requirements of the coming mission and to fight and win in combat; however, Stratman affirmed that his greatest asset was the competency of the battalion's officers and NCO chain of command. Yet this confidence did not afford him any opportunity to rest on his laurels since there were a couple of unexpected challenges he would now have to deal with during the ramp-up to final deployment. A couple of weeks before Christmas and within days of their pending departure, Stratman was approached by his battalion command sergeant major, who provided him with an unexpected and alarming revelation.

"The command sergeant major had previously been a major who was rifted as an officer but was allowed to revert to the enlisted corps to qualify for retirement," stated Stratman. "Here we were, preparing for our combat deployment, and he pulls out a hip-pocket (medical) profile that stated he was not fit for deployment." With a pause to suppress his aggravation the spineless act, he added, "What made it even worse is that there were no other command sergeants major in the division artillery who stepped forward to backfill him. After consulting with Captain Mueller, commander of B Battery, I pulled my strongest first sergeant from my strongest battery, Robert Phillips, and promoted him to command sergeant major."

Any challenges associated with locating a suitable replacement for his senior NCO within the battalion notwithstanding, Stratman soon discovered that he had a soldier attempting espionage during the Persian Gulf War. One day, while sitting in his battalion office reviewing paperwork related to their readiness levels and deployment preparations, there was a knock on Stratman's door by a gentleman who curtly identified himself as an Army Criminal Investigations Division Special Agent (CID).

"When he walked into my office, the agent closed the door behind him and introduced himself. He then said that EUCOM (United States European Command) commanding general had told him to inform me that one of my soldiers has been colluding with the Iranian and Jordanian embassies. The soldier he was speaking about had a wife and several kids, had been struggling financially and was not a very good or reliable soldier anyhow." Chuckling, Stratman added, "At that point, I wondered what can happen to me during an already stressful timeframe."

The CID agent advised Lieutenant Colonel Stratman that the soldier should neither be made aware of their knowledge of his activities nor allowed to deploy while they completed their investigation. Utilizing the excuse that he had too many family concerns to deal with during a deployment, the soldier was told he was being left behind with the rear detachment to take care of his family.

Stratman later learned that the CID had undercover agents play the role of foreign agents willing to pay for information on activities related to the United States' military capabilities. The soldier, Albert T. Sombolay, was a naturalized U.S. citizen born in the African country of Zaire. After the war, he was convicted of espionage and sentenced to thirty-four years in the military prison at Fort Leavenworth, Kansas.[62] It was reported that Sombolay received from a foreign intelligence agent approximately $1,300 dollars for the information he provided.

"Part of the irony of it all is the soldier really didn't know or have access to any critical or useful military information," said Stratman. "The information he attempted to sell to the foreign representatives was documents related to our deployment schedule and examples of the chemical protective equipment that we used in training for deployment."

These momentary distractions fortunately did not impede their progression toward deployment to the Middle East and, only days prior to Christmas, the soldiers of the battalion prepared to say their goodbyes to members of their families and their friends and neighbors at Baumholder. Brigadier General John P. Otjen, the assistant 8th Infantry Division commander who had handpicked Stratman's battalion for deployment, wrote in a brief letter to the departing soldiers on December 19, 1990, "Your unit has been selected to deploy as part of the United States' force in Operation Desert Shield. Your unit was selected because it is highly trained and combat ready." The general further noted, "I am confident in your unit's abilities and proud of your personal professionalism"

Stratman himself wrote a letter to families of the deploying soldiers, seeking to provide those remaining at Baumholder with information on communicating with their soldiers during the absence and assuring them of their loved ones' safety and ability to perform the tasks at hand despite the many uncertainties of the moment. He maintained, "Tentatively, the battalion will deploy to Saudi Arabia prior to 1 January 1991, and take up defensive positions. I assure you the battalion is prepared to accomplish any assigned mission. Our equipment is the best in the world and, more importantly, your

---

[62] The December 5, 1991 edition of the *Gazette* (Montreal, Canada).

(soldier) and his comrades are highly trained, motivated, and professionally led. Regardless of the combat mission we receive once in country, rest assured we will get it done right."

The battalion held their farewell ceremony on Christmas Eve, an event that was full of hugs and tears of sadness, followed by the soldiers traveling by bus to Ramstein Air Base, where they were scheduled to board commercial aircraft bound for Saudi Arabia. Their pending departure, Stratman explained, resulted in an unexpected complication that required him to make the first of many difficult deployment decisions.

"A couple of hours before our departure, they said that our scheduled flight was cancelled because of some issue with the aircraft," Stratman recalled. "We were told they could bus us back to Baumholder or that they could put us up in barracks at Ramstein until the next morning." Pausing, he continued, "I conferred with Command Sergeant Major Phillips and we both agreed that we didn't want to go back to Baumholder because of the emotional goodbyes that had already taken place … we just didn't want to put everyone through all that stress again. That moment," he added, "became my first deployment decision."

As Stratman had previously remarked, propaganda had run rampant during the months leading up to their final deployment day, much of which alleged the destructive capabilities of the Iraqi forces. A great deal of information had been shared to allay any fears among the soldiers in the battalion and their families, as Stratman maintained they were well positioned to overcome any obstacles placed in their path.

"I had every confidence in our training and readiness," he affirmed. "I knew that my soldiers clearly reflected the unit's motto of 'Battle Ready.'"

CHAPTER 6

Operation Desert Storm

"The outstanding 'Battle Ready Soldiers' who professionally answered the call to arms, deployed to Southwest Asia and conducted sustained combat operations for six weeks supporting 1ˢᵗ Cavalry, 1ˢᵗ Infantry, and 3ʳᵈ Armored Division's defeat of Iraq's Republican Guard forces." – From the "Combat Historical Summary" highlighting the participation of 2ⁿᵈ Battalion, 29ᵗʰ Field Artillery in Desert Storm.

During the last week of December 1990, Lieutenant Colonel Stratman and the 607 soldiers of the battalion boarded commercial aircrafts at Ramstein Air Base. Four hours later, they cast first glances upon their new surroundings after arriving at the international airport in the city of Dammam—a province on the eastern coast of Saudi Arabia. Shortly after exiting the aircraft, the soldiers of the battalion boarded buses and were transported to a recently constructed commercial hotel and condominium complex. The massive accommodations, Stratman explained, housed 8,000 U.S. soldiers, was several stories high and vacant of any furnishings. It had been built by the government in an effort to end the wanderings of the country's nomadic populations by bringing them into the cities to urbanize and resettle them in more comfortable accommodations.

"The complex had been nicknamed the MGM Grand Hotel by the troops," Stratman chuckled. "It was situated only few miles from the airport and that is where we resided for several weeks while we waited for all of our equipment to arrive by ships." He added, "There wasn't very much for us to do while we were there and to be honest with you, in my mind, I felt like we were sitting ducks while waiting around without any of our equipment or any way to defend ourselves if something happened."

First Sergeant Robert H. Phillips, left, acting sergeant major for 2nd Battalion, 29th Field Artillery waits in a warehouse in Saudi Arabia with Lieutenant Colonel Stratman for the battalion's equipment and supplies to arrive from Germany.

In his position as battalion commander, it was Stratman's understanding that everything his battalion owned would be arriving in the nearby port aboard three or four ships. To his dismay, he soon discovered that all of their equipment, which included eighty-four tracked vehicles and one hundred thirty-four wheeled vehicles, was being transported on thirteen different vessels. An interesting logistical situation began to evolve when the equipment started to come into the port in a piecemeal fashion a few days later. Fortunately, the first ship to arrive happened to be carrying Stratman's Humvee, a few trucks and several of the battalion's howitzers. Anxious to depart their accommodations in Dammam and make preparations for approaching combat assignments, Stratman was able to coordinate several heavy equipment transports to haul their early receipt of equipment on a two-hundred-mile road march to their first duty location in the desert.

Lieutenant Colonel Stratman and about two hundred soldiers of the battalion departed the MGM Grand Hotel on January 10, 1991. The remainder of the troops remained in Dammam, under the command of the executive officer, to offload the incoming ships, transport the rest of their equipment and meet up at their new base camp in the coming days to reconstitute the battalion. Traveling to a tactical assembly area in the desert spanning no more than twenty acres and situated near the King Khalid Military City (an established Saudi Arabian military camp), Stratman and the battalion set up their own base camp, erected tents and began a limited cycle of training. While there, they entered a self-defense mode of operations while Stratman awaited the battalion's battle orders from higher headquarters. The area was designated "Spearhead" and controlled by the 1st Cavalry Division. Little time was wasted since the battalion fired more than three hundred rounds while calibrating their howitzers as part of their rigorous preparatory training.

While still in Baumholder, Germany, Stratman had the inside stripped of the battalion's "float" M992 Field Artillery Ammunition Support Vehicles (tracked vehicle in foreground) so that it could be converted for use as his command vehicle with multiple communications and mapping capabilities.

"Our camp was located south of Tapline Road in northern Saudi Arabia, a nice paved highway that had been built and maintained by the oil companies and essentially paralleled the border to Kuwait," he said.[63] "By the time we left there, we had pretty much destroyed the road with all of our heavy equipment. I positioned soldiers as lookouts along Tapline Road to flag down the convoys carrying the battalion's equipment. The next few days, we waited for the rest of our equipment and soldiers to arrive and began to figure out how to navigate in the area. We didn't have the benefit of any GPS (global positioning system) devices when we first arrived and

---

[63] Tapline Road is a major two-lane highway that stretches from east to west the entire length of Saudi Arabia. The highway became a major supply route during the Persian Gulf War. The highway "runs roughly 25 to 75 miles south of the Saudi-Kuwaiti border." February 1, 1991 edition of the *Fort Worth Star-Telegram*.

we often had to travel by the seat of our pants. That's how we came up with the acronym LID—lost in desert," he laughed. "The desert was very unforgiving if you were to become disoriented, which was too often easy to do."

A few weeks later, Stratman recalled, many of the units now in country were provided with a beneficial navigational aid when the oil companies issued handheld devices that calculated their current stationary position relative to communications towers in the region serving as beacons. Many of the navigational problems were identified when the battalion's service battery would attempt to deliver ammunition and supplies at night and could not locate their destination. The rule they operated by in these situations was that when traveling at night and unable to locate the rest of the battalion, the soldiers were to park and remain in place until daylight because navigating in the darkness posed a significant and dangerous challenge.

"Many of the times they got lost, they would have to park until morning and then discover they had only been a mile or so away from us," Stratman said.

Prior to their departure from Germany, Stratman had the interior of the battalion's "float" M992 Field Artillery Ammunition Support Vehicles stripped so that it could be utilized as a fire support coordinator's command vehicle. Often referred to as the "CAT (Carrier Ammunition Tracked)," the M992 was used to store and transport rounds, powder and primers for the howitzers of the battalion. However, Stratman explained that each of the battalions had an extra howitzer and CAT that they referred to as a float since it was intended to serve as a replacement when one of the other CATs or howitzers was undergoing repairs or was down for servicing.

Fortunately, a few weeks later, the battalion was issued seven global positioning systems to aid them in their travels throughout the region. Sometimes, their journeys occurred during the daylight hours while other times it was in the pitch blackness that could fall like a thick, impenetrable blanket across the deserts during the seemingly endless overnight hours.

The battalion's deployment placed them alongside 2nd Battalion 82nd Field Artillery in addition to a 155mm self-propelled howitzer battalion and an MLRS battalion as part of the 42nd Field Artillery Brigade, with the collective mission to reinforce Division Artillery fires in support of VII Corps. Though their role in the battalion structure was critical to the success of the overall combat operations, one of the overriding concerns for Stratman was the safety of each and every soldier under his command. At their assembly area, he noticed that while drawing their ammunition and performing combat uploading of the howitzers by installing fuses on munitions and other miscellaneous duties, many of the soldiers appeared to be getting a little "sloppy." The clearly defined performance standards they had trained on while performing battle drills and exercises back in Germany were now being neglected, he alarmingly observed.

The former battalion commander explained, "They were just being careless with their handling of their munitions ... dropping them in the dirt and sand. That's when I called all of the NCOs together and explained to them in no uncertain terms that there are no shortcuts in this combat zone." Pausing, he firmly added, "I told them that I had made a promise to their wives, mothers and children that I would bring every one of them back home and that I couldn't fulfill that promise on my own. I made it clear to the section chiefs that they were not only responsible for their howitzers' operations, but for the safe return of soldiers in their section, placing much of the responsibility on their shoulders."

The intensity of combat operations escalated on January 17, 1991, at which time several strategic and operational Iraqi targets were attacked during air strikes. On this date, Operation Desert Storm began in earnest and heralded the approach of ground combat operations for the battalion. It was also on this date that 2nd Battalion, 29th Field Artillery began the first of many combat wedge formation movements in support of operations being planned in concert with the 1-82nd Field Artillery, 1st Brigade, of the 1st Armored Cavalry Division. Remaining imminently prepared to provide reinforcing artillery fires wherever and whenever called upon, the soldiers of the 29th Field Artillery spent the next three weeks refining their movement patterns, training with chemical protective equipment and stockpiling the assortment of supplies and munitions that might be necessary to sustain them throughout the coming weeks. Stratman had his service battery draw extra ammunition and supply an ammunition supply point forward of any battalion movements to ensure they did not run short of ammunition while maneuvering to make contact with any elements they were assigned to support.

In an effort to protect themselves from rocket and artillery attacks, particularly while they were sleeping, the soldiers of 2nd Battalion dug large trenches to set their tents inside. The excess sand was then piled around the perimeter of the tent for added protection.

When setting up their camps—often referred to as dug-in positions— Stratman noted that great level of care was taken in erecting their tents in a layout that provided his soldiers with the best defense possible against potential Iraqi rocket and artillery attacks. Their tents, he said, were placed inside trenches that were often times dug three feet deep, using the excess sand and dirt excavated from the trenched area to pile in a protective berm around the entire perimeter of the tents. In the unfortunate circumstance that a rocket or similar explosive projectile were to land near the tent, the occupants would have some protection; however, such a set-up provided little defense in the unusual circumstance that a rocket was to fall directly upon the tent. Their equipment, another critical component of their offensive capabilities, was protected by sandbags and berms as well.

The austere and threatening living conditions in which they were immersed on a daily basis were not absent the occasional moments of unexpected humor. One morning, Stratman exited his tent only to find their camp littered with thousands of leaflets that had been dropped overnight by aircraft of the United States Air Force. The leaflets, featuring assorted designs, were covered in Arabic statements that encouraged those fighting in the Iraqi military, or those supporting the Iraqi cause, to give up their arms and surrender. With a grin, Stratman quipped, "When I found them laying all around our area, I thought to myself, 'I hope the Air Force is more accurate in dropping munitions than they were in dropping those leaflets.'" (See *Appendix D*.)

The 1st Armored Cavalry Division, to whom they were temporarily attached, had two primary missions during the early phases of the war—first, to defend against any Iraqi attacks that might occur down the Wadi al Batin, a river forty-five miles in length that had been acknowledged as the western boundary between Iraq and Kuwait since 1913. Secondly, the division was to conduct feint operations into a sector of Iraq that created the deception that the main effort of the VII Corps offensive operations would unfold in the area of the Wadi al Batin. Elements of the division conducted their feint attack across the border, reaching fifteen to twenty kilometers into Iraq while encountering very little contact with the enemy. But as the calendar moved to mid-February, Stratman received notice regarding the details of the critical role his battalion would play in the overall efforts of the division.

Advised that one of his three batteries was needed to provide artillery support in an upcoming operation, Stratman stressed to the direct support artillery commander that "we don't do battery-level operations," but that he had an entire battalion available to support the division's fire missions. The offer was accepted and instead of bringing eight howitzers, which represented one of his batteries, all twenty-four of his battalion's howitzers would be used to support the division. On February 13, 1991, with the fire support mission having been received, Stratman positioned his artillery battalion forward of the main elements of the division to range potential deep targets, utilizing their radars to detect any counterfire from enemy forces once they started launching their rounds downrange.

Stratman said, "As soon as the battalion was staged, I went forward to the border between Kuwait and Iraq and linked up with an infantry lieutenant who was a fire support team chief in the First Cavalry. He was in an FSV (fire support vehicle, an armored personnel carrier) and was using a Ground-Vehicular Laser Locator Designator to observe and locate enemy vehicular activity three kilometers inside Iraq."[64] He added, "The FSV had a large sight mounted on it that he was also using to surveil activity along the border. I coached him a little and told him that he could engage by sending a request for fire mission through his chain of command since we had an artillery battalion well within range of the Iraqi target."

Permission was granted by 1st Cavalry Division Artillery for a standard fire order—battalion's three rounds of Dual-Purpose Improved Conventional Munitions (DPICM), the first of which was fired shortly after 3 p.m. local time on February 13. This type of artillery round was utilized "[f]rom the mid-1970s to the mid-1990s ... and would be fired in volleys ... over personnel or vehicle formations to achieve fragmentation and penetration effects upon impact." In the 1980s, smart technology was added to these projectiles, including "two sensor-fused munitions, which, after expulsion from the carrier, scan the ground during descent for armored vehicle targets. Upon impact, they fire an explosively formed penetrator (EFP) through the target's roof, defeating the vehicle."[65] The battalion's twenty-four 155-millimeter howitzers fired two, three-round volleys, accounting for a destructive 144 artillery rounds decimating

---

[64] The FSV Stratman refers to here is a track vehicle that is a variant of the M981, considered "[a] versatile target acquisition vehicle ... [that] can 'talk' to artillery command posts by voice or digital message." The Ground-Vehicular Laser Locator Designator "finds the range, azimuth and elevation of targets ... [and] can project an invisible, coded laser spot to guide munitions ... on to targets." Field Artillery, Field Artillery Equipment and Munitions Update, 68-69.

[65] Burke, *The King of Battle Gets Stronger*, https://army.mil.

four of the enemy's heavy equipment transport vehicles. Any demonstrated successes of their first artillery engagement of the war notwithstanding, Stratman noted that the performance of his soldiers left marked room for improvement.

Each battery within 2ⁿᵈ Battalion, 29ᵗʰ Field Artillery utilized M109 Self-Propelled Howitzers. Initially fielded in the 1960s, the M109s are tracked vehicles armed with a 155-millimeter main gun and a .50-caliber machine gun.

"The lieutenant and I were watching as the artillery rounds were coming in—the first volley was right on target," he said. "Then the second volley came in about twenty seconds later and, in about another twenty seconds, the third volley arrived. Within about a minute, we put all of those rounds on an area about the size of two football fields."

The pride he maintained for his battalion's abilities in accurately launching artillery rounds on designated targets was mitigated by an unexpected occurrence. The last several rounds, he explained, fell dangerously close; between five hundred and one thousand meters in front of them, from the high point of ground where he and the lieutenant were observing the enemy vehicle activity.

"I never knew for sure what exactly happened … either one of the NCOs had a fuse setting error or someone got sloppy with their quadrant setting. When I got back to the battalion, all of the guys were high as a kite, giving high-fives and feeling good about their recent shoot. My S-3 officer said, 'You missed it, sir.' I replied, 'No, I didn't.'"

Just as he had done a couple of weeks earlier when witnessing some of his soldiers getting sloppy with their handling of artillery rounds, Lieutenant Colonel Stratman called together all of his section chiefs to discuss the performance he had just witnessed. Reading them the "riot act" and stressing that there was absolutely no margin for error under combat conditions, Stratman made sure they understood that safety was key since he did not want to witness fratricide on the field of battle. Despite any recent performance flaws in their firing, Stratman soon discovered that his battalion earned a special distinction for their efforts on January 17, 1991— they became the first element within the 42nd Field Artillery Brigade to launch rounds in support of combat operations in Operation Desert Storm. Although this was emboldening news for a battalion yet to be truly tested in battle, it did not in any way lessen the details of a commitment he had made weeks earlier.

"I let them know some of the sections chiefs had failed and that we needed to ensure we were performing our tasks just as we had been trained to do and not to take any shortcuts. We were becoming the best artillery battalion there and it was a process of learning, but as I had promised their families back in Germany, we were all going to come home and would be proud of our fire support performance."

G-Day

"Most of the artillery units that were deployed to the Middle East had come from stateside locations and weren't as modernized as our battalion since we had been on the front lines of the Cold War in Germany," Stratman explained. "We weren't perfect at first, but every time we maneuvered and fired, we got a little better. By the time G-Day (Ground Day) arrived, we were 'Battle Ready,' our unit motto," he added.

With the major ground offensive of the war quickly approaching, Stratman made arrangements for any soldier who wished to call home to have the opportunity to do so. The soldiers were loaded in five-ton trucks and shuttled a distance of about forty miles to a location where MCI telephone tents that had been set up. It took about three or four days to get all of the soldiers to a telephone, but this simple effort not only allowed the men of the battalion to briefly reconnect with their families back home, but it also helped maintain a high level of morale within each individual battery and the battalion overall.

A common sight found by U.S. soldiers during the Persian Gulf War consisted Iraqi tanks destroyed or disabled by artillery, bombs or fire of the superior M-1 Abrams tanks used by the U.S. The Iraqi tanks were of Soviet manufacture and most often the T-55 or T-72 models.

"At the same time all of this was happening, the Air Force was conducting air strikes to soften up certain targets in the region," he said. "Sometime in mid-February, while we were still attached to the First Cavalry, we moved in a wedge formation for twenty miles well forward of the friendly defensive line so we could range Iraqi positions.

This mission provided the battalion another moment in a litany of opportunities to build upon some of the skills they had developed prior to their deployment, specifically, those related to forward and rearward passage of lines, which soon became a critical component of their combat activities. The mission was given to 29th Field Artillery to move forward through friendly forces within visual distance of the border between Saudi Arabia and Iraq, and to conduct an artillery raid. Passing through friendly maneuver forces, Stratman affirmed, was a task with no margin for error because fratricide might be the unfortunate outcome if any of his battalion members were misidentified as enemy forces. Successfully completing their fire mission, he recalled that the tension was multiplied on their return since darkness had fallen around them. Noting that there were tankers and other maneuver units set up in defensive positions, comprised of young soldiers armed to the teeth and possibly jittery with a heightened level of anxiety, Stratman said that success depended partially on having sent his operations officer to coordinate with the headquarters of the friendly units. This would ensure that information was quickly and accurately passed down their chain of command to prevent the soldiers of 2nd Battalion from being mistaken for enemy troops upon their return.

"The coordination and planning worked like it was supposed to but one of the howitzers broke down on the way back," he explained. "Part of our SOP (standard operating procedures) was ensuring that we had recovery capabilities in such instances. This vehicle was the last to make it back through friendly lines— the rearward passage of lanes—and I was a little nervous until all of my forces cleared friendly lines. But, again, it was just like we had trained to do in Germany, which benefitted us in our combat mission—you fight as you have trained."

In an official memorandum summarizing the battalion's combat activities during Desert Storm, Lieutenant Colonel Stratman wrote in the weeks after the war: "On 16 Feb(ruary), following the feint attack with MLRS (Multiple Launch Rocket System, a self-propelled, multiple rocket launcher), 155 (self-propelled) and AH-64 (Boeing AH-64 Apache, an attack helicopter) fires, we were chopped …to the 1st Infantry Division and moved 80 (kilometers) west to provide fires for the breach and assault on G-Day. We were positioned 2 (kilometers) from the border and 200 meters behind the maneuver screen line. We were so far forward that other artillery units … would move in amongst the battalion area, fire their artillery raid and then withdraw out of the enemy's counterfire range. We just dug our foxholes in deeper in anticipation of counterbattery that never came. Just prior to G-Day the air strikes were so close they shook our tents and woke us up."

In next few days, the battalion occupied designated positions under the guidance and authority of the 1st Infantry Division, executing artillery raids against targets that included Iraq's 48th Infantry Division and its subordinate infantry platoons and supply points. However, the next memorable moment of the war thus far occurred on February 24, 1991, with the launch of G-Day. "Coalition ground forces struck powerfully, especially on the western flank in the Iraqi desert," wrote John T. Correll in an article appearing in *Air Force Magazine*. "Air strikes continued. Within a day, the Iraqis were in general retreat. Following their instructions from (General Norman) Schwarzkopf, though, soldiers and airmen continued to destroy as many enemy tanks as possible so they could not be used in some future conflict."[66]

The first day of the ground offensive (February 24), the 229th Field Artillery accompanied the 1st Infantry Division as they moved north into Iraq. There was a flurry of activity unfolding as the attack progressed much more quickly than was initially anticipated since there was little resistance encountered and the breach lanes were opened ahead of schedule.

"The entire brigade moved to the 1st Infantry Division sector in preparation for the breach," Stratman said. "They had to clear sand

---

[66] Correll, *Air Force Magazine*, https://airforcemag.com.

berms—grading and plowing them with dozers—for us to travel along. The lanes were about three miles thru enemy fortifications," he added. "We had planned for a ninety-minute preparation by twenty artillery battalions but this was shortened to thirty minutes due to a lack of targets and Iraqi opposition."

Arriving at their designated firing point for the preparatory fires, Stratman was informed by his operations officer that they were still awaiting receipt of their assigned targets from higher headquarters even though the preparatory time on target was now only thirty minutes away. Stratman called the operations officer for the 42nd Field Artillery Brigade, who told him that the applicable target coordinates had already been sent to all twenty subordinate battalions.

"It was a tense moment and I told them to send them again and we'll figure out what happened regarding the break in communications later," he said. "My battalion fire direction center received the targets within minutes of having to fire. It would have been extremely demoralizing to miss the preparatory fires and I am glad we avoided it."

Though encountering marginal resistance, it was time for the battalion to move deeper into Iraq as part of the divisional force, and, as Stratman recalled, they were the first artillery battalion to progress through 1st Infantry Division breach. The movement through the breach lanes was done after nightfall in multiple columns through areas they suspected had the potential of being mined with explosives. The lanes, he recalled, had been cleared for a distance of only about three miles but his battalion's assigned position was still several miles further north. Whether the mines had for the most part been cleared, or few had been placed along the route they were traveling, remains uncertain. Initially, the battalion followed tracks in the sand of those traveling before them but when the 1st Infantry Division veered east towards Kuwait, Stratman led his battalion north and deeper into Iraq, and made it to their assigned firing point around midnight.

"The Humvee for the executive officer of my A Battery ran over something that exploded and damaged the left front tire," said Stratman. "When it was reported to me over the radio, I thought that it was either DPICM dud or a minefield. I told everyone in the batteries to stay in their vehicles and to avoid any external movement until morning so that we could determine what we were dealing with. When morning came, we found that it was one of the unexploded bomblets from our DPICMs rounds that they had driven over and fortunately no one was hurt." He added, "Since it was only A Battery that had been impacted, the other batteries remained where they were; we positioned A Battery about a kilometer outside of the dud zone."

Stratman noted that A Battery had come upon an impact site where, only hours earlier, the MLRS battalion had launched a heavy barrage of artillery against Iraqi positions. The rounds they fired— DPICMs or more protractedly known as "Dual-Purpose Improved Conventional Munitions"—was a form of cluster bomb with each round containing submunitions called bomblets that were often referred to as "steel rain" during the Gulf War. He estimates that his battalion experienced a dud rate of around ten percent, with the bomblets failing to detonate when striking the softer sands of the desert, but often exploded under the pressure of a vehicle tire or the weight of a soldier.

Once completing their movement through the breach, Stratman noted, the battalion's commitment to the 1st Infantry Division was terminated and they were attached to the 3rd Brigade, 3rd Armored Division, on the morning of February 25. Their new mission was to provide artillery support for 3rd Armored Division's end-around sweep to attack Iraq's elite Republican Guard forces. Since the brigade was already on the move to engage enemy targets, 29th Field Artillery headed in a northeastern bearing to connect with them, linking up with the brigade on the move after a road march of about two hours. Upon arrival, it was only a few hours before nightfall and the brigade paused to refuel since their intelligence indicated they were drawing closer to elements of Iraq's Republican Guard. The following morning, while monitoring radio traffic on the brigade fire support net, Stratman heard Colonel Nash tell his direct support artillery battalion commander, "Dick, you can't shoot." This was followed by Colonel Nash calling Stratman's call sign, "Pathfinder Six!"

The brigade commander, Colonel Nash, had three deep targets that he wanted immediately engaged.

"I told him give me the grid coordinates and what order you want them fired," he stated. "Each of our twenty-four howitzers fired three DPICM rounds, three times on each of the three targets identified by the brigade commander."

He was later informed by the commander of the Bradley Battalion that one of the volleys they had fired fell upon an Iraqi counteroffensive force that was preparing to attack the flank of his brigade formation. The artillery volley disrupted the Iraqi plans and once the smoke cleared from artillery detonations, the brigade's Bradley Fighting Vehicles and Abrams tanks finished off what was left of the Iraqi forces.

"We were heroes after that and I moved forward in my command track and joined the brigade commander's tactical command post," Stratman softly remarked. "Colonel Nash said, 'When I want to fire deep targets, your battalion will fire them.' Then he told Dick, the direct support artillery battalion commander who I had previously reinforced, that he would fire task force missions. I shot every mission the brigade commander wanted shot and the direct support battalion fired task force missions. This was not fire-support doctrine, but it was how he wanted to fight with fires in his brigade combat team, and did so very successfully I might add. We were able to send artillery downrange within two to three minutes of a fire order because we had already been doing this for a month in Saudi Arabia."

The 3rd Armor Brigade kept moving and making contact with reconnaissance elements of the Republican Guard. Later in the evening of February 26, Stratman's battalion participated in their biggest engagement of the war when the brigade commander called upon them to conduct multiple fire missions, resulting in firing artillery for nearly forty minutes straight against enemy targets.

"We fired so much in that brief period that the tubes of the howitzers were glowing red and residue was dripping out of the end of the barrel like lava," he enthusiastically remarked. "Our battalion was responsive, fast and accurate. Most of the brigade's fighting took place at night because we had night vision capabilities."

2nd Battalion fires had been used to soften up Iraqi forces that were arrayed within a big valley through which the brigade would soon pass. Once their fire missions were complete, Stratman recalls the strangely colorful glamour of combat that erupted in a land full of the bland tones of barren desert. The next part of the engagement was turned over to the M1 Abrams, Bradley Fighting Vehicles, Apache helicopters and infantry soldiers. Red tracer rounds were lighting up the darkness as they zipped through the air toward elements of Iraq's 17th and 57th Divisions, while the occasional green tracer round flashed past the American positions.

"The green tracers were the Soviet rounds, but basically all of the arms and military equipment the Iraqis had was from the Soviet Union. The Iraqis didn't stand a chance and we didn't lose a tank or a Bradley."

The success in achieving their combat missions, followed by the brief period of calm that came when reaching their objective, was supplemented by wonderful news arriving on the morning of February 28, 1991. It was on this date the soldiers of the 229th Field Artillery were advised that President George H.W. Bush had declared a cease-fire only one hundred hours after the ground war had begun.

For the next couple of weeks, the battalion performed maintenance on their equipment since it had been running the gauntlet of combat operations for nearly six weeks. The greatest threat to their safety following the cease-fire was avoidance of the duds of various types of munitions that appeared to litter the landscape. On March 11, Stratman was advised that his battalion would be assigned to 2nd Brigade of the 3rd Armored Division, who had the mission of defending the demarcation line between opposing forces that had been established in southern Iraq. When Stratman questioned the reason why his battalion had received this lackluster assignment instead of the other 155mm battalion in the brigade, he was advised by the 42nd Brigade commander that the hard-to-please 2nd Brigade commander had refused to accept the reinforcing battalion that had committed fratricide during 2nd Brigade's offensive. The following day, they embarked upon the 100-kilometer trip to their newly-assigned sector.

General Norman Schwarzkopf, who has served as the coalition commander, met with Iraqi generals on March 3, 1991 "to discuss the terms of the ceasefire, focusing on the lines of demarcation between opposing forces, the mechanisms for exchanging prisoners of war, and an order by Schwarzkopf that Iraq not fly fixed-wing aircraft."[67] A request was made to Schwarzkopf by an Iraqi general that they be allowed to fly helicopters to ferry government officials, clinging to the excuse that the war had resulted in the destruction of many important roads and bridges throughout the country. Regrettably, this request was granted and would have unfortunate repercussions in the coming days.

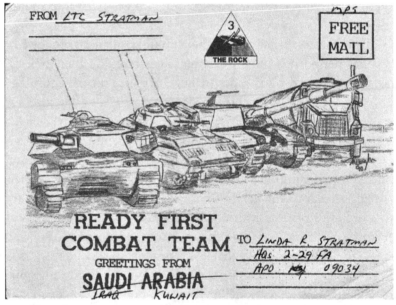

On March 6, 1991, several days after the cease-fire, Stratman used this locally produced postcard to send a note to his wife under the free postage program authorized through the Military Postal Service. At the time, 2nd Battalion was still attached to the First Brigade of the 3rd Armored Division and Stratman wrote that he foresaw his battalion's return to Germany no later than June 1, 1991.

---

67 Zenko, *Remembering the Iraqi Uprising Twenty-five Years Ago*, https://cfr.org.

As part of their duties along the demarcation line, the 229th, while still attached to 2nd Brigade, 3rd Armored Division, remained in a ready position to defend their sector against attack while also interdicting and destroying Iraqi equipment and munitions. The battalion repositioned on March 22, 1991 with 3rd Battalion, 8th Cavalry Regiment along the western Kuwait border. For the next three weeks, they maintained their combat capabilities in defense of Kuwait although the call for a fire missions remained unlikely. It was during this period, Stratman recalled, that they began to witness firsthand the consequences of Schwarzkopf's decision to allow the Iraqi government to continue to use their helicopters.

"The Iraqi's decided to send their helicopters to attack the Shia in the south and the Kurds in the north since they had rebelled against government forces at the end of the war. While we were conducting our defense of Kuwait, my medics occasionally treated many of the Shia refugees that were injured during these attacks."

During the ground war, Stratman explained, prisoners of war were a rare occurrence. His standing orders to the troops of his battalion was that in the circumstance they encountered an Iraqi soldier wishing to surrender, ensure they were disarmed, provide them with some food and water and instruct them to head south where they would be apprehended and processed by rear echelon forces.

"While we were involved in the ground war and had firing missions, we always seemed to be on the move and did not have the time or available personnel to deal with prisoners," he explained.

One of the most interesting developments during the deployment were the uniforms Stratman's battalion wore during their combat operations—the traditional woodland camouflage uniforms. The logistical systems appeared to work well with regard to food, water and munitions for their howitzers, but the uniforms stood out against the tan backdrop of the deserts that surrounded them. Many of the units from the states with whom they worked during combined arms operations had received their desert uniforms early in the deployment cycle, while others had them in their war reserve stocks. However, the soldiers of 2nd Battalion would continue to wear their out-of-place green uniforms well after the end of the war since they had deployed from Europe and did not have a combat stock designed for a desert environment.

"It was really not an issue for us, but since we were one of the last units to deploy, we didn't even receive our issue of desert camouflage uniforms until after the cease-fire and shortly before returning to Germany," he said. "The rumor going around was that the Iraqi forces feared the green-uniformed U.S. forces that came out of Europe because we were equipped to fight the Soviets and … the Iraqis had primarily Soviet weaponry." Smiling, he added, "So maybe having the green camouflage uniforms wasn't such a bad thing and may have worked out for the better."

Since they were one of the last units to arrive in Saudi Arabia, 2nd Battalion was likewise slated to be one of the last to depart. The battalion finally made the move back to King Khalid Military City in northeastern Saudi Arabia on April 16, 1991, days after Iraq signed the formal cease-fire agreement with the United Nations. A few days later, the battalion returned to the port at Dammom, Saudi Arabia, to prepare for redeployment back to Germany.

"While we were in Dammom, I sent Major Zook, my battalion operations officer, back to Baumholder with about half the battalion to make arrangements to receive the remainder of the battalion," he recalled. "I intentionally remained in Dammom with the rest of the battalion so that we could clean up the equipment and turn it over to stevedores to be loaded on the ships to begin the return trip to Germany," he added.

The first week of May 1991, Stratman and the soldiers of the battalion who remained in Saudi Arabia, awaited the arrival of the commercial flight that would fly them back to Germany. Disheartening news arrived when Stratman was approached by an Air Force officer responsible for the scheduling of the flights, informing the lieutenant colonel that his departure would be delayed since they were having difficulty locating an available aircraft. Lieutenant Colonel Stratman told his executive officer, Major Kirby, to inform the soldiers that the flight home had been delayed.

"The news was not something we wanted to hear because everyone was ready to get back home," he said. "But thirty minutes to an hour later, the Air Force guy came and informed me that they had found an aircraft and we would be leaving soon," Stratman added. "I carried this good news to the troops and they may have assumed I influenced the situation somehow, but apparently there was an aircraft crew who had heard about our delay and they all volunteered to come and get us. I can't remember what airline it was, but they all treated us like first-class heroes."

In a letter dated April 28, 1991, that was sent to General John P. Otjen, commander of the 8th Infantry Division in Germany, Colonel Morris "Morrie" J. Boyd, commander of the 42nd Field Artillery Brigade, praised the pre-deployment training and combat performance of the soldiers of 2nd Battalion, 29th Field Artillery. Boyd wrote, "As 2-29 begins their redeployment to Germany, I thought I would take the opportunity to thank you … for providing the 42nd FA (Field Artillery) and VII Corps Artillery with such a highly-trained and superbly led group of soldiers. LTC Hank Stratman and his soldiers led the way from the alert last November to the redeployment we are now executing." Boyd added, "The 2-29th consistently drew praise from brigade and division commanders. You do not get this good in a few months."

Colonel Boyd would formalize his impression of Stratman's combat performance in his *U.S. Army Officer Evaluation Report* for the rating period of November 10, 1990 to April 14, 1991. As his rater, Boyd noted that Stratman "has rendered one of those truly rare, one-of-a-kind performances matched by only a select few in the Army today. Under his superb leadership, the 'Battle Ready' battalion amassed a record in combat marked with extraordinary distinction." On the same evaluation form, Brigadier General Creighton W. Abrams Jr., VII Corps Artillery Commander and Stratman's senior rater, wrote, "Probably the best artillery battalion commander of some 20 (that) I observed in Desert Storm. Hank Stratman overlooks nothing, believes emphatically in 'train hard, fight easy.'" [68]

---

[68] *U.S. Army Evaluation Report* of Lt. Col. Henry Stratman covering the period of November 10, 1990 to April 15, 1991.

Following a direction essentially reverse of their initial deployment months earlier, Stratman and the remaining soldiers of the battalion departed Saudi Arabia at the end of the first week of May 1991, flying into the air base at Rammstein, Germany. From there, they were bussed back to the military base at Baumholder and were soon celebrating their return from war in the embrace of loved ones they had not seen for more than six months. A ceremony welcoming the soldiers back was held at the gymnasium on the base with a grand turnout from not only the family and friends of those who had deployed, but members of the community wanting to congratulate the battalion on a successful and safe overseas deployment. The accolades, though deserved and welcomed, was only a momentary respite for Stratman since he had another year remaining in command of the battalion. He realized there was still much work to be done reestablishing the combat readiness of the 229th Field Artillery in Germany.

One of the most momentous experiences that arose following his return to Baumholder was being asked to deliver the commencement address for his son's graduation from high school on June 7, 1991. Held in the Wagon Wheel Theater on Baumholder, Stratman used his remarks to stress to his son and his fellow classmates on how to establish a plan and pursue success in their lives while drawing upon some of his personal experiences in decision-making that had impacted hundreds of soldiers during his recent service in the Persian Gulf War.

"Regardless of how good your plans or intentions are, your execution of the plan and the decisions you make over time will directly influence the outcome. I have a really simple decision-making process that I want to share with you: normally there are at least two viable options when a decision is required. One option is usually easier to do than the other. I have found that the easier option almost always proved to be the wrong thing to do, while the most challenging and demanding option provided the best solution." He emphasized: "Does that mean I always do things the hard way? No, it means I try to do things the right way."

Closing his remarks, he added, "Every parent in this theater wants their child to be successful. Why? Because we don't want you to return home to live with us," he grinned. "No … that's not the real reason why. We love you, and it is you who carry forward our dreams and hopes for a better world. You are our future."

CHAPTER 7

Climbing the Ladder

Linda and Jon Stratman smile during a ceremony in May 1991 to welcome home the soldiers of 2ⁿᵈ Battalion, 29ᵗʰ Field Artillery from their service in the Persian Gulf War. Lt. Col. Stratman explained that although he was excited to be back at Baumholder, Germany, he still had a year of battalion command time remaining with a lot of work yet to be accomplished.

With a successful record of performance during the Persian Gulf War, the soldiers of 2nd Battalion, 29th Field Artillery were finally back home in the arms of their loved ones at Baumholder, Germany, having earned a few welcome moments of rest and relaxation. But despite any hopes among the soldiers for a break in activity, the next few weeks remained a busy and transformative period for the battalion since there were many soldiers rotating into new assignments while others troops were arriving to fill the vacancies their departures had left. For Stratman and the members of his command staff, there was little time to pause for celebration since extensive maintenance recovery plans needed to be executed for the equipment returning from the Middle East along with training developed for the unit's newly assigned personnel.

"As the commander, it was my goal to be able to report as combat ready within ninety days ... and we were able to accomplish that because of the hard work and dedication of the soldiers in the battalion," he said. "We had a sister battalion who had also been deployed to the desert that wasn't able to do that and, at the commander's change of command a year later, they still were not mission capable with regard to their maintenance capabilities and overall readiness status. You," Stratman stressed, pointing to himself, "as a leader, must set high expectations of your soldiers but at the same time provide them with adequate resources and training to accomplish that mission."

Their assorted military responsibilities and duties in the ensuing weeks were interspersed with several important events, the highlight of which was a Desert Storm awards ceremony held on July 2, 1991. Stratman remarked that no one was any prouder than himself of all the respectable accomplishments of the battalion in the recent war. In his remarks at the ceremony, he stated that his soldiers "competently conducted sustained combat operations for six weeks in support of 1st Cav's feint up the Wadi Al Batin, 1st Infantry's attack and breach, and 3rd Armored Division's defeat of Iraq's Republican Guard forces." He also stressed to those in attendance that the troops had earned the right to "stand tall and proud," while wearing their combat patch on their right shoulder in addition to the Southwest Asia campaign ribbons and awards. In addition to the scores of deserved awards Stratman presented to the soldiers of his battalion in recognition of their distinguished performance, he was personally awarded the Bronze Star Medal for his "superb leadership and extraordinary courage when inspiring the battalion's personnel throughout the critical phases of Operation Desert Storm...." His focus on training and dedication to his soldiers both before and during the war also earned him the Legion of Merit—a military decoration awarded for exceptional meritorious conduct and achievement.

But as Stratman explained, the accomplishments of the battalion notwithstanding, there was much work yet to be done. In addition to bringing all their maintenance capabilities to the highest levels attainable in a brief period of time, the battalion was also scheduled for a technical proficiency inspection to certify them for the handling of nuclear weapons. The battalion spent countless hours preparing for the inspection and underwent their detailed evaluation a few months later. Prior to the inspection, it was widely understood that the government of the Soviet Union was essentially in shambles and the reason for having tactical nuclear capabilities in Germany was quickly disappearing. The *New York Times* explained that President George H.W. Bush had made the announcement that the prospect of an invasion of Western Europe by the Soviets was unlikely, meaning there was "no longer a realistic threat." The President added, "We now have an unparalleled opportunity to change the nuclear posture of both the United States and the Soviet Union."[69]

"On the day of the out-briefing for the battalion, when we were scheduled to be informed as to our performance and whether we had passed the inspection, the Army announced they were no longer in the tactical nuclear weapons business," said Stratman. "It was aggravating because we had put in all of this work preparing for the inspection when someone in my leadership chain should have known that it was not necessary."

The finality of the defensive posture that had defined much of 2nd Battalion's role in Europe came to an end following a relatively

---

[69] September 28, 1991 edition of the *New York Times*.

anticipated announcement several weeks later—a historic milestone that heralded the final nail in the coffin for the Soviet Union. On December 25, 1991, notes the United States Department of State, "the Soviet hammer and sickle flag lowered for the last time over the Kremlin, thereafter, replaced by the Russian tricolor. Earlier in the day, Mikhail Gorbachev resigned his post as president of the Soviet Union, leaving Boris Yeltsin as president of the newly independent Russian state. People all over the world watched in amazement at this relatively peaceful transition from former Communist monolith into multiple separate nations."[70]

Maj. Gen. John Otjen, left, commander of the 8th Infantry Division, holds the flag of 2nd Battalion, 29th Field Artillery, while Lt. Col. Hank Stratman assists his wife, Linda, in attaching the second of two battle streamers the battalion earned for their role in the Persian Gulf War.

---

[70] Department of State: Office of the Historian, *The Collapse of the Soviet Union*, https://history.state.gov.

Early in January 1992, still reeling from the reflections of historic world events that had recently transpired, Stratman and the 29th Field Artillery paused for another recognition that had ties to their participation in the recent Persian Gulf War. In a ceremony at Baumholder, Major General Otjen, the 8th Infantry Division commander who had made the decision to send the battalion to the Middle East a year earlier, presented the battalion with two battle streamers. During the ceremony, Gen. Otjen had Stratman affixed the first battle streamer to the battalion's flag and then, recognizing the role spouses and family fulfilled during the deployment, requested that Linda Stratman come up in front of the battalion and assist her husband in attaching the second battle streamer to the flag. As Stratman noted, the first streamer represented the battalion's participation in the "Defense of Saudi Arabia" while the second was for the "Liberation of Kuwait (Desert Storm)."

"This represented the first battle streamers earned by the battalion since the Vietnam War," said Stratman, "so it was really a big deal for all of us."

In his remarks to the battalion, Gen. Otjen referenced how the soldiers' demonstrated success in the recent war helped redirect the public's opinion of the military following what many citizens of the United States had years earlier perceived to be rampant shortfalls in Vietnam. "You fired for three divisions and helped destroy what was once the fourth largest Army in the world. You were participants in a great endeavor, one that has earned this battalion a proud place in our Army's history. The professional excellence you have always been known for, bore the fruits of a victory that won more the war—you helped win back our national confidence." He concluded, "You endeared yourselves to a newly freed people; and most significantly, to those of us here in Germany, you all returned home safely. The nation fell in love with its military once again."

Between the changes that had occurred with regard to the recent dissolution of the Soviet Union and removal of the nuclear weapons mission, 2nd Battalion experienced another profound moment on January 17, 1992. During ceremonies held at Baumholder, the 8th Infantry Division was formally redesignated the 1st Armored Division.

The change was the result of the shifting political climate in Europe since reinforcing and defending the border in Germany was no longer a mission focus. The new division would focus on training, and, as the former 8th Infantry Division commander, Gen. John P. Otjen, remarked of the new division: "Its singular, most important mission is to maintain itself in a trained and ready posture." He added, "Highly trained, able to deploy either on the European continent or elsewhere, and to demonstrate expertise in doing so that it is indeed a credible force anywhere in the world."[71] The new division headquarters were moved to Bad Kreuzenbach, Germany, while Gen. Otjen moved to the Pentagon to allow Maj. Gen. William M. Boice to assume command of the new European-based 1st Armored Division.[72]

The inactivation of the 8th Infantry Division heralded an end to a proud legacy that began with the division's activation at Camp Fremont in Palo Alto, California in World War I. The division had long held the title of "Pathfinder" from the namesake of Camp Fremont—John Fremont, an explorer and soldier who is credited with opening the Oregon Trail. The division

During a ceremony held at Baumholder, Germany on January 17, 1992, the 8th Infantry Division was redesignated the 1st Armored Division.

---

71 January 18, 1992 edition of the *Stars and Stripes*.

72 A native of Texas, William Milton Boice graduated from the United States Military Academy in 1963. He commanded an armor company in Vietnam and went on to complete a number of interesting and career-progressing staff assignments. From December 1987 to August 1989, Boice was the Assistant Division Commander for the 1st Armored Division followed by service as Deputy Commander of the United States Army War College and Chief of Staff of United States Central Command. The recipient of a Defense Superior Service Medal and Legion of Merit, Boice retired at the rank of major general.

provided soldiers for American Expeditionary Forces that were sent to Siberia in the summer of 1918, and, more than a quarter-century later, supported the fighting in Europe during World War II. Later in the war, they proved their mettle during the Battle of the Bulge and helped liberate a concentration camp, eventually earning the distinction of three Medal of Honor recipients. Although it was deactivated after the war, the division was resurrected in 1950 and made its move to Germany in 1956. Another significant milestone came in the midst of the Civil Rights Movement in May 1972, when Major General Frederic E. Davidson assumed command, becoming the first African American division commander. The soldiers of the division witnessed many historic moments such as the fall of the Berlin Wall and making the transition from a defensive posture to an offensive structure during the Persian Gulf War. However, with the history of the 8th Infantry Division coming to a close in the early days of January 1992, likewise would Stratman's service in Germany in the coming months.

A couple of weeks following the division's redesignation, Stratman was informed of his selection for the Army War College at Carlisle Barracks, Pennsylvania. The college was a distinction offered to few and provides graduate-level courses and instruction to senior military officers from various branches— and civilians— to help prepare them for more advanced leadership roles as general officers. Stratman had excelled in his previous duty assignments and command opportunities, thus earning good ratings on his evaluation reports. These efforts in turn helped identify his potential for senior level positions, and the academic training at the Army War College would prepare him for those senior-level assignments. In a letter to his mother dated February 14, 1992, Stratman remarked that securing a seat at the War College was more difficult than promotion to colonel since only 331 lieutenant colonels out of 5,039 eligible (6.5 percent) were slated to attend. Yet the beginning of his most recent formal military educational opportunity was still months away and he had many responsibilities to fulfill in the interim.

"My remaining months of command in Germany were busy, but we were able to get all of our equipment back to combat readiness standards in ninety days," he said. "Also, I had personnel transitions and received a new S-3 and executive officer who had to be trained. We were still moving forward because shortly after our redesignation, we had training exercises and maneuvers at Hohenfels and live-fire exercises at Grafenwoehr as part of the ARTEP (Army Training and Evaluation Program), which was a means by which to evaluate the brigade." He added, "We had many new soldiers and this was part of the certification we went through every year to ensure we were combat ready."

Based upon observations of challenges experienced during various training exercises and maneuvers, Stratman became integral in the development of the COLT (Combat Observation Lasing Teams). This independent and specially-equipped Humvee provided forward observers with mobility and long-range communications, thus enabling timely and accurate fire support for brigade and taskforce commanders. U.S. Army photograph

This recent training exercise and evaluation, combined with Stratman's observations from exercises prior to their recent deployment, influenced his desire to find the means by which to improve the communication between combined arms within the brigade structure to deliver more timely and accurate artillery fire. The field artillery elements under his command had no difficulties in shooting artillery, but oftentimes the forward observers and scouts were failing to effectively utilize available fire support resources.

"I think a lot of the scouts were not comfortable calling for artillery because they had been primarily trained to conduct reconnaissance and missed opportunities to engage targets," Stratman explained.

In the past, the pervasive practice had been for the forward observers to ride with the company commander, utilizing for communications a backpack radio with a very limited range. However, with many units drawing down after the Persian Gulf War, there was a glut of Humvees now available and Stratman was able to secure many of these surplus vehicles to be assigned to forward observers and fire support officers. This, in addition to improved communications resources, afforded him the resources to train forward observers alongside the scouts to learn the important battlefield process of calling for artillery strikes.

"The concept I named COLT, which stood for Combat Observation Lasing Team," Stratman said. "It updated and improved upon the brigade fire support paradigm since, in the past, they had clung to the Vietnam-era belief that forward observers were necessary to call for and adjust artillery fires when this should have been a combat essential task for all combat arms personnel."

The excess Humvees became COLT-ready by equipping the vehicles with an operations station with the built-in capability of interfacing with field artillery computer systems both digitally and using voice communications. It was also fitted with a targeting station that allowed the user to conduct surveillance and reconnaissance while also able to acquire targets for precision-guide munitions. During their training exercises, this highly-mobile concept helped Stratman's batteries become more deadly and combat-effective since COLT teams could quickly and accurately bring to bear artillery fires when and where the maneuver commanders wanted them. Stratman detailed in several reports to the Field Artillery School at Fort Sill, Oklahoma, the effectiveness of the COLT concept. It would be several years, he noted, before the COLT concept would enter into field artillery doctrine and become widely implemented in a combat role. It would also become a subject that he would visit again in greater depth in the coming months.

When his battalion command came to a close on June 30, 1992, the Stratman family made preparations to return stateside, having all of their belongings shipped from Germany by a moving company contracted by the U.S. Army. Jodie was still attending college in the states and their son, Jon, now graduated from high school, decided to move to Springfield, Missouri and attend Southwest Missouri State University (now Missouri State University). Stratman explained that Jon had remained close to his cousins back in Missouri and looked forward to participating in outdoor activities with them during his time off from his university studies and activities. Linda had been working hard while in Germany, in addition to her involvement in many volunteer activities, and was now looking forward to the break that the transfer to the states would offer. Additionally, her parents were now becoming elderly and this would grant her the opportunity to be located a little closer to them during their golden years.

Army War College to the Pentagon

The Army War College has beginnings dating back to November 27, 1901, when then Secretary of War Elihu Root "established the Army General Staff and Army War College to train staff officers by General Order 155. As an adjunct to the staff, the college would advise the President, devise plans, acquire information, and direct the intellectual exercise of the Army." The focus of the school later shifted to academic studies of war following World War I, and the curriculum soon evolved to share lessons learned from World War II and to prepare leaders for the unprecedented environment of the Cold War. With the fall of the Soviet Union, additional changes to the school's curriculum were introduced that included a focus on strategies of war and is now accredited to award students successfully completing the course a master's degree in strategic studies.[73]

---

[73] Army War College, *Historic Carlisle Barracks*, https://armywarcollege.edu.

This postcard shows the front of Root Hall, the main academic building for the Army War College at Carlisle Barracks. Since 1951, the college has been located at the Pennsylvania base and trains senior leaders on national security policy in addition to strategic and operational warfare principles.

The home of the college, Carlisle Barracks, has a history dating to the years before the Revolutionary War and is currently situated on a five-hundred-acre campus in the Susquehanna Valley in south-central Pennsylvania. In the years after its establishment, it became an active cavalry training location and during the Civil War was used to receive recruits, served as a supply center for Union forces and was even occupied briefly by Confederate forces. Following the Civil War, the barracks was used to provide academic and vocational training to Native Americans but after World War I, shifted into a new direction as a rehabilitation center for troops injured in the war while also playing host to a training course for soldiers assigned to the Medical Corps. Eventually, in 1951, the Army War College was relocated from its home in Washington, D.C. to its current location at Carlisle Barracks.

"When we arrived at Carlisle Barracks (in June 1992), Linda and I were given living quarters in a section of the post that was called 'Smurf Village,'" he said with a grin. "All of the homes in this area looked like Smurf houses—they were very small and had steep roofs. There may have been about a hundred or so of these small homes and I think ours was around 1,200 square feet in size, but it was large enough for just Linda and I."

Classes for the ten-month course began on July 1, 1992. Stratman recalls that one of the first actions that occurred was dividing the initially large group of students into smaller class sections of approximately thirty. Early in their cycle of classes, it became easily discernible who among them was destined to someday become a general officer. The next few months quickly passed as they completed a range of study in interesting topics pertaining to such subjects as regional strategic appraisal, military contingency planning, joint doctrine and coordination that included naval strategy and operations, collective security and peacekeeping operations, air power, and the utilization of intelligence in command-level decision-making.

"Looking back, I seem to remember a lot of the classes explored how the Pentagon functioned along with EUCOM (United States European Command) and CENTCOM (United States Central Command)," he said.[74] "Several of us already had the experience to become brigade commanders, but many of these courses showed us how to successfully operate as staff officers within combat commands in addition to support commands, such as Forces Command, which trains and provides forces to combatant commands and is where warfighting is not so much a focus. This included training on how to work assorted budgets and to understand how certain political fac-

---

[74] United States European Command (EUCOM) was established in 1952 and is currently headquartered in Stuttgart, Germany. Currently, "its area of responsibility comprises 51 countries stretching from Portugal's Azores Islands to Iceland and Israel." Federation of American Scientists, *United States European Command*, https://fas.org. United States Central Command (CENTCOM), like EUCOM, is one of the eleven unified combatant commands of the U.S. Department of Defense. With headquarters in Tampa, Florida, CENTCOM's area of responsibility (AOR) "spans more than 4 million square miles and is populated by more than 550 million people." Additionally, its AOR "sstretches from Northeast Africa across the Middle East to Central and South Asia...." U.S. Central Command, *Area of Responsibility*, https://centcom.mil.

tors can impact a military career." He added, "It was a welcome and needed break for me."

The climax of the months he spent at the War College came with the thesis that was written by each of the students about a military subject of their choosing. For Stratman, identifying a subject that he found interesting and in which he had experience was simple— the explanation and analysis of the implementation of the Combat Observation Lasing Teams (COLTs). In his thesis, it was stressed that the concept of employing these teams in a combat environment already possessed demonstrated results but had yet to become ingrained in field artillery doctrine because "budgetary and force structure constraints, competing deep and counterfire requirements, parochialism, personalities and power brokering...." Not only had Stratman demonstrated the effectiveness of integrating these teams within the brigade structure during combat maneuvers in Germany following his battalion's return from the Persian Gulf War, his thesis described several changes that would help bring the "eyes" of fire support from the company level to the task force and brigade levels while integrating observation, targeting, reconnaissance and surveillance efforts.

"It was one of those things that did not happen overnight, but a few years later, these changes were accepted by Fort Sill and the COLT teams became a widespread reality through the development of the Striker—a Humvee equipped with enhanced surveillance, target identification and designation capabilities along with updated communications."

Her husband's tenure at the War College may have only been a little more than ten months in length, but however short the period, Linda found no reason not to be gainfully employed since it afforded her the opportunities to become involved in the local community. While at Carlisle Barracks, she was hired as assistant manager at the guest house where dignitaries and senior officers stayed when visiting.

While Stratman was embroiled in classes and structuring his thesis at the U.S. Army War College, a listing came down from higher headquarters in the early weeks of 1993 denoting officers who had been selected for a brigade-level command. In Stratman's case, he had made the list but the specific command he was chosen to assume was not scheduled to "turn over" until a year following graduation from the college. As a result, in June 1993, after successfully completing the U.S. Army War College, Stratman was slated to work the next twelve months as an "Action Officer" with Headquarters Department of the Army at the Pentagon in Arlington, Virginia.

"They needed staff officers at the Pentagon, and I needed Army staff-level experience to further my professional development. Linda and I made the move from Carlisle Barracks to a townhouse near Burke, Virginia," Stratman said. "Every day, I rode the metro to and from work and the hours were horrible—often you would get to work at five or six in the morning and sometimes not leave until nine or ten at night. You really had no family time and it was quite the internal bureaucracy."

Within the sprawling Pentagon structure, comprised of what seemed to be endless directorates, Stratman soon discovered some unspoken tension since there were colonels who had not been selected for career-enhancing brigade command time, many of whom were somewhat jealous of lieutenant colonels who were slated for brigade command assignments. Overall, the nine months he spent at the Pentagon were not as personally satisfying as field assignments, but did provide him some insights into the organizational bureaucratic underpinnings and pervasive political influences within the Department of Defense and the U.S. Army.

"The section I was assigned to helped oversee the National Training Center at Fort Irwin (California) and reported the training readiness of all U.S. Army units," he recalled. "I was only there a short time and wasn't given anything important to do other than update some SOPs (standard operating procedures) for countries with whom we did mutual training. It may have not been what I wanted to do at the time, but you couldn't just sit back and say I made it ... you still had to perform. It was a duty I had to tolerate to get to my brigade level command, but I will say that one of the most rewarding aspects of my time at the Pentagon was working for then Brigadier General Eric Shinseki, who became one of my mentors," he added.[75] When speaking of Shinseki, who would later achieve the rank of four-star general and become Chief of Staff of the U.S. Army, Stratman noted, "You just never know when you meet someone, how far they will go in their career and possibly influence your own career."

Shinseki was serving as the Deputy Chief of Staff of Training and reported to the three-star general who was Deputy Chief of Staff of Operations. Although General Shinseki's executive officer was Stratman's senior rater, the two had intermittent contact; Stratman, as a lieutenant colonel, often briefed him on projects that fell under his directorship. Stratman recalls that Shinseki was aware of his battalion's stellar performance in Desert Storm and that he had been selected for a below-the-zone promotion to colonel and for a brigade command.

Stratman remarked, "My time working for him as a lieutenant colonel was the beginning of a mutual respect relationship. He and his wife Patty would stay in touch with us in later years, congratulating me and Linda on my promotions and assignments."

During his brief tenure at the Pentagon, Lieutenant Colonel Stratman intermittently reported to Brigadier General Eric Shinseki (pictured). In later years, Shinseki would rise to the rank of four-star general and serve as Chief of Staff of the U.S. Army. U.S. Army photograph

---

75 Eric Shinseki would become the first Asian-American four-star general and served as the thirty-fourth Chief of Staff of the U.S. Army. A Vietnam veteran who earned two Purple Hearts and three Bronze Star Medals, he served as the Secretary of Veterans Affairs under President Barrack Obama from 2009 to 2014.

When his tour of duty of nine months at the Pentagon came to an end in the spring of 1994, Stratman's evaluation report noted he was "(c)ompletely reliable to drive projects to completion in a particularly complex and politically-charged arena" and highlighted his continued abilities to share "critical information efficiently, ensuring prompt action by senior leaders."[76]

During a ceremony held at the Pentagon in September 1994, General Eric Shinseki assisted Linda Stratman in pinning on the rank of colonel for her recently promoted husband.

The next several weeks were busy as ever since Stratman and his wife finally had a break to enjoy some hard-earned leave followed by the process of once again assisting Linda in carefully packing up all of their belongings so they could make the move to his new brigade command assignment at Fort Riley, Kansas. Prior to departing the Pentagon, Stratman was extended the privilege of being promoted to the rank of colonel by General Shinseki on September 1, 1994. When taking a moment to reflect upon the few months he spent at the Pentagon, it was an experience that did not, at the moment, appear

---

[76] *U.S. Army Evaluation Report* for the period of July 1, 1993 to March 29, 1994.

to have been personally enriching. However, as Colonel Stratman would come to discover through the lessons of time and hindsight, it was a point in his career that bestowed upon him the opportunity to make acquaintances that would help enhance his promotion posture in later years and prepared him for some of the political implications that arose during future deployments and command assignments.

CHAPTER 8

Duty First and Peacekeeping in Bosnia

"Magnificent performance. Colonel Hank Stratman is the absolute perfect DIVARTY Commander and Division Fire Support Coordination Officer. From preparing his brigade for combat, to developing leaders for the 21ˢᵗ Century, to taking care of soldiers and their families, Hank has repeatedly demonstrated the versatility of our future senior leaders." – Major General Randolph House in his comments on Colonel Stratman's Officer Evaluation Report for the period of November 10, 1994 to November 9, 1995.

Colonel Stratman had paid his dues in the frenzied political climate of the Pentagon and was now eager to embrace the most anticipated aspect of his military experiences—brigade command. Beginning his first brigade-level command assignment with the Headquarters and Headquarters Battery for the Division Artillery for the 1st Infantry Division at Fort Riley, Kansas, Stratman was fully prepared to draw upon all of his previous military assignments in an effort to excel in his newest responsibilities. He now had to ensure that his subordinate units (consisting of two cannon artillery battalions, a Multiple Launch Rocket System battery, a target acquisition battery and a chemical company) attained and maintained a high level of material and combat readiness. It had also become increasingly clear, following the end of the Cold War and further revealed during the Persian Gulf War, that his brigade needed to maintain the posture to deploy worldwide, if and when they were called upon, while demonstrating their fire support expertise.

One of the earliest steps in his position as a brigade commander was to equip his two cannon artillery battalions with the COLT he had developed during his battalion command days. Through use of these modified Humvees, they were able to dominate in their performance when participating in training at the National Training Center at Fort Irwin, California, for large-scale battle maneuvers. The COLT proved so effective, that oftentimes the opposing forces would hunt for them during the refit/time-out phase between battles.

"One of the things that I really focused on during this time was marketing the capability of the COLT concept because it really improved the timeliness and accuracy of our fires," he recalled. "Eventually, the Field Artillery School recognized its value and bought into it, which soon led to the fielding of eight of the Stryker fire support vehicles," he added.

When Colonel Stratman was preparing to leave his brigade command at Fort Riley in late 1995, he was honored by the Field Artillery Half Section—a ceremonial unit attired in World War I era uniforms that pulled a cannon that could be fired during special activities and events.

An odd wrinkle in the fabric of the period he spent at Fort Riley was linked to the domestic terrorism activities of Timothy McVeigh, a former U.S. Army soldier who had once been stationed at Fort Riley. It was on the morning of April 19, 1995, that McVeigh "parked a rented Ryder truck in front of the Alfred P. Murrah Federal Building in downtown Oklahoma City. He was about to commit mass murder." The truck contained a bomb made from a number of chemicals and ingredients such as diesel fuel and fertilizer. Following the detonation, the death toll was 168 individuals, a depressing number that included the shocking loss of nineteen children.[77]

Buried amongst the rubble, the Federal Bureau of Investigation soon uncovered clues that revealed the Ryder truck used in the domestic terrorism attack had a vehicle identification number linked to a

---

[77] Federal Bureau of Investigation, *Oklahoma City Bombing.* https://fbi.gov.

body shop in Junction City, Kansas. These clues soon necessitated that the FBI set up a field office in the area of Junction City as they pursued their investigation to acquire McVeigh's identity. Needing a secure area, they chose nearby Fort Riley, establishing a temporary investigation site and field office in a compound that was guarded by soldiers under Stratman's command.

"It was my observation that the FBI was very fearful of the general public at this time, which, I guess, is understandable considering the circumstances," Stratman said. "They closely monitored and controlled access to the compound during the short time they were at the fort."

In May 1995, Colonel Stratman performed the Army Officer Oath of Office, when his son, Jon, was commissioned a second lieutenant through the ROTC program at Southwest Missouri State University in Springfield, Missouri.

During his command time, Stratman recalled, he remained in good company within the 1st Infantry Division since two of the officers with whom he had recently attended Army War College were now in command of sister maneuver brigades. These former classmates he considered friends, and Stratman looked forward to developing his leadership in tandem, watching as they all grew their command abilities and progressed forward in their Army careers. Normally, a brigade command assignment was slated for two years in length and, throughout his first year, Stratman strived to train his troops for the evolving threats of modern combat situations, such as those faced in the Persian Gulf War. Yet a year into the brigade command assignment, he was advised that the 1st Infantry Division was slated to move to Germany in late 1994 and, despite being a new colonel in his first brigade command, he anticipated reassignment to the Pentagon because division artillery in Germany already had a commander in place.

"That was not a prospect I was looking forward to because the Pentagon was too cliquish for my taste, along with all of its entrenched and exhaustive political networks," he said.

His brigade command time at Fort Riley was supplemented with two important events in the lives of their children. In May 1995, their son, Jon, graduated with the bachelor's degree in administrative management from Southwest Missouri State University (now Missouri State University) in Springfield. While in college, his son participated in the Reserve Officer Training

Jodie Stratman and Richard Bonett were married during a ceremony held at Fort Riley, Kansas in September 1995. This caricature of the couple was printed on the front of the bulletin provided to guests prior to the ceremony.

Corps program, just as Stratman had done more than two decades earlier at Lincoln University in Jefferson City. Colonel Stratman was able to travel to the commissioning ceremony, and was extended the privilege of conducting the Army Officer Oath of Office during his son's promotion to second lieutenant. Jon went on to spend four years in the active-duty U.S. Army with subsequent time in the Army Reserve, achieving the rank of captain.

Next came an exciting event for their daughter, Jodie, who had graduated the previous year with a bachelor's of science degree from the University of Michigan in Dearborn. She was now living in Washington, D.C., and was engaged to marry Richard Bonett, a young man from Long Island, New York, working in the commercial construction business. The Stratmans agreed to host their wedding at Fort Riley since it would be closer for Hank and Linda's family to attend while also being much more affordable. The wedding was conducted at the main post chapel and the nearby Officer's Club was rented for the reception. As had been the case with the marriage of both Hank and Linda more than two decades previous, in addition to many in the Stratman family, Hank's uncle, Father Ambrose Stratman, served as the officiant.

While living at Fort Riley, Stratman recalls that he and his wife resided in a large stone house that sat above the post parade field. He quickly recognized that the field, which was named "Artillery Parade Field" was conspicuously absent any displays that might denote its professed connection to the field artillery.

"I made the arrangements to have colonial-era cannons that my battalions fired during ceremonies on post to be displayed on the field," he said. "My daughter and family visited Fort Riley in 2015 and confirmed that the cannons were still there."

Operation Joint Endeavor - **Bosnia**

Colonel Stratman was soon approached by Major General Bill Nash, who had been his commander when his battalion was attached to the 3rd Armored Brigade during the Persian Gulf War. General Nash was now in command of the 1st Armored Division in Germany, which had been given the unenviable mission of deploying to Bosnia to enforce provisions of the Dayton Peace Agreement. Impressed with Stratman's performance and that of his battalion during the war, General Nash now wanted the colonel to assist him with an assignment that was unique not only for the division, but the U.S. Army as a whole.

Father Ambrose Stratman, Hank's uncle, was a Catholic priest and the officiant in many wedding ceremonies within the Stratman family to include Hank and Linda's marriage and that of their daughter, Jodie.

"General Nash said he wanted me to come work for him as his chief of the Joint Military Commission," said Stratman. "This was going to be part of a new peacekeeping initiative in Bosnia and something that the U.S. Army didn't want to be involved in. My division commander and the assistant division commander both advised me against accepting the assignment because they thought it would ruin my career, since this type of peacekeeping mission probably wouldn't enhance my record or my potential for getting promoted." He further explained, "But General Nash asked me for help, and I had fought for the guy in the Gulf War. I admired and respected him, and could not in good conscience decline his request to be his Division Chief for the Joint Military Commission, even though I had no idea what the job entailed."

Lieutenant General Daniel Bolger, U.S. Army retired, wrote, "… communist Yugoslavia had collapsed into a ferocious civil war with Serbs, Croats and Bosnians killing each other in great numbers." He further described the reluctance of U.S. military brass wanting to become embroiled in the conflict, noting, "The former

Yugoslavia teemed with terrorists, insurgents, 'ethnic cleansers' and militias in civil dress, factions atop factions all hungry to slay each other. It looked to be the wrong kind of war for America's armed forces."[78]

Much of the resulting bloodshed had been instigated by Slobodan Milosevic, who had served as the president of Serbia since 1989 and "took advantage of the vacuum created by a progressively weakening central state and brutally deployed the use of Serbian ultra-nationalism to fan the flames of conflict in the other republics and gain legitimacy at home."[79] Previously, there had been a cohesion in

Major General William Nash, center, commander of the 1ˢᵗ Armored Division and Colonel Stratman's senior rater during Operation Joint Endeavor, is pictured in Bosnia in January 1996, shaking hands Colonel Andrić, Chief of Staff for the Serbian Drina Corps Faction. Colonel Stratman is on the far right.

the region because of Soviet influence, but once this was removed with the collapse of communism in Eastern Europe in 1989, the former Yugoslavia dissolved into constituent states while cultural and religious differences between various ethnic groups soon led to widespread carnage and the settling of old scores dating back decades previous.

It is estimated that the war in former Yugoslavia claimed the lives of 250,000 between 1992 and 1995, inspiring the United Nations to intervene. Several nations including the United Kingdom, France,

---

[78] Bolger, *ARMY magazine*, 54.
[79] Department of State, *The Breakup of Yugoslavia*, https://history.state.gov.

Canada and the United States sent forces to help quell the slaughter that continued and also to encourage the Serb, Croat and Bosnian leaders to reach an amicable resolution. Known as the United Nations Protection Force (UNPROFOR), their primary mandate was to monitor and stabilize the situation. Stratman explained that the efforts of the UNPROFOR resulted in failure since the mandate was too limited in scope with very little military capability to compel a peaceful coexistence.

Following NATO air strikes, the Dayton Peace Agreement was signed on December 14, 1995, providing the framework for the beginnings of peace and mandating a cessation of hostilities that required the leaders of the warring parties to separate within specific zones in the next thirty days. NATO stepped in with the Implementation Force (IFOR) to compel compliance.

"When I agreed to serve under General Nash, I had two weeks to join his division in Germany," he said. "Linda decided to remain in our home at Fort Riley, where she had friends and I knew that I would only be gone for six months."

Arriving in Germany in November 1995, Colonel Stratman embarked upon the mission of serving as the special assistant for General Nash under the Joint Military Commission. The Joint Military Commission [JMC] defined and organized the meetings that took place between leaders of the warring factions in an effort to enforce the Dayton Peace Accord, disseminate the intent and instructions, and, most importantly, to resolve disagreements. The efforts of the commission fell under the auspices of the Operation Joint Endeavor, the NATO-led peace enforcement mission in Bosnia-Herzegovina. Stratman explained that it was a daunting task since he would soon be saddled with an assortment of unique responsibilities, nothing like those he had performed as a warfighter. As a component of the Implementation Force's peacekeeping mission in Bosnia, he would need to organize, train and lead brigade-level operations for the JMC under the command of "Task Force Eagle."

There wasn't any doctrine and virtually no "staff to speak of," Stratman recalled. Another challenging aspect of his upcoming assignment was receiving only a few pieces of information from a recent training exercise the task force held in Germany prior to their departure for Bosnia. Their destination was the United Nations Headquarters established at Tuzla, a large city in northeast Bosnia. Stratman accompanied, Brigadier General Stanley F. Cherrie (the assistant division commander), the division command sergeant major, a major who spoke the local language and a couple of security guards, when they attempted to fly into the airfield at Tuzla on December 15, 1995, to take over operations from the United Nations. Tom Brokaw, the renowned journalist who wrote the book *The Greatest Generation*, was also on the flight to report on the historic event. When the Air Force plane approached the airfield, the cloud cover and fog was so thick within the valley surrounded by mountains, that their aircraft was unable to land.[80]

---

[80] Raugh Jr., *Operation Joint Endeavor*, 16.

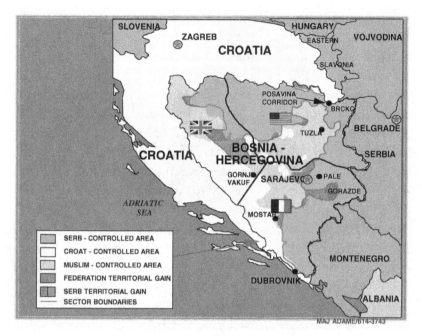

While deployed to Bosnia as part of Operation Joint Endeavor, the
Operations Section for Task Force Eagle prepared this topographic map
showing the respective sectors assigned to the U.S., French and British
forces in addition to the areas controlled by the warring parties.

"The Air Force had not certified the field yet for instrument landing," said Stratman. "After several attempts, we flew into Sarajevo and the British then flew us into Tuzla at night on one of their helicopters." Rubbing the back of his neck in an expression of disbelief at past events, he added, "It was the seventeenth day of December, and we walked up to the U.N. Headquarters that was right off the airfield in Tuzla, and it was simply a building with a U.N. vehicle sitting outside. There was only one person inside and he handed General Cherrie the keys to the building, walked out to the vehicle and drove away ... and that was the handoff we received from UNPROFOR!"[81]

---

[81] Stanley Cherrie graduated from Rutgers University in 1964 and enlisted in the U.S. Army. During his second tour in Vietnam, he lost his right leg after stepping on a land mine. Despite the disability, he remained in the United States Army and climbed through the ranks, serving in the Persian Gulf War

The next big movement in the operation was the scramble to get the airfield at Tuzla up and running to facilitate the arrival of General Nash and all of the equipment that would be needed to support their mission in the coming months. The heavy fog that had prevented their earlier landing permeated the field in the months of December and January. The Air Force had installed a radar for instrument landing but it was yet to be calibrated and certified for its intended purpose. A couple of days after Stratman and the handful of 1st Division staff took over the operations at Tuzla, the Air Force was finally able to test and certify the radar system so aircraft could begin bringing in personnel and equipment. Soon General Nash was able to fly in on a Blackhawk helicopter under the intimidating escort of two heavily-armed Apache helicopter gunships. Within a short period of time, transport aircraft began to deliver the command teams in addition to vehicles such as Humvees.

"One of the focuses of those early days was on the Sava River Bridge in northern Serbia, which was needed to bring in heavy equipment such as the M1 Abrams tanks and Bradley Fighting Vehicles," Stratman remarked, reflecting on the logistical challenges posed by the landlocked terrain of Bosnia.

The Sava River formed a border between Croatia and Bosnia and was taunting the U.S. forces by remaining at flood stage and delaying any plans for crossing. Between a medley of freezing and thawing, the effort to install a floating ribbon bridge continued to experience delays. While transport planes delivered supplies and equipment that was destined to make its way into Bosnia, engineer reconnaissance teams were focused and dedicated on making the crossing a reality as soon as climatic circumstances allowed.

"The engineers battled the icy waters and relentless rain and snow to piece together the bridge," wrote Lieutenant General Daniel Bolger. He added, "As things seemed just about done, the skies opened with a torrent. On December 28, the Sava overtopped its

---

and in Bosnia-Herzegovina. The recipient of several awards to include the Distinguished Service Medal and the Silver Star, Cherrie retired in 1998 after having achieved the rank of brigadier general. Rutgers University, *Stanley F. Cherrie*, https://alumnni.rutgers.edu.

banks, inundating the 16th Engineers' base camp. That scale of flooding on the Sava hadn't happened for 70 years," Bolger concluded.[82]

Persistence would yield the desired results, and the bridge was soon completed and busy with the traffic of the equipment of the 1st Armored Division. In the days after this arrival at Tuzla, while the soldiers of the division were busy moving equipment into Bosnia to support the expanding peacekeeping mission, Stratman was focused on working with the British Special Forces troops that had been assigned to their headquarters since they had previously worked with the leaders of the three warring factions in Bosnia. In his duties with the Joint Military Commission, at the brigade level, Stratman became immediately involved in implementing the Dayton Peace Agreement. The layout of the operations, he added, consisted in establishing a cohesive effort between the U.S. sector in the north, the British in a sector in the west toward Croatia in addition to the French sector in a southern area of what had once been Yugoslavia.

The Organization for Security and Co-operation in Europe explained that the "General Framework Agreement for Peace in Bosnia and Herzegovina, also known as the Dayton Peace Agreement (DPA), Dayton Accords, Paris Protocol or Dayton-Paris Agreement, is the peace agreement reached at Wright-Patterson Air Force Base near Dayton, Ohio … in November 1995, and formally signed in Paris on 14 December 1995." The accords helped usher a resolution to three and a half years of war that had consumed the former Socialist Federative Republic of Yugoslavia. Article I of the fifty-eight-page agreement noted the warring parties "shall fully respect the sovereign equality of one another, shall settle disputes by peaceful means, and shall refrain from any action, by threat or use of force or otherwise, against the territorial integrity or political independence of Bosnia and Herzegovina or any other State."[83]

Stratman explained, "The warring parties were within rifle range of one another and had become accustomed to fighting in the

---

[82] Bolger, *America Takes on Difficult Mission in Balkans*, 56.
[83] Organization for Security and Co-operation in Europe, *Dayton Peace Agreement*, https://osce.org.

previous three or four years," he recalled. "They had managed to establish entrenched fighting positions in this mountainous, rural area of the country, and they had employed mines along the perimeters in several areas." Boldly, he added, "It was an ugly place and, as I mentioned before, the accords called for separation of the parties within thirty days, which was going to be no easy task."

Major Eugene Maggioncalda, a deputy of the Military Commission Office who had previous experience as a Yugoslavian foreign area officer, noted, "There's no U.S. manual on JMC (Joint Military Commission) that I'm aware of. There have been a lot of studies and research and on-the-ground experience but no compilation of it into one coherent pattern."[84]

The implementation of the Joint Military Commission in the Bosnian theater of operations occurred at five levels of commands— the lowest was the company level, followed by battalion, brigade, division and finally, at the zenith, was the theater and corps level. Each of these echelons, Stratman recalled, had specific duties and responsibilities as part of Operation Joint Endeavor and the implementation of the Dayton Peace Agreement. Assigned to the Joint Military Commission at the division level, Colonel Stratman had a bevy of duties that introduced him to the unique challenges of peace enforcement. Learning to comprehend, analyze and integrate complicated political and military aspects of their peacekeeping operations, Stratman was walking on new ground since he had to develop policies and procedures to help compel compliance among the warring factions. Other times he was deeply involved assisting the commanding general in preparing correspondence and the planning and facilitation of bilateral and joint negotiations with Muslim, Croat and Serb corps commanders. Additionally, with United Kingdom special forces troops attached along with support from Russian Nordic and Turkish brigades, Stratman had to integrate into his operations, friendly forces from varying cultural backgrounds and possessing differing military competencies, while at the same time supervising six field-grade officers.

---

[84] Roache, *The Talon*, 5.

"Communication was a key aspect of my daily duties because I had to pass down through our chain of command, to our brigades, the specifics of our daily mission so we all shared the same voice when working with the warring factions," he said. "An inconsistent message might cause one of the parties to lose faith in the peace process or believe that you favored another party. Honestly, many of us were reluctant at first because we were warfighters, and peacekeeping missions weren't part of our military vocabulary, but we were there to perform the mission that we had been given. Failure was not an option."

The communication process was aided by the translation assistance of two U.S. soldiers—one a former citizen of Yugoslavia whose father had worked for Josip Broz Tito, the former president of the Socialist Federal Republic of Yugoslavia. Tito gained great popularity and has been praised for "turning Yugoslavia into one of the most prosperous communist countries," however, there was a darker side to his legacy as many "critics highlight his jailing of political dissidents and his repression of the historical grievances between communities that surged back with a vengeance in the 1990s."[85] Approximately a decade following his death, there unfolded the descent of Tito's beloved country into a bloody civil war. Not only would the translation assistance of this soldier lend a presence at the peace conferences that provided a living connection to a more stable and beloved past, it also bequeathed the American forces a translator able to effectively communicate between the warring factions.

One of the earliest steps of the peace process was establishing what was designated as "Zones of Separation (ZOS)" between the warring parties, and to begin the process of pushing them away from one another. These zones were structured to extend approximately two kilometers on either side of cease-fire lines that had been agreed upon at Dayton, Ohio, weeks earlier. The Bradley Fighting Vehicles and Abrams tanks that had been brought across the Sava River were used to enforce the ZOS with checkpoints established to discourage the parties from any attempts to engage in any renewed hostile

---

[85] Barron's. *Grandson Reveals Late 'Regret' of Yugoslavia's Tito*, https://barons.com.

actions. Stratman noted that Abrams tanks were often stationed on hills overlooking the various checkpoints with their gun turrets aimed toward high traffic areas, providing a level of intimidation that ensured any planned skirmishing did not become a reality.

"Little by little, we began to push the warring parties away from one another," said Stratman. Then, the next phase was disarmament. Following that, we had to encourage the factions to remove mines from the area and eliminate all of the munitions hazards, which proved to be quite challenging since the former Yugoslavia had been one of the biggest producers of munitions for the Soviet Union." He added, "The U.S. was prohibited from any of the demining activities because the United Nations had that mission."

President Bill Clinton visited U.S. troops supporting the peacekeeping operations in Bosnia as part of Operation Joint Endeavor on January 14, 1996. U.S. Army photograph

Security in the region reached its crescendo on January 14, 1996, when President Bill Clinton packed a day full of visits to troops in Bosnia, Italy, Hungary and Croatia. Following his arrival at the tarmac in Tuzla, Clinton spoke to 850 American soldiers, praising them as "the veterans of Tuzla mud" who had worked alongside "NATO troops in rain and flood to lay the groundwork for the fragile peacekeeping mission," reported the *Daily News* on January 14, 1996. The article also explained, "(President Clinton) noted the struggle to build a bridge across the Sava River, and said 2,000 vehicles have rolled across it in the last two weeks." During his trip, the president was accompanied by Stratman's supervisor and the commander of U.S. forces in Bosnia, Major General William Nash. General Nash stressed to the president, "Sir, we are committed to do our duty and we will succeed."[86]

Reflecting on the president's visit, Stratman remarked, "While the president was visiting Tuzla, we provided him with presentations on the implementation of the Dayton Peace Agreement. He appeared uneasy and somewhat disinterested in our military operations and did not stay very long in Tuzla. When the commanding general took the president back to the airfield to fly out, I went down to the office of the commanding general to visit with his aide about an issue. There was a middle-aged man waiting in his office wearing civilian clothes … nice western attire."

Stratman took a few moments to himself in an attempt to search his memory and determine the gentleman's identity, since he looked familiar and was perhaps Secret Service; however, he was soon overcome by curiosity and asked the man, 'Who are you?'

"He looked at me rather shocked and responded, 'Why I'm Dan Rather.' He looked to be somewhat hurt that I didn't recognize who he was," Stratman laughed. "He had been waiting there to interview General Nash, so I did a little tap-dancing to cover up not knowing who he was by inviting him to visit with my staff while he waited for the general to return." Grinning, Stratman added, "My apology to him was that I was so busy with our peacekeeping mission that I didn't really have time to watch television, which was certainly the truth."

At Fort Riley, Linda Stratman experienced some of her own unexpected, yet interesting, moments during her husband's overseas deployment. When she was not engaged in volunteering with the local Red Cross chapter or assisting in the organization of community fundraisers, she and a couple of military spouses with whom she had become friends, often walked and jogged along a small trail that that had been created around the NCO Club on post. During one of their outings, Linda spotted some plants that had the appearance of something she had seen in pictures.

---

[86] The January 14, 1996 edition of the *Daily News* (New York, New York).

"We were jogging early on morning and the light was coming up," Linda recalled. "I spotted these plants and asked one of my friends what they were. She said she didn't know but I told her they looked a lot like marijuana plants; they both just laughed me off," she added.

A short time later, one of the spouses told a military policeman whom she knew about the plants, and it turned out Linda's suspicions were confirmed—there was a healthy patch of marijuana plants growing on Fort Riley. She was later informed that in the months prior to the discovery, word had reached some soldiers stationed on the base that there was going to be a raid of their residences by military policemen. Before they were caught with the illegal plants they were growing; they decided to dump them behind the NCO Club and the seeds soon took root and spread.

Back in Bosnia, dignitary visits provided Colonel Stratman opportunities to brief the mission and continued success of U.S. troops in Bosnia. On February 3, 1996, an entourage including Secretary of State William Christopher and Secretary of Defense William Perry, were accompanied by General George Joulwan, the commander-in-chief of the United States European Command. The group was there to visit with U.S. soldiers involved in the peacekeeping mission in addition to Secretary Christopher's visit with Alija Izetbegović, President of Bosnia and Herzegovina and Slobodan Milošević, president of Yugoslavia.

"While giving them the briefing on our mission and measures of success, Secretary Christopher asked me, 'Where did you learn to do this?' At first, I was kind of shocked by the question but responded by telling him that's what the military does, we solve problems and make it happen."

The peacekeeping mission faced many challenges, but Stratman notes that, although regrettable, the division lost only one soldier. Stratman reiterated that it was not the mission of the U.S. to remove or disarm the deadly mines that were sprinkled across the region. Sadly, this became a prohibition that one soldier chose to ignore. Sergeant First Class Donald A. Dugan, disobeying orders, attempted to defuse a mine that had been pointed out to him by a local Bosnian family. Not being trained on the intricacies of mine disarmament, Dugan inadvertently triggered the device and was killed instantly in the resulting explosion.

Colonel Hank Stratman shakes hands when greeting First Lady Hillary Rodham Clinton on her visit to see the operations in Tuzla on March 25, 1996.

"That situation prompted a crackdown on all of the U.S. soldiers in Bosnia to make sure they didn't try the same thing, and themselves become casualties," Stratman stressed.

A senior representative of one of the warring factions who was party to the Dayton Agreement was not overwhelmingly appreciative of Colonel Stratman's dedication to the enforcement of the various nuances of the agreement. On January 21, 1996, an interesting letter was sent to General Michael Walker—the British general commanding NATO's Allied Rapid Reaction Corps (ARRC) Headquarters in Sarajevo since his deployment to the Balkans in 1995—from General Ratko Mladic, a Bosnian Serb who had served as the commander of the former Yugoslav People's Army and was at the time the chief of staff of Army of the Republika Srpska (Bosnian Serb forces). In his letter, Mladic claimed that he had been informed that Colonel Stratman was "demanding from them to submit the most detailed information concerning their respective areas" and that it was his belief the colonel "does not have the authority to give new tasks concerning this issue…."

When reflecting on the letter, Stratman affirmed, "General Walker told me to keep it up because we were doing what we were supposed to do in order to compel compliance with the terms of the Dayton Agreement. In fact, we had placed the same requirements on all parties involved in the peace process." As affirmation that he was performing his military duties as expected, Stratman was proud to have received this complaint from Mladic.

In an interesting twist of fate, Ratko Mladic, who had complained about Stratman's efforts, was arrested and, in 2017, convicted of war crimes and genocide by the International Criminal Tribunal, receiving the sentence of life imprisonment. Known as the "Butcher of Bosnia," Mladic's crimes against humanity unfolded during "the blood-soaked breakup of Yugoslavia in the 1990s." A year-long siege of Sarajevo resulted in an estimated 10,000 dead while Mladic's forces were reportedly responsible for "8,000 Muslim men and boys as young as 12 (who) were herded to the slaughter, their bodies tossed into mass graves." [87]

High profile situations continued to define much of Stratman's service in Bosnia since only a few weeks after the visit of President Bill Clinton, the division welcomed other guests of international notoriety—First Lady Hillary Rodham Clinton and her sixteen-year-old daughter Chelsea. While visiting the operations in Tuzla on March 25, 1996, Clinton and her daughter visited with the soldiers of Task Force Eagle and delivered "hundreds of long-distance phone cards, dozens of movie videos and 22 boxes of donated toys for soldiers to distribute to local children." Prior to her arrival in Bosnia, Clinton had traveled to Baumholder, Germany, and visited with the children and spouses of many of the deployed soldiers.

---

[87] November 23, 2017 edition of the *Los Angeles Times*.

Stratman said, "Although President Clinton hadn't appeared to be genuinely interested in what we were doing in Bosnia, Mrs. Clinton and her daughter seemed quite engaged and asked a lot of questions about our operations."

The next few weeks remained as busy as the previous while Stratman continued to assist in the coordination of meetings and conferences between members of the former warring parties. Throughout the entire peace process, Stratman affirmed, the Serbs, Muslims and Croats were treated the same and there were not any favorites in the peace process. As he recalled, the key to their success was to treat everyone fairly; however, this achievement would be compromised by a subordinate officer who later caused Stratman a delay in receiving a hard-earned promotion.

"I had a reserve lieutenant colonel assigned from the Pentagon to my commission about two months into my assignment," said Stratman. "He thought he knew it all and was pro-Bosnian, and many of his actions revealed that. We had to maintain an environment of impartiality between the parties involved in the peace process. Since this colonel didn't respond to counseling, I had to relieve him." Stratman added, "He was obviously angry over being relieved and told me, 'You'll never make general officer … I'll see to that!'" Little credence was lent to this threat and Stratman continued to focus on the mission before him.

Regardless of the distractions that came from some of the personnel issues with which Stratman had to contend during the deployment, the accomplishment of his peacekeeping duties remained his primary focus. A sad moment arose when U.S. Secretary of Commerce Ronald H. Brown accompanied a delegation of business executives to explore business opportunities in the war-torn region. Brown had become the first African-American to hold the commerce secretary position when appointed by President Clinton in 1993. Sadly, on April 3, 1996, he was killed when his plane crashed into a mountain near Dubrovnik, Croatia. General Nash's operations center coordinated locating the wreckage and the extrication of the remains.

Stratman tirelessly toiled to get everything organized and his staff properly trained before he handed over his position to Colonel

David Fastabend in the latter part of May 1996. In the evaluation of Colonel Stratman's performance in Bosnia, Major General Nash glowingly wrote, "His willingness to coach, mentor, share assets and advice made (the) brigade level joint commissions more successful. One of the keys to Joint Endeavor success," Nash concluded.

In a farewell note to Colonel Stratman, Brigadier General Stan Cherrie wrote, "Best of luck in the future, to my top teammate, and fellow ZOS (Zone of Separation) warrior!"

Summarizing a peace-keeping mission that had been packed with several months of new and never-before-experienced assignments and interactions, Stratman, in his modest, no-nonsense and direct style of communication, remarked, "It was a non-standard mission but we managed to do it right."

CHAPTER 9

Promotion to General Officer

"Great potential for senior command. Promote to brigadier general. Assign as an Assistant Division Commander. More stars to follow." –Major General William Nash in his comments on Colonel Stratman's Officer Evaluation Report for the period covering his service in Bosnia with the Joint Military Commission.

A joint assignment was one of the blocks that needed to be checked if Colonel Stratman were going to acquire the necessary background and experience to be considered as a candidate for promotion to brigadier general. This assignment came in the form of his transfer to the Defense Security Assistance Agency in the latter days of May 1996. The agency was commanded by Lieutenant General Thomas Rhame, who had served as the commander of the 1ˢᵗ Infantry Division in Operation Desert Shield/Storm. Initially slated to fulfill the role of Deputy Director of Operations for the Middle East, Asia and North Africa Directorate, he worked with a team that coordinated foreign military sales to allies of the United States. His staff consisted of a few long-term civilian government employees who understood assorted U.S. policies toward any given country through coordination with such entities as the State Department, National Security Council, military departments, and congressional staffers.

"It was certainly interesting because we had to make sure that equipment being sold had been approved for technology release," he said. "There were also political considerations, especially when it came to ensuring a specific nation wanting to purchase items from us were not prohibited from doing so because of terrorist activities or that it might violate U.S. national security objectives."

When beginning this assignment, he and Linda leased a townhouse in Springfield, Virginia, which was accessible by the Metro (Washington Metropolitan Area Transit

During his assignment with the Defense Security Assistance Agency, Stratman worked for Lieutenant General Thomas G. Rhame. Years earlier, General Rhame commanded the 1ˢᵗ Infantry Division during the Persian Gulf War. U.S. Army photograph

Authority) so Stratman could easily make the trip to and from his office. The location of their new home was fortuitous since their daughter and son-in-law lived only a short distance away. On July 31, 1996, they joyously welcomed into the world their first grand-child, a boy named Richard (Richie) Francis Bonett Jr. During the Christmas holiday of 1997, their second grandchild was born, a girl named Eucolona. Hank and Linda invited their daughter and her family to celebrate the holidays at their new home. It was then that the grandparents noticed something slightly amiss with the eighteen-month-old Richie's health, who seemed to appear rather listless.

Stratman explained, "We encouraged Jodie to get him checked out by a doctor and he was diagnosed with aplastic anemia—his immune system had shut down. They ended up putting a stint in his heart and he almost died. Jodie had to make a decision on his treatment and researched a number of doctors and treatment options—both clinically tested and experimental," he added.

Richie, left, the first-born grandchild of Hank and Linda Stratman, is pictured in late 1997 with his younger sister, Lona.

Hank and Linda were able to get out of the lease for their townhouse and moved in with their daughter and son-in-law to provide some assistance with household chores and other associated domestic tasks for the remainder of time he was assigned to the Defense Security Assistance Agency.

"The only real cure they noted for our grandson was a bone marrow transplant," said Stratman. "Jodie and our son-in-law Richard had their daughter, Eucolona (which was Linda's birth name in German), because a sibling might be the best DNA match. Unfortunately, she wasn't a match for her brother. As time passed and they continued to look for a medical solution, they had another son, Andrew, who turned out to be a perfect DNA match."

Jodie worked diligently to study and identify all medical treatment options available for her young son, locating a doctor in whom she placed a significant amount of trust. Utilizing an experimental stem cell treatment, Stratman recalls that the doctor was able to reverse their grandson's immune deficiency after about six months, and has since been in remission, never requiring the bone marrow transplant from his younger brother.

While in the middle of searching for a medical solution for their grandson, another difficult moment arose with the passing of Linda's adoptive father, John Deakins, on January 12, 1997. Making the trip back to Missouri, Hank and Linda were present when the seventy-five-year-old U.S. Army veteran was laid to rest in the Dripping Springs Christian Church Cemetery in the community of Columbia, where he and his wife had resided for the last several years.

"They had built a home near Columbia to be closer to family because two of his sons were employed as police officers there," said Stratman. "He had been in failing health for some time since he had suffered a brain aneurism and later developed Alzheimer's." He continued, "During the Korean War, he commanded an all-Black mobile assault hospital unit. At his funeral, his honor guard from Fort Leonard Wood—through happenstance—was comprised of all black soldiers, which was a fitting final tribute."

Returning to the East Coast, the next few weeks were quite busy with his military duties while Linda continued to help her daughter and son-in-law around the home. In April 1997, Colonel Stratman had the unexpected pleasure of returning to Missouri to receive an honor from his alma mater linked to his many years of dedicated service in the U.S. Army. The Military Department at Lincoln University holds an induction ceremony for individuals commissioned through their Army ROTC program who "best exemplify the ideals of Lincoln University, the concepts of the University Oath and who have upheld the Army Values by high achievements and valuable contributions for the betterment of the community, Lincoln University, the nation and themselves." [88]

Colonel Hank Stratman is pictured with his mother, Mary, during his induction into the Hall of Fame of Lincoln University's Military Science Department at Jefferson City, Missouri in April 1997.

Stratman was one of three colonels inducted into the university's hall of fame during a ceremony in Jefferson City, Missouri on April 19, 1997. His sisters and mother made the trip to the university to support their brother during the receipt of the coveted honor. When asked to speak to the attendees, primarily the cadets still coming up through ROTC program, Colonel Stratman explained that his experience at Lincoln University, more than two decades earlier, helped to form and cultivate within him traits related to self-discipline, competitive spirit, teamwork, and leadership.

---

[88] Lincoln University, *ROTC Hall of Fame Induction Ceremony*, https://lincoln. edu.

Additionally, he added, it provided the environment where he learned what it meant to be a minority while attending the historically black university.

"... I learned to measure a man's worth by his character and performance and not by the color of his skin," he remarked to those in attendance. "Good leaders in the Army treat all soldiers with dignity and respect." He added, "Soldiering is not just a job—it's a calling to serve this great country. The motto of the First Infantry Division says it best: 'No mission too difficult. No sacrifice too great. Duty first!' Commit this simple but powerful slogan to memory and let it be the basis for your actions. Good luck cadets and best wishes for a great career!"

The month following his honor at Lincoln University, Stratman was moved from the position of Deputy Director of Operations with the Defense Security Assistance Agency to the new role of Principal Deputy Director. His additional responsibilities for the next four months included working with twenty-five joint service military and civilian personnel that assisted with the coordination of $70 billion in arms transfers to sixty-five countries that supported U.S. national security objectives. His senior rater, Lieutenant General Michael S. Davison Jr., remarked of Colonel Stratman's performance: "My best of eight joint billet colonels in this agency.... A natural leader with exceptional political-military skills and commitment to excellence."[89]

While with the Defense Security Assistance Agency, Stratman was given the assignment by his three-star boss to develop a new name for the agency since some of the country's allies took offense to the word "assistance" in the agency's title.

Within less than a day of pondering this new responsibility, Stratman concluded the agency should use the word "cooperation" instead of "assistance" in its title. At the time this was all unfolding, the song *YMCA* remained a popular song, and since the abbreviation for Defense Security Cooperation Agency [DSCA] rhymed with the song, the name change became and easy sell and approved by

---

[89] *U.S. Army Evaluation Report* for the rating period of May 22, 1997 to September 30, 1997.

the Secretary of Defense without reservation. The new designation of Defense Security Cooperation Agency was now established and became well received by the nation's allies.

His period of a joint assignment was not only interspersed with the death of this father-in-law and the challenges regarding his grandson's health, but also included his undergoing the detailed process of consideration for promotion to brigadier general. Stratman explained that boards for officer promotions, up to and including the rank colonel, were completed using a secret ballot. For promotion to brigadier general, it consisted of an open forum for discussion, publicly summarizing the strengths and potential of colonels under consideration. The key to promotion to the level of one-star general, Stratman maintained, was performance-based—having the right mixture of challenging duty assignments in one's file while conducting oneself professionally and insightfully in the execution of those duties.

Fortunately for Stratman, two of his former senior officers were members of the brigadier general board. The first was Major General John Pickler, for whom he had worked at 3rd Corps Artillery when Stratman was only a major and who accepted him for assignment as an operations officer with the 8th Infantry Division in Germany. The second was Major General Bill Nash, the 3rd Armored Division commander in Desert Storm and Stratman's boss during his first deployment to Bosnia. Reflecting on the composite of the promotion board, Stratman explained that decisions matter in the course of one's career because had he not accepted Nash's request to deploy to Bosnia, he would not have been selected for general officer. Major General Pickler was able to validate Stratman's field artillery expertise while Major General Nash confirmed his fire support performance in combat and his potential for increased levels of responsibility.

"In my earlier deployment to Bosnia, there was a colonel that I had to relieve from my staff because he was biased in his performance. When he was reassigned, he told me that he would make sure that I would never receive promotion to brigadier general." Stratman continued, "He filed a complaint when I was up for the promotion board, claiming that I was biased against him because he was a reservist and not active duty."

Part of the process, Stratman recalled, consisted of an investigation into the merits of the complaint. When the initial list came out for promotions to brigadier general, Stratman's name was not on the list. Fortunately, many of the senior officers involved in the promotion review process realized the lack of merit in the complaint that had been filed, and advised Stratman to "sit tight, it will all work out."

He said, "It really took the wind out of our sails because I had worked so hard for this and always strived to perform the mission in the most competent way. But when the investigation was concluded and I was back-briefed on the results— the allegations were clearly unfounded and everyone that had been interviewed spoke highly of my leadership and potential; even the investigating officer remarked, 'I want to work for you someday.' This lieutenant colonel was simply being vindictive and essentially delayed announcement of my promotion by a few months," Stratman added.

Colonel Stratman became the first and only colonel who worked at the Defense Security Cooperation Agency to be selected as a general officer.

Brigadier General

On July 1, 1998, Colonel (Promotable) Stratman assumed the position of Assistant Division Commander—Support for the 3rd Infantry Division, whose headquarters was at Fort Stewart, Georgia. The position was being vacated through the transfer of Brigadier General (Promotable) Alfred A. Valenzuela, who had been Captain Stratman's supervisor years earlier during his assignment in Korea. In this new assignment, Stratman received his initial exposure to the larger support structure but with a new emphasis in power projections, logistics and sustainment. The 3rd Infantry Division, he explained, was part of the 18th Airborne Corps and was considered a rapid deployment force that could quickly respond to emerging threats anywhere in the world.

"There was certainly a lot to learn because I had been a field artillery and fire support expert, but when you become a general officer, you have a to broaden your competencies well beyond your basic branch qualifications," he said. "With our mission, we had to ensure a high standard of preparedness and training to be able to rapidly deploy worldwide and on short notice."

The rapid deployment component of their mission consisted of several tiers that included having a company ready to deploy within twenty-two hours, a battalion combat team within forty-eight hours and a bridgade ready force prepared to set sail in seventy-two hours. Part of Stratman's responsibilities were to make sure the division's personnel and sustaining materiel were coordinated and prepared for movement by land, sea, or air. Referred to as "Strategic Power Projection," it was a mechanism by which rapid

Stratman, left, is pictured with his wife, Linda, and William Webster during both soldiers' promotions to brigadier general at Fort Stewart, Georgia, on November 2, 1998. Webster, a graduate of West Point, served with Stratman multiple times during his career.

deployment was executed through cooperation with several military installations under the umbrella of the overall National Military Strategy.[90] Fort Stewart, and Fort Benning, Georgia, are in a region

[90] The National Military Strategy (NMS) "was established by precedent in the Goldwater-Nichols Department of Defense Reorganization Act of 1986 (Public Law 99-433), which charges the Chairman of the Joint Chiefs of Staff, the President, and the Secretary of Defense with providing strategic direction for the armed forces. The Chairman of the Joint Chiefs of Staff produces the NMS based on consultation with the Combatant Commanders and members of the Joint Chiefs of Staff. It serves as a strategic framework for how the armed forces

that has quick access to multiple modes of transportation needed to deploy in addition to the facilities and resources that can facilitate the transport and storage of significant amounts of resources and equipment that might be unique to rapidly deploying forces. The deployment "nodes" consisted of a network of such components as an ammunition supply point, general purpose warehouse, container handling facility, rail marshallin~ ~~~~ ~~~ ~~ ~~~~~~~~.

He explained, "The division had an infantry brigade at Fort Benning and there were two armored brigades at Fort Stewart, and an aviation brigade with attack lift helicopters. (Although not in his direct chain of command, there was also an Army Ranger battalion and a Joint Special Operations helicopter battalion stationed at Hunter Army Airfield, of which he had oversight.) "Linda and I lived at a small officers housing area on Hunter Army Airfield near Savannah, Georgia, which was a good hour and fifteen-minute drive from Fort Stewart.[91] Fortunately, I was often able to get a Blackhawk (helicopter) flight to work, and that worked out quite well because it only took about ten minutes to get to Fort Stewart and our pilots and crews required the flight time."

The 3ʳᵈ Infantry Division, whose patch is pictured, earned the nickname "Rock of the Marne" for their distinguished combat performance in the face of a major German assault during the Aisne-Marne Offensive in World War I.

---

will execute the overall policy goals laid out in the most recent National Security Strategy and National Defense Strategy. Office of the Secretary of Defense, *National Military Strategy*, https://history.defense.gov.

[91] Hunter Army Airfield was identified by the National Aeronautics and Space Administration as an alternate landing site for the Space Shuttle missions.

Within thirty days of beginning his new assignment, Stratman noted that an aviation tragedy occurred that had major consequences for some of his fellow senior-level officers in command positions. The aviation brigade was augmenting the Drug Enforcement Agency as part of a counterdrug mission in the Bahamas. The previous command climate allowed some of the pilots to bring their spouses down for a week or two, as a vacation of sorts. However, on one occasion, a pilot and his co-pilot decided to take their wives on a Blackhawk helicopter for a joyride.

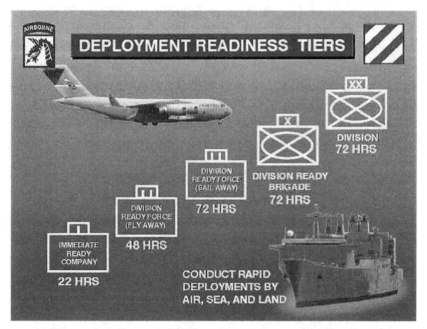

This visual shows the deployment readiness tiers for the 3rd Infantry Division. At the time of Stratman's service as the Assistant Division Commander—Support, they had the mission of deploying to a contingency area by air, land or sea, to conduct mobile, combined arms offensive and defensive operations worldwide.

"As the sun began to set over the Bahamas ... two experienced U.S. Army pilots, apparently treating their wives to an unauthorized ride over the deep blue waters, crashed their Black Hawk helicopter," reported the *Washington Times* on July 8, 1998. "The two women were killed and the three male crew members seriously injured, defense officials said yesterday."[92]

Stratman noted, "The pilots were court-martialed, and the battalion commander was relieved of his duty," Stratman remarked. "There was a big investigation, but fortunately, both I and the aviation brigade commander were brand new and unaware of the spousal visit policy. It was ugly. The entire incident did not have any bearing on me professionally, but we tightened up the standards and expectations for our aviation personnel."

The date of November 2, 1998 was a memorable occasion for Stratman for a couple of reasons. First, it was on this date that he, along with Colonel William Webster, the Assistant Division Commander for Maneuver, received the much-anticipated promotion to the rank of brigadier general.[93] What made the moment even more special for Hank and Linda was their son, Jon, served as the platoon leader of the Field Artillery platoon that fired the ceremonial thirteen-round salute during the promotion ceremony. When given a moment to make a few remarks after he was pinned with the rank of one-star general, Stratman said, "Linda and I are extremely honored by this opportunity to serve in the 'Rock of the Marne' Division as its Power Projection and Force Sustainment Assistant Division Commander. We join the Marne team well rested and eager to take on new challenges and responsibilities that await us at Fort Stewart, Fort Benning and Hunter (Army Airfield), and wherever this great division is deployed in support of national security objectives." General Stratman went on to pledge his "undaunting loyalty, dedication to soldiering, and a staunch commitment to excellence in every endeavor—large or small."

---

[92] July 8, 1998 edition of the *Washington Times*.

[93] William G. Webster later became the commander of the 3rd Infantry Division and concluded his military service as Deputy Commander of United States Northern Command and Vice Commander of the United States Element, North American Aerospace Defense Command. Webster retired in 2011 at the rank of lieutenant (three-star) general. During Operation Iraqi Freedom, Major General Stratman again served with Webster as deputy commanding general of operations for Third Army.

Like she had done during many of her husband's previous military assignments, Linda chose to remain actively involved at the local level by volunteering with the Red Cross at Fort Stewart. Additionally, she participated in planning functions with the division's wives' club while also supporting an array of fundraisers. She also assisted in teaching citizenship classes for soldiers of the division (and oftentimes their spouses) who were going through the naturalization process as part of the pathway to U.S. citizenship, which could be accelerated through their service in the military.

General Stratman had knowledge and experience in working with infantry, armor, and artillery, but in his new assignment, he quickly gained an in-depth understanding of integrating aviation assets into the combined arms environment. He also acquired critical knowledge in utilization of such resources as supply, fuel, and maintenance assets at the division support command level. One component of the division's worldwide deployment capabilities included maintaining a forward deployed headquarters in Kuwait. Since the end of the Persian Gulf War, the division maintained a battalion in the Middle East that helped train and prepare the Kuwaiti military for any developing threats in the region.

In the fall of 1998, Saddam Hussein announced that Iraq would no longer cooperate with weapons inspectors from the United Nations. These inspectors were part of the United Nations Special Commission (UNSCOM), which had been established after the end of the Persian Gulf War in 1991. The UNSCOM operated under the following mandate: "…to carry out immediate on-site inspections of Iraq's biological, chemical and missile capabilities; to take possession for destruction, removal or rendering harmless of all chemical and biological weapons and all stocks of agents and all related sub-systems and components and all research, development, support and manufacturing facilities; to supervise the destruction by Iraq of all its ballistic missiles with a range greater than 150 km and related major parts, and repair and production facilities; and to monitor and verify Iraq's compliance with its undertaking not to use, develop, construct or acquire any of the items specified above." [94]

---

[94] United Nations Special Commission, *Mandate*, https://un.org.

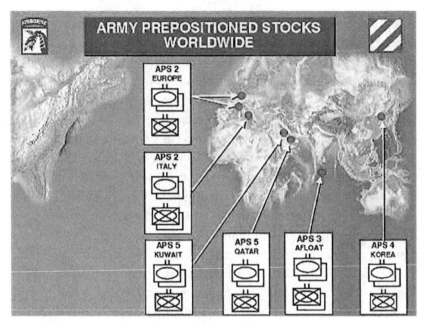

Stratman maintains that an important part of his experience with the 3rd Infantry Division was acquiring knowledge about prepositioned stocks. Army Prepositioned Stocks consist of equipment sets such as tanks and armored vehicles strategically positioned in climate-controlled facilities worldwide. According to Stratman, knowledge of these stocks was important during his deployment to the Middle East during Operation Iraqi Freedom.

Hussein's act of defiance caused great alarm among the international community, heralding to the world that the dictator intended to rebuild his chemical weapon capabilities while also potentially developing the country's nuclear capabilities. Apprehensions reemerged since he might then use these destructive capabilities against neighboring nations. On some occasions, Hussein even ordered the removal and destruction of documents related to weapons resources and development programs prior to inspections by UNSCOM representatives.

"Saddam was giving us all kinds of problems during this time and had also been violating no-fly zones, threatening to shoot down our planes," said Stratman. "What unfolded was 'Operation Desert Thunder.'"

This operational mission, which covered the period of January 24, 1998 to December 15, 1998, evolved in response to Iraqi threats to shoot down aircraft performing reconnaissance under the auspices of UNSCOM. Within a short period of time, "troops from 11 countries, including Canada, deployed to Kuwait in a show of force."[95]

Stratman explained, "In early November (1998), I was deployed to Camp Doha in Kuwait as the lead element to establish the logistical infrastructure for the introduction of the 3rd Infantry Division into the region. Upon my arrival, I went to the forward headquarters to report to the 3rd Army Commander, Lieutenant General Tommy Franks. I informed him of who I was … that I was representing the 3rd Infantry Division, told him what we were doing to support his mission and then asked him what his expectations were for us."

Less than two years following this initial encounter, General Franks achieved the rank of four-star general and went to finish out his military career as Commander of the United States Central Command. General Franks had served with the field artillery during the Vietnam War and was an Assistant Division Commander with the 1st Cavalry Division in the Persian Gulf War. He had heard about Stratman's performance in the Persian Gulf War, and bluntly advised Stratman that what he had in mind for him was an entirely different type of mission, one that would bequeath him with a unique set of responsibilities.

"He looked at me and replied, 'Stratman, you're my land component commander.' That immediately quadrupled my responsibilities because then I would have been given oversight of all land components including the Marines and coalition partners."

Although there had been a significant buildup of land, sea, and air forces in the region, the threat soon subsided because of effective coalition air strikes against Iraqi military targets. Within two weeks after his arrival, it was determined there would be no need to deploy the 3rd infantry Division since ground forces were not deemed

---

[95] Government of Canada, *Operation Desert Thunder I and II*, https://canada.ca.

necessary. Shortly thereafter, Stratman returned to his duties at Fort Stewart.

"While I was in Kuwait, I believe I had three or four meetings with General Franks," said Stratman. "I really liked him; he was a straight-shooter and, as a general officer, knew how to lead. He was often considered a maverick because, like me," Stratman paused, "he wanted you to give him the mission and then get the hell out of the way. He had a great reputation as a warfighter."[96]

The next months were a medley of training exercises and planning sessions to ensure the division maintained its worldwide deployment capabilities. In June 1999, he received notice that he was slated for a second deployment to Bosnia. Each assignment, with increasing levels of responsibility, drew a little deeper upon the specialized training he had received earlier in his career, providing him with a broader understanding of the "big picture" in the nation's ability to both wage war and, at times, enforce and implement protocols for peacekeeping.

Reflecting on the time spent with the "Rock of the Marne," Stratman noted, "I gained an in-depth understanding of our military's Power Projection capability, and the extensive training that is necessary to rapidly deploy a division-sized force in a short timeframe. This," he unflinchingly added, "became knowledge that I would use when setting up the theater posture in Kuwait for Third Army and Operation Iraqi Freedom."

---

[96] Stratman explained that more information on the military story of General Tommy Franks, specifically that related to his time with U.S. Central Command, can be found in the book *American Soldier*.

CHAPTER 10

Stabilization Force in Bosnia

General Stratman arrived at Sarajevo, Bosnia in early July 1999 to assume the position of Assistant Director of Operations of the Multinational NATO Coalition Forces for Stabilization Force Rotation 7. Stratman is pictured in Bosnia with General Montgomery Meigs, the four-star general who was commander of United States Army Europe, while concurrently serving as commander of the NATO Stabilization Forces in Bosnia.

With notice of less than two weeks, General Stratman was advised in mid-June 1999 to make the necessary preparations to deploy to Sarajevo in Bosnia and Herzegovina, to serve as a member of the stabilization forces. One of the most pressing and immediate of his concerns became making the arrangements for Linda to relocate to Virginia, so that she could stay with their daughter and son-in-law for the next year. This would not only provide Linda with the opportunity to spend time with her grandchildren, but to assist their daughter in babysitting, thus affording their daughter, Jodie, adequate time to work the necessary number of hours to maintain health coverage for Richard, who was still undergoing treatment for aplastic anemia.

Linda Stratman traveled to Virginia to live with her daughter and son-in-law after Hank deployed to Bosnia in the summer of 1999. This afforded Linda the opportunity to assist her daughter and to spend time with their grandchildren, who are pictured in 2000.

"When I asked what I was supposed to do with my wife on such short notice, I was bluntly told that it was not the Army's problem," said Stratman. "It was a last-minute situation, but the more senior you are in the U.S. Army, the less the system cares about your spouse. It all worked out in the end; by this time Jodie had four children and I felt comfortable with Linda being there during my absence."

Scrambling to get his affairs in order, Stratman reported to his duty assignment in Sarajevo by the first of July. Montgomery Meigs, the four-star general in command of the United States Army Europe was concurrently serving as the commander of the NATO Stabilization Forces in Bosnia. General Meigs, like many with whom Stratman met during his years in uniform, chose to carry forth a proud legacy of military service since his father had been a tank commander in World War II and was killed in action a month before the birth of his son. Additionally, Meigs had been named in honor of General Montgomery C. Meigs, his great-great-granduncle who served as Quartermaster General of the U.S. Army during the Civil War, and who helped establish Arlington National Cemetery.

During this feverish period of acclimating to this new and unique assignment, Stratman explained, the United States had a dual role in the formerly war-torn region: first, to maintain peace and stability. There still existed British, French, and U.S. sectors, all of which were working to ensure the situation did not devolve into bedlam between the former warring factions. Second, the U.S. had the mission of capturing individuals who were indicted by the International Tribunal for war crimes, which NATO and U.S. forces referred to as PIFWCs (Persons Indicted for War Crimes).

Upon his arrival, General Stratman discovered there had recently occurred a major restructuring of SFOR senior leadership, and, although only a one-star, he was now slated to replace a two-star general while assuming additional responsibilities for civil affairs as well as overall security operations in Bosnia. His primarily U.S.-based staff had also been downsized, further challenging accomplishment of the additional responsibilities assigned to him. General Meig's multi-national staff consisted of a deputy who was a French three-star general along with a British three-star general, German one-star general, Spanish one-star general and an Italian one-star general. Stratman's focus was running security operations and civil affairs that included oversight of plans and operations within the stabilization forces command structure. There was little opportunity available for him to settle into his new position before a major event was announced that resulted in some unanticipated excitement involving a French soldier, the president of the United States and a near tragedy that fortunately failed to work its way into the international news feeds.

"Word came down from the Department of Defense that NATO made the decision to hold a European peacekeeping summit in Sarajevo, right when I was beginning to figure out my new position and responsibilities," said Stratman.

"There was to be twenty-nine heads of state in attendance and part of the job of my staff was the security of Zetra Stadium, where the summit was to be held, along with providing security for the route to and from the airport," he added.

A press release on the NATO website notes the primary function of the Peace Stabilization Force (SFOR) during the summit was "to support security activities, working alongside the more than 4,000 Federation and Republika Srpska police who will be securing the main routes and facilities employed for the summit." It was added, "SFOR personnel have been working behind the scenes to help plan many aspects of the summit and are assisting with such things as transportation, communications, emergency medical response, and air traffic management." [97]

The Sarajevo summit was held at the Zetra Olympic Sports Complex, which was a location that was used in the 1984 Olympics. Many news outlets were hailing the selection of Sarajevo for this historic summit of world leaders because of its symbolism, noting that "[v]iolence in Sarajevo triggered World War I, after the two brutal Balkan wars of 1912-1913" and the city was "still recovering from the horrific Serbian shelling of 1992-1995..." [98] Any concerns with symbolism aside, Stratman recalled the detailed plans that had to be made and implemented, while coordinating with multiple embas-

---

[97] NATO, *SFOR Troops Play Supporting Role in Balkans Summit*, https://nato.int.
[98] July 30, 1999 edition of the *Miami Herald*.

sies, all of which was to ensure the world leaders in attendance made it safely from the airport and to the sports complex through a dangerous route that had been coined "Sniper Alley." Sniper Alley was part of the city's main boulevard, surrounded by high-rise buildings and hills that had, in years past, been used by snipers, while the city was under siege, to pick off civilians, firefighters and United Nations peacekeepers. Many civilians had learned to dart quickly across streets to avoid becoming a stationary or slow-moving and easy target for the snipers.

While assigned to the Stabilization Force in Bosnia, Brigadier General Stratman worked with senior officers representing a multi-national coalition force. Pictured, back row, from left: French Colonel Vleeschouwer; Brigadier General Hank Stratman; Spanish Colonel Domenech; and Italian Brigadier General Enrico Mocellin. Front row, from left: British Brigadier General Charles Le Gallais; Brigadier General Bernd Diepenhorst, German army; French Lieutenant General Charles-Henri De Monchy, and; British Lieutenant General Michael Willcocks.

***General Stratman is pictured while working in Ilidza
with plain-clothed members of one of the "Civil Affairs"
teams that had the dangerous job of apprehending
"Persons Indicted for War Crimes" in Bosnia.***

Stratman said, "We put Special Forces teams on key buildings along Sniper Alley. One of the biggest issues that came up in that part of the process was an accidental discharge of a firearm by a member of the protective forces when the Croatian head of state was traveling through Sniper Alley, but fortunately, no one was injured. However, the greatest concern," he continued, "unfolded after the arrival of President Clinton."

The airport at Sarajevo, Stratman explained, had a two-story terminal building. On the second floor of the building, journalists and news outlet employees scrambled to get a good view of dignitaries arriving for the televised summit. On the roof of the buildings, Special Forces personnel, Secret Service and CIA agents were "armed to the teeth" and scanning the area for potential threats. When President Bill Clinton arrived at the airport for the summit on July 30, 1999, the ramp lowered on the Air Force C-17 aircraft, he exited the aircraft and began walking toward the terminal about one hundred yards away.

"The surveillance people on the roof observed a French soldier across the tarmac who was aiming his weapon at the president," Stratman recalled. "The only reason he wasn't immediately taken out by the Special Forces and Secret Service was because he did not have his finger on the trigger. We immediately got communications to the French and they quickly relayed a message to the soldier to drop the weapon, stand up … or else he was dead. Apparently, he was peering through his scope to get a good look at President Clinton, like he was a tourist, but that almost got him killed." With a sigh of relief, he flatly added, "Exciting times."

The incident was not publicized by the Secret Service. Stratman noted that had a burst of fire come from the roof to take out the French soldier, it would have made international news and become a humiliation for the French government. Fortunately, cooler heads prevailed with the Secret Service and Special Forces personnel making the right call in the tense situation. Tragedy may have been avoided but the moment was not absent consequences for the French soldier.

"Although it wasn't publicized, it was embarrassing for the French SFOR military leadership," Stratman said. "I don't know for sure what happened to that soldier, but he was out of theater within twelve hours and on the way back to France. But overall, the peacekeeping summit and operation were successful, mostly because the U.S. was involved. That," he concluded, "was part of the reason they decided to hold this summit in Sarajevo."

While at the summit, "President Clinton joined over 40 leaders from Europe and North America in reaffirming our shared commitment to support the reconstruction, development, democratization, stabilization and integration of Southeast Europe by formally launching the Stability Pact." The president announced that not only was the United States committing $10 million toward promoting "democracy in Serbia," but recognized that the summit demonstrated the great lengths toward recovery made in Bosnia since the Dayton Peace Accords had been signed three years earlier.[99]

Following the departure of the dignitaries, General Stratman and his team returned their focus to the second component of the responsibilities they had been given under SFOR—the capture of war criminals. The process of capturing criminals, Stratman described, was highly secretive and not shared outside the U.S. chain of command. Despite any intended secrecy, Stratman explained that he worked in the same office area with Italian, Spanish, French and British senior officers, who easily could have ascertained that PIFWIC capture operations were underway. Through multiple intelligence sources, Stratman and his teams were able to identify where and when war criminals were supposed to be in certain areas, and then developed a plan of apprehension utilizing Special Operations personnel that were referred to as 'Civil Affairs Teams.' One of the overarching concerns of this detailed planning events was to not only apprehend, but to mitigate any collateral damage to the civilian population. The process for receiving approval for an apprehension was both detailed and cumbersome, Stratman recalled.

General Wesley Clark, a four-star general who later became a Democratic nominee for president of the United States, was at the time serving as Supreme Allied Commander Europe, making him the overall command authority for NATO forces operating in Europe. When an apprehension plan was developed by General Meigs and his Special Operations Forces team, General Clark had to grant the approval.

"General Clark tended to be very risk aversive and asked a lot of questions," said Stratman. "We would brief him on a capture plan and its risks, and he would then brief the Secretary of Defense, who would then go on to brief the president for approval. It was a very cumbersome process to get the final approval through all the levels in our chain of command." He added, "I was essentially the middleman between the intelligence community and Special Forces, working to

---

[99] The White House, *President Clinton: Promoting Stability for Southeast Europe*, https://clintonwhitehouse4.archives.gov.

get the final approval from above and then overseeing the execution of the mission."

The daily grind of military activities in Bosnia was interspersed with USO-sponsored celebrity visits. Stratman (back row, center), is pictured with members of the Washington Redskins cheerleaders in Ilidza. Stratman quipped, "It was a tough job, but someone needed to do it!"

Upon completion of a PIFWC apprehension mission and the safe return of the Special Operations teams to the base, Stratman's job was to manage the consequences and inform the NATO allies, United Nations ambassador, U.S. ambassador and SFOR members. When a war criminal was apprehended, they were immediately flown to the Netherlands and turned over to the custody of the International Criminal Court in The Hague for prosecution. Stratman explained that concurrent to the U.S. missions to apprehend war criminals, the British Special Forces teams were conducting the same types of operations in their sector. One of their missions, he noted, was considered a "textbook example" of how such a mission should be accomplished through a highly responsive and cooperative spirit.

"On a Friday, our U.S. intelligence sources received information that a war criminal was going to be in the British sector visiting his parents that weekend," Stratman said. "We got the information to Lieutenant General Michael Willcocks, British three-star general that I worked for, and they developed a capture plan. The British special forces were not in country, but within twenty-four hours, they flew in, staged everything needed and rehearsed the operation. When the war criminal was leaving his parents on Monday, the capture force carefully designed and executed a trap along the road and apprehended him without any collateral damage. For us," he said, releasing a sigh of exasperation, "it would have taken a week to get the approval through our chain of command, but the British didn't have the same kind of bureaucracy to go through."

While he had been in Bosnia three years earlier as a member of Task Force Eagle, Stratman recalled, he had flown to a meeting held between the warring factions in the Zone of Separation. He arrived aboard a U.S. Blackhawk helicopter that was escorted by two Apache attack helicopters—a very impressive show of force. He remarked, "No one dared to even think about challenging our forces."

Three years later, while running SFOR's multi-national operations, the helicopter support took on a less threatening appearance. Ukrainian aviators were flying the older Huey helicopters that were provided by the U.S. government through foreign military sales, which, ironically, Statman had helped to coordinate during his time at the Defense Security Assistance Agency (later renamed the Defense Security Cooperation Agency). The Ukrainians flew Stratman and his security team to a meeting with Serbs at their camp, located on the east side of the Drina River that bordered Serbia. During the flight, General Stratman thought to himself, "I hope the Huey navigational avionics work, because how would I explain to my wife, and the Army, what I was doing in a Huey helicopter, piloted by Ukrainian Aviators, in the event we strayed into Serbia and were forced to land …or worst case, shot down for penetrating their airspace?" The mission was successfully flown, leaving Stratman highly impressed with the pride and professionalism of the Ukrainians pilots, who had maintained their aircraft in pristine condition. Additionally,

Stratman observed, the aviators appeared to be very proud to fly a U.S. general, whom they in some way associated with helping secure their country's freedom from the Soviet Union years earlier.

One of the few privileges the troops enjoyed while serving in Bosnia were the occasional USO-sponsored morale and welfare visits by celebrities and other notable individuals, who often posed for pictures and signed autographs. Stratman remarked that one of the visits that raised a lot of eyebrows among the soldiers serving with SFOR were the Washington Redskins and Dallas Cowboys cheerleaders. But another important visit came when General Stratman had the opportunity to conduct a personal briefing for former NFL Player turned coach, Don Shula, and his wife, Mary Ann. Not only had Shula ascended to legendary status within the NFL after earning the title of winningest coach in NFL history and was inducted into the Pro Football Hall of Fame in 1997, he also possessed a military background from having served at Fort Polk, Louisiana, with his National Guard unit during the Korean War.

During a USO visit, General Stratman provided an operations briefing to Don and Mary Ann Shula. Two years earlier, Don Shula was inducted into the Pro Football Hal of Fame and holds the distinction as the winningest coach in NFL history.

"I had the opportunity to provide them with a general overview of our operations in Bosnia," said Stratman. "They were very gracious, polite and a pleasure to be around. Shula had been the head coach for the Miami Dolphins, and he and his wife invited Linda and I to come visit him in Florida after I left Bosnia. We were never able to make it," he added.

The ninety-year-old Shula passed away on May 4, 2020.

During the first part of his tour in Bosnia, Stratman worked out of the headquarters that was established in an old hotel and resort in the city of Ilidza. But with NATO's long-term commitment to security and stabilization in the Balkans, it was soon necessary to have a modernized facility, resulting in a move to a site near the Sarajevo International Airport. The new headquarters at Butmir was more spacious, technologically advanced and had such protective implementations as bulletproof windows.

"Part of that process was establishing communications and security in the new complex," he said. "Basically, we tripled our working space in the move and my staff helped oversee the transition while at the same time continuing to run our security stabilization operations."

Another transition came during the final six months of Stratman's time in Bosnia—the appointment of Lieutenant General Ronald Adams as the new commander for the Stabilization Force in Bosnia and Herzegovina. There were also occasional visits to the operations staff by Lieutenant

Throughout his military career, Stratman formed many close friendships with fellow officers, including General Bryan "Doug" Brown, who retired in 2007 as a four-star general in command of U.S. Special Operations Command. US Army photograph

General Doug Brown, who had previously served as Stratman's commander for about six months at Fort Riley, at which time he was a one-star general and assistant division commander.

Lieutenant General Brown was the Joint Special Operations Commander during Stratman's second tour in Bosnia and had command of all the special operations forces that supported their operations in the region. Stratman noted that General Brown was highly respected by those who served both with him and under his command.

"I've really met a lot of great people who have been part of my life, both professionally and personally," said Stratman. "At the top of my list of great Americans and friends are Doug and Penny Brown," he added.

The close of his one-year tour in Bosnia approached in June 2000, and Lieutenant General Adams expressed his appreciation of General Stratman's performance, presenting him with the award of a Defense Superior Service Medal followed by the award of the international military decoration known as the NATO Medal. Arriving in country to take over Stratman's duties was Brigadier General Eldon Bargewell. During the Vietnam War, Bargewell had served as a non-commissioned officer with a reconnaissance team. Years later, Bargewell served as a member of the Special Operations group known as Delta Force during the failed rescue attempt of fifty-three diplomats and Americans who were taken hostage by Iran under the presidency of Jimmy Carter.[100]

Prior to his departure, Stratman had received approval for an in-country leave. He was able to fly Linda into the airport at Sarajevo and embark upon a much-needed vacation to several interesting locations. Initially, Linda was given a tour of their former operations center in Ilidza, where Hank had spent most of his time during the deployment. He had formed a relationship while working with members of the Central Intelligence Agency as a component of the mis-

---

[100] Spending several years as an enlisted soldier, Eldon Bargewell would go on retire at the rank of major general in 2006. He was seventy-one years old when he passed away on April 29, 2019, and is interred in Fort Mitchell National Cemetery in Alabama.

sion of apprehending those convicted of war crimes. Stratman and his wife were graciously provided with the use of the CIA safehouse in Sarajevo as lodging during part of his leave period. The house, he recalled, sat on a hill and granted a stunning view of Sarajevo from its elevated perch.

"The Italians had a brigade that they provided for SFOR's mission—a paramilitary quick-reaction force called the Carabinieri," he said.[101] "I had become close with their commander, Colonel Renato Scuzzarello. He offered to host Linda and I at the Carabinieri resort on the island of Ischia off the coast of Naples, Italy." He continued, "We also had an offer from the British I worked with to stay at one of their R&R

During his second tour in Bosnia, General Stratman became friends with many officers from the multi-national forces with whom he worked. He is pictured with Colonel Renato Scuzzarello, the commander of an Italian quick-reaction force known as the "Carabinieri."

(rest and recreation) compounds in Split, Croatia and a safehouse in Dubrovnik."

---

[101] The "Carabinieri" are one of Italy's primary law enforcement agencies and carry out domestic policing duties, however, are considered a military force. Their name originates from the "carabina," which was the rifle members of the organization carried. Carabinieri are several decades older than modern Italy and were established by Victor Emanuel I, Duke of Savoy and King of Sardinia. According to an article by the BBC, "When Italy was unified, the royal corps of carabinieri remained a nationwide military presence performing law enforcement duties so, in many ways, functioning as a duplicate police force." Mitzman, *It's 200 Years Old, But What is Italy's Carabinieri?*, https://bbc. com.

Located on the eastern Adriatic Sea, Split was near Dubrovnik, a city that served as a tourist destination in Croatia. Stratman explained that while he was busily engaged in successfully performing the mission of SFOR in Bosnia, many United Nations and U.S. Embassy personnel assigned in-country were able to enjoy extended weekends in Dubrovnik. Oftentimes, he remarked, they would depart Thursday night and not return to their work duties until Monday.

"We were left to run the country and maintain law and order," he laughed. "But I had always wanted to see Dubrovnik and finally got to do so, spending a few days there with Linda."

When the end of his leave approached and it was time to return to the United States, Stratman had a general officer's 9-millimeter pistol that he had been issued and carried with him while overseas. The Carabinieri assisted him in registering it at the airport and it was placed in a lockbox in custody of one of the airline pilots. When arriving back in the states, Hank began wandering around the airport to find with whom he should speak to retrieve the locked case containing his handgun. While he was away from the baggage claim area, a pilot came up to Linda and said he was looking for someone to whom he could hand off the box. Linda stated it was her husband's.

"He handed the box with the 9-millimeter Beretta over to me with no questions asked," Linda mirthfully recalled. "That really seemed odd to me, but this was before 9/11." Hank added, "It's kind of a fluke that the gun even made it back to me."

The year he served in Bosnia as a member of the Multinational Stabilization Force was rich in many valuable experiences for the general, becoming the first time in his career that he worked directly with the National Guard at the divisional level during a deployment. Mobilized in support of SFOR was the 49th Armored Division of the Texas National Guard along with brigades from North Carolina, Oklahoma and Georgia. General Stratman fulfilled the role as their "go-to-guy" at the headquarters in the American sector, working to ensure the citizen-soldiers were successful in their appointed missions. The Texas National Guard division performed admirably in the large-scale operation, which was highly attributable to the great working relationship between all parties.

The deployment also opened Stratman's eyes to the national intelligence collection capabilities that were employed in the apprehension of war criminals and used to monitor the activities of warring factions. The intelligence gathered, which was then used in their Special Forces operations, stands out in his memory as part of a mutually supportive process that ensured successful outcomes in their missions. This timeframe, Stratman explained, also bore witness to the teamwork and camaraderie that developed between the different Coalition military forces, while also demonstrating that certain political influences could complicate the manner in which missions were approached.

"It was fascinating to be able to work directly with a multi-national staff and to learn about the United Nations, in addition to the politics and hidden agendas of the various European nations in the Coalition," he said. "There were some historic linkages of which we had to be wary, and we also learned to recognize the partners that were the most trustworthy, such as the British." Stratman continued, "The national interests of our NATO allies don't always align with interests of the United States, which made coordinating 'Unity of Effort' among the twenty-nation SFOR Coalition quite a challenge at times. I observed that most NATO military leaders were very 'risk averse' and too often reliant on their country's ambassador for political approval. Some of these NATO allies spent more time monitoring and collecting intelligence on US Forces, than they did the Bosnians, Serbs and Croats."

There were circumstances, Stratman recalled, when difficult decisions needed to be made because of suspicions regarding the dedication of certain NATO senior personnel to the success of the overall SFOR mission. On one occasion, Stratman explained, there was a French colonel who worked for him as a chief of planning officer. The colonel frequently failed to perform the tasks he had been given and demonstrated an uncooperative spirit.

"We were attending a party where this colonel got drunk and began running his mouth, stating he and the French government would cherish the day that the U.S. failed in Bosnia, just as the Roman Empire had failed in the past. Essentially, he intended to help facilitate the country's demise. Due to his grievous revelation and failure to follow instructions, I reported his insinuations to his French boss, Lieutenant General de Monchy and, with no questions asked, this colonel was relieved of his duty."[102]

Stratman concluded, "His replacement, who was also a French colonel, was certainly more politically astute and respectful."

---

[102] Lt. Gen. Charles-Henri de Monchy served as deputy commanded of SFOR and was Chief of French troops in Bosnia and Herzegovina.

CHAPTER 11

Global War on Terrorism

"General Abrams was able to return to TRADOC quickly and, the next day, sent me to the Pentagon to see if TRADOC could offer any assistance putting the Army staff back together," Stratman said. "I was able to catch a Blackhawk to Fort Belvoir (Virginia) and then carpooled to the Pentagon. The Pentagon had been damaged by the aircraft that had crashed there the previous day..."—Stratman describing his activities the day following the 9-11 terrorist attacks.

While he was stationed at Fort Riley, Kansas, a few years earlier, Brigadier General John Sylvester had served as senior rating officer in then-Colonel Stratman's chain-of-command. A short time later, when he deployed to Sarajevo as a member of the Stabilization Force (SFOR), Brigadier General Stratman served as the SFOR operations officer, filling the position that had recently been vacated by then-Major General Sylvester. Since General Stratman had through his Bosnian service become a fellow soldier with "Balkan mud on his boots"—and was familiar to many in senior leadership positions—when General Sylvester was making preparations to depart his position with the U.S. Army Training and Doctrine Command (TRADOC) in the summer of 2000, he selected General Stratman to backfill his position at Fort Monroe, Virginia.

"When I got orders to return to TRADOC, I quickly concluded that it was because of (General Sylvester)," Stratman remarked. "Previously, I had worked in combat development but, in this new assignment, I was now working within the agency that had responsibility for overall doctrine development; the agency that worked to determine how the overall force structure will look in ten to twenty years, and then developing the best path on how to get there." He continued, "We worked with the different military schools, such as those for the armor, infantry and field artillery, assessing the capabilities being sought (i.e., new tanks, artillery rounds), and then coordinating with the defense industrial complex that would go on to develop, produce and deliver the equipment that we forecasted might be needed in future warfighting."

Throughout his year assignment with TRADOC, General Stratman and his wife resided in a nice home on Fort Monroe, Virginia. Their home overlooked the waterfront and was situated near the Chamberlain Hotel, where Linda had worked years earlier. However, this time, Linda chose not to seek employment opportunities. Since she was now the spouse of a general officer, Stratman explained, it was generally frowned upon for Linda to have a job; rather, it was the unspoken understanding that she and the other spouses of general officers should focus their efforts on volunteering and military family assistance endeavors.

The next few months served as yet another busy period of his career since Stratman remained busy integrating into the unique responsibilities of his new duty assignment. His professional activity, he recalled, was briefly suspended after his eighty-four-year-old mother, Mary Catherine Stratman, passed away at her home in Vienna, Missouri on May 8, 2001.

"My oldest sister, Georgena, had been looking after our mother because her health had been declining for some time," Stratman said. "After we were informed that she had passed, Linda and I drove back to Missouri and stayed for a little more than a week," he said. "Jon and Jodie also came home for the funeral, which was a traditional Catholic service and burial. Mother was laid to rest with our father in Visitation Cemetery in Vienna," he added.

Not long after returning to the East Coast, his duties at TRADOC culminated in an event known as the Army Transformation Wargame 2001. Stratman noted this wargame focused on the speculation that U.S. forces were engaged in military action against Syria and Iraq. A component of the implementation of the exercise was to ensure the U.S. Army possessed the training and resources to strategically respond to threats, embracing the right mix of hardware and troop levels to attain the lethal force deemed as necessary in future warfighting demands. It was during these wargames that the use of drones was first explored for use as a reconnaissance tool. The findings of the weeklong wargame exercises helped senior leadership design an overall force structure "with the striking power, staying power, and agility to win major theater wars ... (and ensured the Army was) capable of applying selective force throughout the spectrum of conflict." Additionally, the wargames explored the implementation and benefit of future combat systems designed to increase the force's agility, versatility, lethality and survivability. These wargames revealed the compelling need for certain types of combat capability systems, and oftentimes fell victim to funding limitations.[103]

"One of the interesting things identified in the wargames was the need for a protected vehicle to protect our soldiers because all

---

[103] Army Transformation Wargame 2001, *Vigilant Warriors*, 2-3.

we really had at the time were a few up-armored Humvees," he said. "But despite this need, an up-armored vehicle did not make the final funding cuts. They soon discovered there was a dire need for such a vehicle in Iraq, which led to the hasty development of the Mine-Resistant Ambush Protected vehicle (MRAP)."

With honest and reflective self-appraisal, Stratman explained that his position at TRADOC was more of an academic and theoretical position that did not provide a great deal of professional interest; he was more focused on the immediacy of warfighting and not what might be necessary years in the future. Although he did not view himself to be the best fit for his current assignment, just as he had done in previous situations, he applied himself to the tasks given and simply "made the best of it" while learning from his mentors.

This timeframe also resulted in the opportunity for Stratman to participate in a learning initiative that was a capstone course mandated by Congress for those who achieved the one-star rank. Consisting of six weeks of training with similarly situated generals and flag officers from the other branches of the military, Stratman traveled to the East Coast, beginning his participation in the professional development program with his counterparts from the U.S. Navy.

"As part of the program, we basically spent one week learning about each branch of the military," Stratman said. "They flew us on a fixed-wing aircraft called a CHOD, which landed on an aircraft carrier somewhere off the East Coast and we spent some time exposed to naval operations and capabilities." He continued. "Then, to learn some about the Air Force, we departed Virginia aboard a C-135 tanker that had seats in the back. While traveling to Nellis Air Force Base (Nevada), I got up and went to the back to bullshit with the boom operator. During our chat, a B-52 Stealth bomber from Whiteman Air Force Base was to be refueled in flight. It was very interesting to watch the boom operator make that process happen for some pilots who were flying out of Missouri."

During their brief stay at Nellis Air Force Base, Stratman and his fellow general officers in training were taken to a bombing range and witnessed several demonstrations on air firepower that included close air support from fighter aircraft. Also, he had an opportunity to get a close-up view of the Stealth Bomber that had been refueled in flight, visiting with the pilots and their crew.

He recalled, "These were all twenty-five- or twenty-six-year-old Air Force captains and lieutenants operating these high-dollar aircraft. At that moment, it really struck me just how much responsibility we entrust to these young men and women."

The final component of the professional development training consisted of the individual officer selecting a region of the world they wanted to visit in order to acquire a broader understanding of existing military and political conditions. Stratman, already possessing European and Middle East experience, chose Southwest Asia. He would travel to locations in Singapore, Japan, Thailand, Malaysia and Hawaii, where he was given demonstrations of regional strategic war plans and was provided with situational awareness of the military strategic role in the Asia-Pacific region he was observing. He affirmed that although it may have had the appearance of a vacation—visiting exotic foreign lands with little responsibility other than learning about U.S. national security intents in the region—an important aspect of the educational journey was forming relationships with classmates from different branches of service.

"The entire purpose of this training was to help us recognize the capabilities each branch of service brings to the fight," he said. "As general officers, we were now part of the joint warfighting team. It came late in my career and didn't help me get to where I was, but it was a fascinating experience and a much-needed break."

Stratman explained that it was never his intent to remain at TRADOC for very long ... and he did not. Thirty days before 9/11, he was selected for the rank of two-star (major general). The promotion list was released toward the end of August 2001 and his name was on it for assignment to Third Army (later designated Coalition Forces Land Component Command—CENTCOM).

He noted, "Third Army was known as 'Patton's Own' from their service back in World War II under General George Patton."

Major General John Sylvester, Stratman's boss at TRADOC, received his promotion to the rank of lieutenant general and was reassigned shortly before the 9/11 attacks. While Stratman was waiting for his official transfer to his new appointment at Third Army, he was selected to replace General Sylvester as the chief of staff at TRADOC. During this "temporary" assignment, the 9/11 attacks unfolded and abruptly shifted the arc of Stratman's military career.

September 11, 2001

Stratman explained that at the time, General John N. Abrams, the son of a U.S. Army Chief of Staff who served through multiple wars and for whom the historic M-1 Abrams tank was named, was the four-star general fulfilling the role of commander of TRADOC.[104] His brother, Creighton Abrams III, had served as Stratman's senior rater during the Persian Gulf War. The morning of September 11, 2001, General John Abrams was in Arizona visiting the military intelligence school. Stratman was in Virginia and in the process of playing host to a foreign general, a NATO ally, when his aid burst into his office to advise him that an airplane had just struck the World Trade Center in New York City. The meeting was immediately halted and they switched on a television just in time to gasp in shock as the second airplane crashed into the Twin Towers. Immediately, Stratman got on the phone and contacted his boss, General Abrams, to advise him of the situation that was unfolding.

---

[104] Creighton Abrams was a 1936 graduate of West Point and revealed himself to be an aggressive armor officer during World War II, which included his command of an armor regiment in the Battle of the Bulge. He would go on to command military operations in the latter part of the Vietnam War, eventually achieving the rank of four-star general and serving as Chief of Staff of the United States Army until his death on September 4, 1974. In 1980, the M-1 Abrams tank was named in his honor. His son, John N. Abrams, for whom Stratman worked at TRADOC, also achieved the rank of four-star general. The younger Abrams retired as TRADOC commander in 2002 and passed away in 2018. Like his father, he was laid to rest in Arlington National Cemetery.

*One of the four commercial aircraft hijacked by terrorists
on September 11, 2001, was crashed into the Pentagon.
The following day, Stratman was sent to the site to
determine whether TRADOC could offer any assistance in
the aftermath of the attack. U.S. Navy photograph*

The tragic events that occurred on the morning of 9/11 shook the entire nation and almost immediately ended the country's widely-held belief that terrorism was a concern only for underdeveloped foreign nations. It was on this day that members of an Islamic extremist group hijacked four commercial aircraft, employing them as weapons used in a coordinated attack against the United States. Two of these airplanes were flown into the Twin Towers of the World Trade Center, and a third crashed into the Pentagon. A fourth passenger airplane, United Flight 93, crashed into a field near Shanksville, Pennsylvania, after passengers bravely stormed the cockpit in an act of defiance against their captors. On that tragic and fateful day, more than 3,000 people were killed, earning it the sordid distinction as the greatest loss of life to occur on American soil as the result of a foreign attack. In the coming months and years, America's response to the attacks would evolve into a major, worldwide military operation that was designated the Global War on Terrorism, during which Brigadier General Stratman would come to play a significant role.

"General Abrams was able make it back to TRADOC quickly, and the next day sent me to the Pentagon to see if we could offer any assistance putting the Army staff back together," he said. "I was able to catch a Blackhawk to Fort Belvoir (Virginia) and then carpooled to the Pentagon. When I arrived, the Pentagon was a wretched sight … it had been significantly damaged by the aircraft that had crashed there the previous day," he paused, "and the corridors reeked with the smell of burning rubble, smoke and fuel … something I'll never forget." He continued, "I spent the day there visiting with a number of officers, some friends of mine and contemporaries. It was a very uncomfortable situation because there was a stressed relationship between TRADOC and the Army staff. They didn't seem interested in any assistance from our agency because the Army command center was underground and undamaged, so I came back to Fort Monroe and briefed General Abrams on my experience."

The smoke of the attacks had barely begun to dissipate when Stratman shifted his focus on this new assignment with 3rd Army. Prior to 9/11, he had been slated to replace Major General Warren C. Edwards, who was retiring as the deputy commanding general of operations for 3rd Army.[105] Given the circumstances of a nation that was now on war footing, the general, who was to retire, instead made the decision to remain in his position, resulting in Stratman being appointed the deputy commanding general of support. Every two years, the command participated in a large scale, multi-national exercise held in Egypt that was known as "Operation Bright Star." Scheduled to occur just weeks after the unexpected horror of the terrorist attacks, a high-level decision was made to move forward

---

[105] Warren C. Edwards is a graduate of the University of Richmond (Richmond, Virginia), earned a Masters of Military Arts and Sciences from the U.S. Army War College and holds a Master's of Science in International Studies from the U.S. Naval War College. Following his retirement as a major general from the U.S. Army, he served as a Chief Operating Officer for Oak Ridge Technology and later became a Senior Fellow at the Community and Regional Research Institute.

with the exercise and have General Stratman oversee its successful execution. For approximately six weeks, Stratman remained in Egypt, encountering the good fortune of having a staff trained to do the "heavy lifting" and resulting in a sound and successful training outcome.

"The entire Third Army command deployed to Camp Doha in Kuwait and 3rd Army became the Land Component Command in the overall mission to capture or kill Bin Laden, who was being harbored in Afghanistan," Stratman said. "When I came home from Egypt, it was only for a day or two; I kissed my wife goodbye, confident she had good, safe quarters on post at Fort McPherson, Alabama (the headquarters for U.S. Army Forces Command or FORSCOM, which is the command that provides land forces to combat

Following more than 28 years on active duty, Stratman received promotion to two-star general while deployed to Kuwait during the Global War on Terrorism.

commanders). From there, I deployed to Kuwait," he added. "It was interesting to note that when I was still at Fort McPherson, the Third Army soldiers were the only ones wearing desert camouflage not any of the FORSCOM soldiers."

Shortly after his arrival in Kuwait, Stratman was promoted to major general (two stars) on December 8, 2001. He spent the next few weeks "wrapping his head" around the logistical support aspects of their new mission assignment, an interesting situation, he said, considering the challenges presented by the landlocked country of Afghanistan. At the time, the United States was invested in building up forces in the country, setting up forward operating bases in

Uzbekistan and Pakistan. Early in the endeavor, special forces personnel worked to establish Bagram Air Base, a site that had once been used by Soviet forces during their occupation of the region years earlier. As soon as the area for the base had been secured from Taliban threats, Army engineers were deployed to clear the area of any obstacles and establish useable runways for C-130 transport planes. Through every step of this process, Stratman worked closely with his counterpart in the Air Logistics Command since air support was recognized as a critical component in transporting supplies, personnel and equipment into the rocky, difficult to navigate terrain that defined a large swath of Afghanistan. Within a short period, the base was up and running, being utilized as a base camp for Special Forces operations throughout the dangerous region.

Stratman, second from left, along with other 3rd Army senior leaders, wave during their promotion ceremony at Camp Doha, Kuwait in December 2001. It was during this ceremony that Stratman was promoted to the rank of two-star general [major general].

"The 10th Mountain Division headquarters was deployed to Uzbekistan, but there appeared to be a political reluctance by the

U.S. Army to deploy ground forces to Afghanistan because of what they viewed as substantial training and equipment requirements that had not been met," he explained. "There was a belief that emerged that our special operations teams could work with the tribal factions in the north to apprehend Osama Bin Laden, who had been trapped in Tora Bora (complex network of caves in eastern Afghanistan). The request was made for the 82nd Airborne rapid reaction force to come in, but the Army leadership would not approve this. Based upon the Army's reluctance, CENTCOM turned to the Marines Corps, who deployed a Marine Expeditionary Unit to Afghanistan."

Pausing, he added, "By the time they deployed the U.S. Marine ground forces to Kandahar—a Taliban hotspot—Bin Laden had already managed to escape from the region. At that time, that entire area of the country was reminiscent of the wild, wild west."

The British forces, Stratman recalled, were working to establish a new government in Kabul, the capital city of Afghanistan. Stratman worked with the U.S. ambassador to Afghanistan in an effort to reinstate diplomatic relations in Kabul. Additionally, his charge included oversight of the soldiers responsible for running and guarding a small base in Pakistan used by the Central Intelligence Agency. The base was a falcon hunting camp for an Emir from the Persian Gulf region, but had been contracted by the CIA for the purpose of launching armed predator drone reconnaissance and strikes into Afghanistan.[106] Although General Stratman's primary duty location was in Kuwait, he flew to Bagram and Pakistan repeatedly in C-130s and C-21s, working to ensure his troops had the necessary supplies and equipment to be successful in their security missions, while also remaining as safe as possible when executing the critical orders they were given.[107]

---

[106] "Emir" is a title of nobility or royalty that has been used by several countries, oftentimes Middle Eastern nations. Falcon hunting has been around for centuries and involves using falcons to hunt for assorted types of small mammals and waterfowl.

[107] Transport aircraft utilized by the United States Air Force.

Major General Stratman shakes hands with one of the many dignitaries he worked with during his deployment in the Global War on Terrorism. He is pictured during a discussion with United States Ambassador to Afghanistan, Ryan Crocker, in 2002.

"Flying into Bagram was an interesting experience because you approached at an altitude of around 15,000 feet, and then the aircraft would corkscrew down to the airfield because of the threat of surface-to-air missiles," Stratman said. "We would fly in at night and the pilots were wearing night-vision goggles. When we flew out," he added, "they would use the same corkscrew procedure when gaining altitude until they were out of range of any air defense missiles."

The relationship he had fostered with his Air Force counterpart met with a "hiccup" when, two months into his duties of developing bases in Afghanistan, the Air Force general he had been working with was replaced. Suddenly, Stratman recalled, the air support they had come to appreciate seemed to fizzle away. He soon discovered that the Air Force was still operating on peacetime deployment cycles, rotating air wings in and out of country after only about ninety days. Stratman, as were many of his Army counterparts, was deployed for the duration of the mission, which provided a high level of continuity in their operations. However, when he had the opportunity to meet the four-star general serving as the Air Force chief of staff during a visit to the Middle East, Stratman was not reserved in expressing his dissatisfaction with the deployment cycles of his counterparts in the Air Force.

"I gave the general a piece of my mind, but was professional and tactful about it," Stratman said. "I explained how their ninety-day deployment schedules negatively impacted us in successfully accomplishing our missions because we relied upon their air support since Afghanistan was landlocked." With a grin, he added, "It wasn't long after that little encounter that the Air Force set aside their peacetime posture and extended their deployment cycle to six months and eventually a year."

Major General Stratman recalls traveling to the base at Bagram for a week or two at a time, especially during the initial stages since the base camp and its operations cycle were being established. He also made a trip to Jalalabad in eastern Pakistan, to participate in a meeting with his counterpart in the Pakistani military.

"About twenty-five percent of my time was supporting the effort in Afghanistan, otherwise, there were scores of us working in developing a plan to invade Iraq and topple the regime. Honestly, 9/11 just shook us to the core because, what troubled us the greatest, is that it was an attack against the civilian population. If anything," he continued, "I expected our military to be attacked because that's the kind of business we are in—but to have our civilian population attacked was utterly disturbing. We wanted revenge and a big part of that was to capture or kill Bin Laden. This effort is what escalated into the Global War on Terrorism."

In the weeks following Bin Laden's escape into Pakistan in December 2001—an unfortunate result of the Battle of Tora Bora in eastern Afghanistan—a parallel mission began to evolve for the U.S. military. In an interview conducted by David Josar for *Stars and Stripes* magazine printed on February 8, 2002, Major General Stratman remarked that the mission in Afghanistan had entered what he defined as a "sustainment phase." Stratman said, "There are a few pockets of resistance remaining, and we're going after them. It's difficult sorting them out … there's still a lot of unrest." He would go on to clarify that the military forces of the United States were committed to Afghanistan "for the duration of the mission to bring peace and stability to this failed nation-state," adding that he had in previous days made visits to several military compounds in Afghanistan to ensure they were prepared to support the stabilization efforts.

Preparations for *Operation Iraqi Freedom*

General Stratman and his fellow senior officers had enough experience under their collective belts that they were able to "read the tea leaves," agreeing that although the stabilization of Afghanistan remained an ongoing concern, the invasion of Iraq was imminent. What came out of their planning sessions was a preparatory task list of equipment and personnel that would likely be needed in support of such a major military operation. Eventually, this list of necessities was submitted through channels to the Secretary of Defense for approval and funding. For 3rd Army, this list came with an approximate price tag totaling $550 million. It consisted of nearly forty items, Stratman recalled, that included seaports and airport upgrades in addition to the construction of base camps in Kuwait with the resources to accommodate a major surge of forces in the region. The other service branches, he said, compiled and submitted their own lists of perceived needs through their internal channels to the Department of Defense.

"Before we ever received any approvals for the funds we'd identified and requested, the Central Intelligence Agency provided me with some seed money to begin building an airfield that could accommodate C-130s and the agency's predator drones," said Stratman. "It amounted to about seven million in CIA money and we began building the airstrip in Kuwait in the September to October (2002) timeframe. In March 2003, the U.S. Army staged 435 Apache attack helicopters for Operation Iraqi Freedom."

The construction project for the CIA ensued without receiving direct approval from the Kuwaiti government. It was not long after an area of the desert was being excavated that Stratman was contacted by Kuwait's Minister of Defense, who indicated he was needing an explanation regarding the work that was underway.

"I informed the minister what purpose the airfield would be used for when it was completed and he said that the project was acceptable, but wished we would have advised him initially so that he could have informed the Royal Family," Stratman said. With a grin, he added, "That's when I explained to him how much easier it is, at times, to ask for forgiveness rather than permission. Anyhow, it was all approved because Kuwait was willing to go to great lengths to get rid of Saddam Hussein and had not forgotten all of the help that the U.S. provided their country during the Persian Gulf War.

In his wartime capacity, Stratman essentially began to assume the role of a contracting officer—reviewing, approving and signing off on many big-dollar construction and purchasing contracts. While utilizing the CIA seed money for the airfield construction initiative, he and his staff continued to work with Central Command to acquire approval on the funds requested from the Department of Defense, an outcome that would allow them to make the preparatory upgrades they had delineated in their submitted critical task list. Throughout this process, Stratman worked with operations and planning staff at CENTCOM, primarily Major General William Mortenson, a personal friend whom he recalls initially challenging most every request he and his staff submitted through channels.

"Finally, it reached the point where I had suffered enough of the endless questioning and told him to get over here to the desert and I'd show him *why* we needed the items. He replied, 'No, no, … that's alright.' Grinning, Stratman, added, "After that interaction, everything seemed to go a lot more smoothly between us."

The process of negotiating the funds necessary to invade Iraq was interspersed with the departure of Lieutenant General Paul Mikolashek, the commander of 3rd Army. Mikolashek had previously been in command of a light infantry brigade in Vincenza, Italy, and supported operations in Bosnia, where he had come to know Stratman. Prior to the event of 9/11, General Mikolashek selected Stratman to serve as his deputy commander of 3rd Army. However, since he had already served two years in his command assignment,

Mikolashek was scheduled to rotate back to the Unites States in September 2002. This left a window of approximately sixty days in which Stratman needed to fulfill the vacated command role while waiting for Mikloshek's replacement to arrive. When his replacement, Lieutenant General David McKiernan, came to assume command of the 3rd Army, Stratman briefed him on the work they had done in preparing a list of needs for the invasion of Iraq and the money that had recently been approved by the Department of Defense.

Maj. Gen. Stratman (left), the CIA station chief for Kuwait (right), and a Kuwait military officer sip tea while discussing the construction of an airfield to be used by the CIA for launching predator drones.

General McKiernan then made the decision to significantly increase his staff of senior officers to be more reflective of wartime levels. Several two-star generals were requested by name, increasing the staff from three general officers to twenty. The new group of senior officers were soon given the sobriquet of "dream team."

In the book On Point: The *United States Army in Operation Iraqi Freedom*, the approval of funds from the Department of Defense resulted in the U.S. Army's capability to make improvements on "the logistics, training, military support, and command and control infrastructure in Kuwait…. Training improvements included building the Udairi Range complex, located about an hour's drive from Camp Doha and situated in a wide-open expanse of desert. The Army steadily enhanced and upgraded firing ranges and training resources, while experienced training support personnel invested countless hours in training support personnel and creating a first-class training facility." These personnel that would soon be operating in the CENTCOM area of responsibility and benefit from improvements to communications and command and control infrastructure, ensuring their ability to comply with any wartime requirements. Stratman remained heavily involved in the building of theater infrastructure while "Third Army worked to developed the capability to receive and sustain units in Kuwait and elsewhere in theater."[108]

The dream team of senior generals may have represented the "cream of the crop" available within U.S. Army leadership circles; however, Lieutenant General McKiernan was inclined to lean heavily upon General Stratman since he had already been in the Middle East for a year, possessing critical regional knowledge and contacts with Kuwait government officials. His earlier experience as the assistant division commander for the 3rd Infantry Division had also been an important part of his professional development since he had been introduced to U.S. Army prepositioned stocks. These stocks were brigade level combat sets, positioned prior to the events of 9/11 that consisted of equipment such as tanks and armored vehicles. The sets were strategically stored as a latent resource in climate-controlled facilities and aboard ships stationed in worldwide locations so as to increase the ability of U.S. forces to rapidly deploy. The brigade sets were brought into a centralized location in Kuwait to equip the U.S. forces that were brought in from the USA in preparation for the invasion of Iraq. As Statman noted, the 3rd Infantry Division would fight using this equipment.

Prior to 9/11, the Kuwaiti government began working toward moving U.S. forces out of Camp Doha since the area was ripe for

---

[108] Fontenot, Degen & Tohn, *On Point*, 31.

commercial development. In demonstration of their continued support for maintaining a strong U.S. military presence in the region, they constructed Camp Arifjan in the south of Kuwait near the Saudi Arabian border. The host government had gone to great expense in the process, erecting buildings complete with plumbing and electrical installed, but lacking the main trunk line hookups to the local utility grid. Soon, work was underway to bring the camp into an operable condition and it became the primary logistics hub for planning and executing the pending invasion of Iraq. Most of the work, Stratman reiterated, was completed by contractors from several different nations.

Another identified concern was the challenges that arose in ensuring there was a reliable source of diesel fuel. An inordinate amount of fuel was consumed by the vehicles and equipment of an expanding military force, and needed to be available without interruption. Early in the process of building U.S. military capabilities within the theater of operations, fuel was trucked to the main military bases in addition to the subordinate posts and airfields. With the approaching surge of forces, Stratman and the senior staff realized such as delivery method would not sustain an offensive force.

"There needed to be an underground pipeline with taps for the fuel at the various bases and camps," said Stratman. "But," he paused, "the price tag attached to that was estimated at around $30 million, meaning it was such a cost that it would require Congressional approval, and we knew it would be quite a challenge to navigate through all of those hurdles in a timely manner."

Realizing the Kuwaiti government had a deeply vested and expressed interest in retaining a long-term U.S. presence in the Persian Gulf, Stratman chose to utilize a more streamlined approach in securing the construction of the much-needed fuel pipeline.

"What happened first is that I scheduled a meeting with representatives from the Kuwait National Oil Company in December of 2002, most of whom had direct connections to members of the Kuwaiti royal family," he said. "When I asked them if the company was willing to consider incurring the costs of building the pipeline, they asked me if I could guarantee that the U.S. government is going to topple the Saddam regime. Although I was not in the position to make any guarantees, I stressed to them that every indication we have says 'yes.' After that, they said give us a week to consider it, and then they came back and said the Emir of Kuwait had agreed to build it." Grinning, he added, "I then said, 'By the way, we need this done in *ninety days*.' The following day, they already had equipment excavating trenches, laying pipe, and by the end of February 2003, the pipelines were finished."

In the early weeks of November 2002, with the $550 million received from the Department of Defense, Stratman recalled that his duties as a contracting officer provided him with a "professional high"—the feeling of being an executive of a Fortune 500 company with massive financial resources. This feeling, he added, was the result of having the authority to commit large sums of money to various projects. However, he never lost sight of the fact that he was expected to spend the funds in a responsible and efficient manner that increased the U.S. Army's capabilities through the construction of adequate base camps and facilities. These purchases included the expansion of the command centers at both Camp Doha and Camp Arifjan, upgrading the sites with modern technologies. The command centers at both locations were equipped with three big screen televisions, each measuring approximately thirty feet wide by twenty feet high, while each center also had the capabilities to accommodate approximately three hundred staff members. These modernizations helped ensure senior leadership, though separated by long distances, had access to the same common operational picture when making important operational and strategic decisions in the coming months.

"These large televisions were part of a larger technology upgrade referred to as 'Blue Force Tracking," Stratman explained.

The Smithsonian, in an article detailing the history of time and tracking systems, described the Blue Force Tracking "as a system that gives commanders and troops in the field a real-time picture of the battlefield not possible with conventional maps. This improves situational awareness and reduces the possibility of friendly fire. It also allows headquarters to issue orders much more efficiently than by previous forms of radio communication. GPS positioning provides the main data source for Blue Force Tracking."[109]

Stratman added, "The GPS units were placed in specific vehicles within our maneuver forces. Perhaps the greatest benefit was that by using these large television screens in the command center, we could observe where each company was *live* as they moved into a specific sector. It was the first time we used this new technology and we were very busy fielding the new equipment and providing training on how it was to be implemented."

Another critical step in the process of preparing for conflict, Stratman detailed with clear reflection, came when Lieutenant General McKiernan needed to identify who would become the major warfighting headquarters to be brought into theater. In the end, he chose V Corps Headquarters out of Europe (commanded by Lieutenant General Scott Wallace) based upon a number of weighted factors to include their modernized equipment and the experience and competencies demonstrated by their commanding officer. The first divisional unit to join V Corps was the 3rd Infantry Division, deploying from Fort Stewart, Georgia. Then, in early January 2003, they were supplemented through the deployment of the 101st Airborne Division.

The 82nd Airborne Division, with capabilities to rapidly deploy worldwide, soon received their alert for deployment to Kuwait. With their pending arrival came a slew of preparations to be made, many of which fell under the purview of Stratman's contracting authority.

"We had a large building constructed for the 82nd Airborne at the Kuwait International Airport because we thought we were going to need airborne assault capabilities to secure Baghdad and other locations," he said. "The building had to meet certain size specifications so that they had a drop rig site to prepare and maintain their parachutes and associated equipment. In the end, we didn't use the 82nd for airborne assault; instead, they were mostly used to help provide route security."

---

[109] Smithsonian, *The Blue Force Tracker System*, https://timeandnavigation.si.edu.

One of the many representatives in the Kuwaiti government Maj. Gen. Stratman worked with included Nawaf Al-Ahmad Al-Jaber Al-Sabah, the Minister of the Interior. A member of the country's royal family, he became the Emir of Kuwait on September 30, 2020. Pictured on the far right is U.S. Ambassador to Kuwait Bill Jones.

Under most deployment preparation circumstances, "Units normally arrive in a theater of operation by a combination of surface and air delivery methods," noted the book *On Point: The United States Army in Iraqi Freedom.* "By experience, approximately 95 percent of personnel arrive by air. Conversely 95 percent of materiel arrives by sea."[110] In supporting the corps and ensuring they had the munitions and equipment to sustain their mission, the Joint Logistics Over the Shore (JLOT) was deployed. This reflected a coordination of effort between the U.S. Navy and U.S. Army, wherein strategic sealift vessels were operationally employed to deliver supplies, personnel and equipment onto beaches or through inadequate ports. Another key resource in the ferrying of personnel, supplies and equipment into the ports was the U.S. Army's theater support vehicle (TSV)—a sleek and fast ninety-eight-feet-long catamaran. This structure ensured

---

[110] Fontenot, Degen & Tohn, *On Point,* 75.

dangerous munitions could be stored offshore and away from areas with a concentration of civilians, and were then able to be transported to shore and loaded on waiting trucks for shipment inland to the various base camps.

There were many interesting facets of planning for war, but perhaps one of the most memorable was the result of the relationship Stratman developed with representatives of the Kuwaiti government, many of whom were members of the country's royal family. He explained, "On a professional level, I became really close while working with the Kuwait Minister of Defense, the Minister of the Interior and the Kuwait Navy Chief—all members of the royal family at some level. I served as their single point of contact for coalition forces and we developed a very trusting relationship. In fact, they granted every one of the requests made by our government with the exception of one; they refused our request to build an Iraqi prisoner of war camp in northern Kuwait."

During a major planning phase in early January 2003, Stratman, along with two of his fellow generals, received an invitation from the Kuwait Minister of the Interior Nawaf Al-Ahmad Al-Jaber Al-Sabah to join him for what essentially started out as a picnic in the middle of nowhere.

Stratman recalled, "We were driven out into this huge expanse of desert, where there had been a large tent set up. They had laid down these huge carpets over the desert floor and there was a table set in the center with a young roasted camel as a centerpiece, along with rice and assorted vegetables. There was not any silverware and you had to use your fingers to dig out the piece of meat you were going to eat." He jokingly added, "That was the first time and last time that I ate camel, but it tasted a lot like chicken!"

After the meal, the minster demonstrated hunting techniques using trained falcons that he owned. The group of U.S. military officers were then invited to get in the minster's sports utility vehicle and driven for a tour along the border between Kuwait and Iraq.

"The minster was driving the vehicle and I was riding in the front passenger seat," explained Stratman. "Along the border, he showed us a high-tech electrified fence with guard posts that Kuwait had built after the first Gulf War to keep Iraqis out. The minister remarked that when it came time for us to invade Iraq, that he did not want us to destroy his fence. Because of this meeting," Stratman concluded, "we built it into our operational plans to coordinate with the Kuwait government to take down sections of the fence for us to make our crossings into Iraq and then to be quickly reinstalled."

In early February 2003, Newt Gingrich, former Speaker of the United States House of Representatives, visited Kuwait to assess U.S. preparedness levels for the pending invasion of Iraq. During the two-day visit, he was escorted by Major General Hank Stratman.

Stratman's efforts continued as part of a master plan that ran for a period of approximately six months, containing countless details and redundancies intended to ensure a successful outcome that would soon culminate in the invasion of Iraq. This process included the visit of political representatives who were focused on making assessments of the preparedness of U.S. forces for the approaching combat engagements. In early February 2003, former Speaker of the House of Representatives Newt Gingrich was dispatched by President George W. Bush to visit coalition forces in Kuwait, offering words of encouragement to the troops serving in the Middle East and to assess levels of readiness if the invasion of Iraq was to become a reality.

"Gingrich was there for two days and I was his escort officer—I was with him every minute of the day except for when he was sleeping," recalled Stratman. "We briefed him on master plans at the Operations Center at Camp Doha and then traveled to Camp Arifjan, where he was briefed on the logistics aspect along with additional theater support information. After that, we boarded a Blackhawk helicopter and flew him to visit the 4th Brigade of the 3rd Infantry Division located in the desert, so he could see their attack helicopters, attack drones and receive a demonstration on how they used the Blue Force Tracking."

While the former Speaker of the House of Representatives was in the desert visiting elements of the 3rd Infantry Division, he was also introduced to the commander of the 2nd Brigade—Colonel David Perkins. Several years later Perkins retired as the four-star general in command of the U.S. Army Training and Doctrine Command. Additionally, Gingrich would meet Brigadier General Lloyd Austin, who at the time was the assistant commander of maneuver for the 3rd Infantry Division. Austin also went on to achieve the rank of four-star general and became the first African American Secretary of Defense in January 2021. One of the most profound memories Stratman retained from the brief interaction with the former Speaker of the House during his visit to the Middle East was the constant barrage of unusual and unanticipated questions he frequently posed to members of the senior staff.

"The questions would challenge you mentally in an effort to provide a coherent response," said Stratman. "Keeping up with him and all of his interesting questions made for a mentally taxing two days," he added.

During Gingrich's visit to Kuwait, he had the opportunity to speak with Brigadier General Lloyd Austin, the assistant commander of maneuver for the 3rd Infantry Division. Austin went on to become a four-star general and the first African American secretary of defense.

At the time of Gingrich's visit, Stratman recalls there was talk in Washington, D.C. to provide Saddam Hussein with additional time to comply with U.N. mandates. When Gingrich was preparing to depart Kuwait and return to the United States with his perceptions of the current state of readiness, Stratman made the decision to stress one important point.

"I told Gingrich that we are now at our peak readiness," said Stratman. "The temperatures were now in our favor and there is no way that we can hold this level of warfighting preparedness through the summer months. I strongly advised him to stress to the president that the invasion should take place in March, otherwise it would be detrimental to our readiness."

Pausing, Stratman concluded, "Two to three weeks later, we got the go-ahead to launch the offensive campaign into Iraq."

CHAPTER 12

Establishing the War Footing

"Hank Stratman has been a magnificent workhorse in Coalition Forces Land Component Command (CFLCC)/Third Army during both Operations Enduring Freedom and Iraqi Freedom. Deployed forward virtually his entire tour, Hank understands operational level warfighting, joint/coalition operations and interagency linkages as well as any two-star in our Army. His future contribution to both the Army and joint communities is invaluable."— Lieutenant General David McKiernan, pictured above, far right, describing Stratman in an Officer Evaluation Report covering the period of July 2, 2002 to July 1, 2003. Pictured center is Major General David Kratzer, commander of the 377th Theater Support Command.

Rubbing his fingers across his temple in reflection, Stratman bluntly stated, "The preparation for the invasion of Iraq never seemed to end. Once everything began with the invasion," he continued, "we had to make sure the resources were in place to sustain our forces while they were engaged in combat operations. Likewise, we had the Fourth Infantry Division and the First Cavalry Division flowing into theater to join the fight in Iraq. It was a situation where we never said that something was 'good enough' nor were we ever completely satisfied with the logistical and support structure—we always felt there was room for improvement."

The 377th Theater Support Command, comprised largely of Reserve forces overseen by Stratman, provided transportation and logistical support for the initial staging of forces and sustainment of operations. Stratman also received support from the very competent Major General Claude V. Christianson who, later in his career, achieved the rank of lieutenant general prior to his retirement from the U.S. Army, and was described by General Stratman as being an important member of the "dream team" well versed in the logistics infrastructure of the theater of operations.[111]

During Operation Iraqi Freedom, Stratman worked closely with Major General Claude V. Christianson, who was the Chief, Logistics, Coalition Forces Land Component Command at Camp Arifjan, Kuwait. Christianson would go on to become Army G-4 and achieve the rank of lieutenant general. U.S. Army photograph

---

[111] Claude V. Christianson was a Distinguished Military Graduate of the ROTC program at North Dakota State University in 1971. He went on to serve in positions of increasing responsibility during his U.S. Army career, retiring at the rank of lieutenant general on June 1, 2008 with more than 37 years of

On March 19, 2003, Tomahawk missile strikes against Iraqi defenses signaled the beginning of combat operations in *Operation Iraqi Freedom*. Though the minutiae of operational planning have been extensively reviewed in books and peer-reviewed articles, Stratman summarized that elements of the 1st Marine Expeditionary Force (supplemented by British forces), along with units of V Corps, 3rd Infantry Division, 101st Airborne Division and 82nd Airborne, began the push into Iraq at the opening of the ground war. While these forces were penetrating the Iraqi border through breach lanes that were previously established through agreements with the Kuwait government, the Fourth Infantry Division began arriving in country and moved into staging areas in preparation for operational deployment, if needed. Unlike his previous experiences in the Persian Gulf, Stratman was no longer leading an artillery battalion with a focused fire support mission, but now had the responsibility for big-picture planning and logistical support that would ensure military success of the coalition forces.

"It took about two weeks for our troops to seize Baghdad and topple Saddam's regime with V Corps sustaining one hundred and sixty casualties during some heavy fighting," recalled Stratman. "Defeating Saddam's army was never in doubt—controlling the country would become the greatest challenge. All of the Coalition Forces Land Component Command (CFLCC) staff and planners knew that defeating Saddam's military would be the easiest part of our efforts." He added, "We realized the follow-up support and stabilization operations would, by far, develop into the greatest challenge with DOD and the State Department at odds on how this process should unfold."[112]

---

service. Following his service in Operation Iraqi Freedom with Major General Stratman, he became the Deputy Chief of Staff, G4, Department of the Army.

[112] Donald Rumsfeld served as the Secretary of Defense under President Gerald Ford from 1975 to 1977 and again under President George W. Bush from 2001 to 2006. Due to the separation of his dates of service as the defense secretary, he holds the distinction of having been both the youngest and oldest appointed to the position. Rumsfeld was eighty-eight years old when he died on June 29, 2021.

In the wake of development of a post-war security strategy, Stratman concluded that many at the top levels in the Department of Defense did not possess a clear grasp of the various complexities associated with establishing security in a recently toppled regime. Additionally, it appeared that the defense secretary was unwilling to deploy the forces that many military leaders explained were necessary to most efficiently secure Iraq. An article appearing in the *New York Times* shortly after Rumsfeld's death explained that the former defense secretary was often viewed as "a combative infighter who seemed to relish conflicts as he challenged cabinet rivals, members of Congress and military orthodoxies."[113] Several agencies within the United States government—the Department of Commerce, Central Intelligence Agency, Department of Defense, State Department, et al.—were granted specific roles to play in establishing a functioning government at a time when a leadership vacuum had been created with the removal of Saddam Hussein. However, the greatest failure at the strategic level, Stratman maintained, was that these agencies did not appear to be pulling in the same direction and it really appeared as if the Department of Defense wanted to maintain control of the nation-building process when it had traditionally been considered a State Department role.

"I may be Monday morning quarterbacking here, but the military had their act together and accomplished their jobs well and efficiently," Stratman said. "Most people do not grasp the complexities of the political, economic and military factors and competing dimensions that were in the works and needed to be integrated for everyone to function in tandem as one successful team."

Another interesting development that unfolded in the ensuing weeks was the establishment of the Iraqi Interim Authority (IIA), which was comprised of "Iraqi leaders who would manage Iraqi affairs while simultaneously devising the permanent political institutions for the post-Saddam era," noted a 2008 article featured in the *Boston Review*. The article went on to explain, "From the outset, this project would have an Iraqi face and therefore … likely command

---

[113] June 30, 2021 edition of the *New York Times*.

broad Iraqi support."[114] What Stratman and several military leaders witnessed; however, was a failure of this and other policies that were often the result of the wrong individuals being appointed to key positions of influence and authority. Furthermore, power vacuums and questionable outcomes abounded since it became uncertain as to who would ultimately be granted authority for guiding the restructuring of the post-Saddam government in Iraq.

Turmoil in identifying a clear and concise security posture remained a persistent aggravation for many senior military leaders during this period. When it appeared that the Department of Defense would take the lead in determining the future structure of the Iraqi government, Secretary of Defense Donald Rumsfeld appointed Lieutenant General Ricardo Sanchez as the new commander of V Corps, the Combined Joint Task Force 7 and the Multi-National Force in Iraq, replacing the experienced and insightful Lieutenant General William Wallace, who had been tapped to become the next commander of the Combined Arms Center at Fort Leavenworth, Kansas. Adding to the emerging leadership concerns, many members of the former "Dream Team,"—whose experience and expertise had been critical in the planning and execution of toppling Saddam's regime—were now leaving for their next career-enhancing assignments.

"I had attended the Army War College with General Sanchez after the Persian Gulf War and knew him fairly well," Stratman said. "He commanded a battalion in the 197th Infantry Brigade in Desert Storm and later the 1st Armored Division in Germany. In his biography, he explained that he received little support and clear guidance from Army staff and the Department of Defense. Although he was knowledgeable about what was being planned in Iraqi Freedom, his major problem was he had staff who were neither prepared nor qualified to deal with the range of unique issues associate with securing and rebuilding the country. He kind of lost control of the situation." Sighing, Stratman added, "And what added even greater toxicity to this mix was the fact that Ambassador Paul Bremer disbanded what

---

[114] Bacevich, *Inside Rumsfeld's Pentagon*, https:// bostonreview.net.

was the equivalent of Iraq's National Guard because he had the attitude that we—the U.S.—could not trust any of Saddam's military. We were relying on them to help us keep control." (Paul Bremer was a civilian appointed by President George W. Bush to serve as the Coalition Provisional Authority of Iraq).

Despite the observed political turmoil and leadership vacuums that were developing on the horizon, Stratman spent his remaining time in country embracing a resolve to perform the responsibilities within his sphere of influence. With the security of the country becoming the greatest military focus and concern, Stratman explained that General Christiansen suggested they should consider contracting drivers for the trucks used to haul supplies and equipment to military camps and points in-between. For Stratman, outsourcing transportation did not appear to be a feasible option since he believed they would encounter troubles finding drivers once they began getting shot at by Iraqi dissidents.

"We were really just trying to make sure the military piece of the mission was supported as well as possible," Stratman firmly noted. "It was simply amazing the number of people who had their finger in the pie to influence how things turned out in Iraq, but we were ultimately able to pull it off."

On several occasions, Stratman was directly exposed to the many dangers facing his troops when accompanied by his security team (comprised of military police personnel) to travel supply routes as a means to assess the dangers faced by soldiers during their logistics trips. The team utilized two armored Humvees to travel the routes to Baghdad that had become the line of progression during the initial attack. Although they never came under attack, his team discovered that many deadly dangers still existed, one of which served as an opportunity for one of his non-commissioned officers to reveal the true depth of their mettle and abilities. While on a route assessment, his personal security detachment commander, Staff Sergeant Jamie Outland, demonstrated her leadership capabilities and applied some of her military police training when they encountered an accident along one of the convoy routes.

Major General Stratman and his security team, comprised of Military Police, frequently traveled supply routes within Iraq. The team's chief, Staff Sergeant Jamie Outland, second from left, often impressed Stratman with her demonstrated leadership abilities. They are pictured during an awards ceremony at the end of their assignment in Iraq.

"On our way to a camp, we came upon an accident site," recalled Stratman. "A convoy of National Guard soldiers had been moving in one direction in their HEMTT (Heavy Expanded Mobility Tactical Truck) wreckers; a tank unit was coming the other way. The tank unit had stirred up a significant amount of dust so the lead HEMMT abruptly stopped to wait for it to clear up a little so that they could see the road in front of them." With a mournful pause, he continued, "The HEMTT behind the lead vehicle rear-ended the one in front of him."[115]

---

[115] The Heavy Expanded Mobility Tactical Truck (HEMMT) is an eight-wheel drive tactical vehicle that first entered service with the U.S. Army in 1982 and comes in a variety of configurations to include cargo truck, tanker, tractor and wrecker.

Stratman recalls there was a lot of chaos and hysteria when they came upon the scene. The two soldiers who had been in the HEMTT that rear ended the one in front of them were crushed inside the cab.

In front of a group of more than 300 soldiers during a USO-sponsored visit to Camp Doha, Kuwait in July 2003, movie star Arnold Schwarzenegger changed out of the t-shirt he was wearing to don the shirt of the Coalition Forces Land Component Command.

"Staff Sergeant Outland took over and began giving orders," he said. "She was certainly a leader. Sadly," he concluded, "after the two soldiers were removed from the damaged cab of the HEMTT, they died from their injuries."

Such disheartening moments were an unfortunate reality of operating within a combat environment, Stratman solemnly explained. Similar to what he had experienced when serving in the Persian Gulf War, accidents and unforeseen circumstances were much too often responsible for deaths of many a young soldier. This was a situation that, throughout his career, he diligently sought to avoid by ensuring the troops under his command were properly trained and disciplined, and their non-commissioned officers—and all in positions of leadership—were committed to bringing all of their soldiers safely home.

Yet the good moments tended to outweigh the bad, often bringing some much-needed levity to otherwise difficult circumstances. To help boost morale, celebrity visits provided the occasional moment of excitement during his tenure in Operation Iraqi Freedom. The USO sponsored a trip to the Middle East for famed bodybuilder and movie star Arnold Schwarzenegger in July 2003, shortly before Stratman's departure for his next duty assignment. At the time of his arrival at Camp Doha in Kuwait, Major General Stratman was the senior officer in the area and escorted Schwarzenegger during his brief visit to their location. The movie star visited the command center, posed for photographs with troops and expressed a genuine interest in the operations that were being conducted by forces in the region. While he was at Camp Doha, Schwarzenegger was escorted into a large theater-style area with more than three hundred soldiers who were waiting to hear him speak and answer questions, while scenes from his earlier movies like *Terminator* and *Commando* played on large screens in the background.

"He was a good entertainer and we had a lot of fun while he was there," Stratman said. "When he spoke to the troops in the command center, he was wearing some type of t-shirt he had been given by the USO. We presented him with our own t-shirt representing the Coalition Forces Land Component Command and encouraged him to wear it." With a cunning grin, Stratman added, "He kind of looked toward his handlers and got the nod of approval, and went ahead and took off the USO shirt he was wearing and changed into our shirt in front of everyone. They started clapping and he was really a good sport through it all. And," Stratman concluded, "he declared his candidacy for governor of California about two or three weeks later."[116]

---

[116] The United Service Organization, Inc. (USO) is a private, non-profit 501(c)(3) organization chartered by Congress. The organization coordinates different types of live entertainment for members of the Armed Forces and their families, which includes an impressive list comedians, actors and musicians. The USO

When Stratman's tour in Iraq approached its end in the early part of July 2003, Lieutenant General David McKiernan did not falter in recognizing his subordinate officer's demonstrated skills and competencies as the deputy commanding general of support. General McKiernan explained that Stratman "skillfully planned, coordinated and overwatched the Theater's power projection and sustainment support infrastructure for Operation Iraqi Freedom (OIF). He flawlessly orchestrated execution of … OIF Preparatory Tasks, ensuring timely completion of CFLCC's command and control centers, aviation and logistic facilities and troop staging areas for 250,000 Soldiers and Marines." McKiernan went on to praise Major General Stratman's keen abilities in approaching the host nation in order to skillfully negotiate access to critical air and seaports and training facilities while also helping orchestrate the construction of a reliable pipeline through which their forces had access to free fuel provided by the Kuwait government.

---

has a variety of other programs that provide benefits and assistance to members of the military and their families. https://uso.org.

CHAPTER 13

NATO Command in Turkey

At the conclusion of his assignment with the Joint Headquarters Southeast, Stratman was presented this plaque by Turkish General Orhan Yöney that featured the flags of several of the nations who had been part of the NATO structure in Turkey.

Stratman said, "When my time was up in Iraq, I was apprised by general officer management folks at the Pentagon that I was being assigned as the deputy commander of a NATO Command, the Joint Forces Command Southeast in Izmir, Turkey. They advised me that this tour would be unaccompanied—meaning Linda would not be able to join me." Animatedly, he added, "I told them that I had been unaccompanied for two years in the Middle East and that I wanted to talk to the Chief of Staff of the United States Army about this unaccompanied assignment. For some reason, their records mistakenly showed that I had been stationed at Third Army's peacetime headquarters at Fort McPherson in Atlanta, Georgia all this time."

While stationed in Turkey, Hank and Linda Stratman enjoyed walks along the waterfront of Izmir Bay. One of the nearby sites they enjoyed visiting was the Izmir Clock Tower built in 1901 in commemoration of the twenty-fifth anniversary of Abdul Hamid II's—the thirty-fourth Sultan of the Ottoman Empire—ascension to the throne.

The general whom Stratman was slated to replace in Turkey had been serving in the position since prior to the events of 9/11 and was accompanied by his wife. However, Stratman was informed that after the terrorist attacks nearly two years earlier, Department of Defense policy regarding tours in Turkey was changed and would henceforth be unaccompanied. Recognizing Stratman's unique circumstances and duty performance with CENTCOM, he was granted a waiver and allowed to have his wife join him in his assignment in Turkey.

"They agreed to let me bring Linda … and she was the only spouse there," Stratman explained. "I came back to Fort McPherson for about a month of leave to help Linda place our things in storage, pack and prepare to head to Turkey. Once we arrived in Turkey (in August 2003), we were placed in really nice quarters, which just happened to be on the third floor of a building overlooking a main tourist waterfront along Izmir Bay. It was really a stunning water-front location."

His new position with Joint Headquarters Southeast fell within the NATO structure and was a component of primarily an Air Force-centric U.S. military command (officially designated the Air Component Command). On the local level, Stratman worked with General Orhan Yöney, a Turkish lieutenant general who, like Stratman, had acquired artillery experience early in his career. Turkey was a country of great interest to the United States and allies because of the strategic location of its air bases in proximity to Russia. While integrating into his new surroundings and making observations of the characteristics of the command, Stratman recognized that the existing physical security structure was rife for disaster.

"I lived among the general public but had Turkish conscript guards that sat outside my door for security," he said. "The American troops lived in the Hotel Hilton complex in the middle of town with no security to speak of, but were enjoying themselves and living high on the hog." He added, "Here I was, coming from the Muslim extremist threat of post-9/11 and into an environment where no one appeared to be that concerned with potential threats to their safety. I spoke to the Air Force commander and said the whole situation is another Khobar Towers bombing just waiting to happen."[117]

Determined to ensure the safety of all military personnel under his command, Stratman was granted permission to move his troops into a secured area within a walled camp in an industrial area. Acknowledging that his actions were not viewed in a popular light by the troops who had been enjoying their resort lifestyle in an exotic country, Stratman observed the conceivable threats to his troops and made every reasonable effort to provide for their safety through a defendable base camp.

---

[117] On June 25, 1996, a truck bomb was detonated near Khobar Towers in Saudi Arabia, which was being used as a housing complex for members of the coalition forces who were helping enforce the no-fly-zone in Southern Iraq as part of Operation Southern Watch. U.S. courts determined that Iran and members of Hezbollah were responsible for the attack that resulted in the deaths of 19 U.S. Air Force personnel.

"Then, Linda and I moved out of our own first-class accommodations and into a small home within a gated community used primarily by foreign contractors," he stated. "Some of our military policemen were used to create our own security detachment, rather than relying on the Turkish guards that had previously been provided to us."

The weekends afforded Stratman opportunities to visit various points of interest with Linda, who had thus far experienced a significant number of foreign cultures while accompanying her husband throughout his military career. Oftentimes, they would visit gypsy markets, purchasing vegetables that were not only excessive in size, but were quite tasty as well. On another occasion, while Stratman was deeply involved with his duties as a general officer, Linda was accompanied on a trip to the Vatican in Rome by her husband's military aid. After entering the holy site, she recalls receiving an unexpected tap on her shoulder.

"It was a Vatican security guard, or whatever their official title was, and he motioned for me to come with him," she animatedly recalled. "I was wearing a very short-sleeved blouse, nothing risqué, but apparently it failed to meet their standards of dress and I was escorted out of the Vatican."

Hank added, "My military aid accompanied Linda and I several times to tour some of the beautiful Catholic churches in Italy. He was a Protestant, but later married a Catholic girl and converted to Catholicism."

Clinging to the moments to spend time with Linda after many years of separation during his military career, walks along the waterfront of Izmir Bay provided them opportunities to discuss their plans for his retirement from the Army in the near-term. During one of these enjoyable excursions, they were passed by a gentleman in Turkish garb who said, "Good evening, General Stratman."

He explained, "We were in civilian clothes, so it really gave us pause because we didn't know who he was. We just kept walking and didn't respond. Later," he added, "we found out that it had been one of the local CIA security officers for the U.S. embassy."

In late 2004, by chance, Stratman met former Secretary of State Madeleine Albright in the Turkish airport's VIP lounge. This was around the time, he recalled, when the Democratic Party was levying personal attacks against President George W. Bush, which, in Stratman's view, undermined his presidency. Stratman approached Albright and introduced himself as a consul officer and then challenged her on her party's flagrant assault on the commander in chief during a time of war.

"I asked her if she had any appreciation for the damage her party's disparaging antics were having on the morale of the troops fighting in Iraq," Stratman said. "She listened politely to my tirade, but made no rebuttal! Apparently, my concerns fell on deaf ears."

In Turkey, General Stratman's assignment devolved into a less than engaging situation especially when compared to the pace of activities in his previous duty positions; however, he affirmed, "I did what I was supposed to do, made the best of it and, most importantly, every one of my soldiers made it through without any casualties."

Since the dissolution of the Joint Force Command was pending, it resulted in a situation where training with multi-national forces was curbed and he grew somewhat dissatisfied with working in a military environment that seemed to underutilize his background and skills as a general officer. On many occasions, when he had the opportunity to visit with senior leaders who might lend him a sympathetic ear at meetings and briefings, Stratman described to them how the Turkish assignment was not challenging since there was so little to be accomplished. A couple of months later, in early summer 2004, after speaking to General John Abizaid, commander of CENTCOM, regarding his desire for a more challenging and rewarding work, Stratman was advised that he had been selected to return to Baghdad and fulfill the duties of Deputy Commanding General (Political-Military) under the auspices of the Multi-National Force-Iraq (MNF-1). This reminded him of the adage, "Be careful what you ask for!"

When making the necessary preparations to depart Turkey and embark upon his new duty assignment, arrangements were quickly coordinated for Linda to return to Missouri. Her new focus, when back in the states, would be to begin the preparations for her husband's approaching retirement from the U.S. Army. Their Turkish experiences had provided them with several occasions to discuss their future plans for a post-Army life, and that time appeared to be soon. In 1975, the couple had the opportunity to purchase a tract of eighteen acres of land located north of the community of Holts Summit in Callaway County, only minutes from the state capital of Jefferson City, Missouri. At the time, Stratman was convinced that he would complete his initial tour in the U.S. Army and then return to Missouri to build a house, family and career. But since he grew to enjoy his daily responsibilities as a leader of soldiers, he chose to pursue a career in the Army but held onto the property, realizing it would be where he and his wife would eventually return in their retirement years.

Fortuitously, the property was situated only a short drive from the homes of Linda's two brothers and mother, who were living the vicinity of Columbia, Missouri. Additionally, Stratman's uncle, Father Ambrose Stratman, who was the priest that had married the couple, was elderly and resided in a nursing facility in St. Louis. With Linda returning to Mid-Missouri, she would be in proximity to visit her family and Father Ambrose while she waited for her husband to finish his career. Their property contained a small brick home and Linda began the arduous process of renovating and cleaning it, recognizing that it could serve as their temporary home while they built a larger, more modern and spacious home in the coming years. While the brick house was undergoing improvements and occasionally unlivable, Linda was able to spend short periods of time staying with her mother and brothers.

"Linda was always very self-sufficient and was on her own a lot because of my different military assignments," Stratman lovingly noted of his wife. "She never complained and, whatever the situation we faced, she found a way to make everything work out."

CHAPTER 14

Iraq Governance

"Magnificent groundbreaking work by a talented and resourceful officer. His work as the Deputy Chief of Staff for Political-Military-Economic integration was remarkable and established a completely new standard for interaction between Departments of State and Defense – Hank mastered the inter-agency process."—General George W. Casey Jr., pictured above, describing Stratman in an Officer Evaluation Report covering the period of June 16, 2004 to June 15, 2005.

Stratman's arrival back in Baghdad occurred within a period of intense political scrutiny and a short time after news of the Abu Graib prison scandal broke on national news networks. Television viewers worldwide were fed a depressing view of U.S. involvement in the torture of Iraqi prisoners, which summarily inspired a number of recommended changes to the command structure of General Ricardo Sanchez's headquarters, coming from the highest levels within the Department of Defense. The leadership breakdown eventually resulted in several unnecessary and depressing circumstances while Stratman was serving in Turkey, with the Abu Ghraib prisoner torture and abuse becoming the most publicized. Abu Ghraib was an enormous prison complex that had been used by Saddam Hussein to house Iraqi prisoners, but later transitioned into a detention facility for prisoners of war. The Central Intelligence Agency and the U.S. Army garnered unfavorable headlines when investigations revealed a situation that devolved into a pattern of assorted tortures and abuses—and in one circumstance, death—of prisoners in U.S. custody. Many U.S. personnel were prosecuted for the identified crimes, some of whom were given prison sentences for the more egregious offenses.

One outcome was the placement of a four-star general in command of Iraq and making the Coalition Ground Forces a major subordinate command, leading to a more robust staff and providing the benefit of greater capabilities and resources. This new force structure was intended to foster an environment in which military and political efforts were implemented at the strategic level. General George Casey was selected to succeed Lieutenant General Sanchez, becoming the first commander of the newly devised Multi-National Forces-Iraq (MNF-1).[118] General Casey had most recently served as the Vice Chief of Staff of the U.S. Army prior to his newest post. Stratman recalled that he first met General Casey when the now-four-star gen-

---

[118] General Ricardo Sanchez went on to become commanding general of V Corps in Germany after relinquishing command to General George Casey. He retired at the rank of lieutenant general (three-star) on November 1, 2006, possessing thirty-three years of service with the U.S. Army.

eral had been a two-star assigned as the Director of Strategic Plans and Policy with the Joint Staff at the Pentagon a few years earlier.

Ambassador John D. Negroponte was brought into the country to represent the State Department and was saddled with the daunting task of establishing a diplomatic structure, a traditional U.S. embassy and new Iraqi government. Raised in New York City and Long Island, Negroponte graduated from Yale University and attended Harvard Law School before transitioning to the government sector with his role in the U.S. Foreign Service. His early government career included posts in Ecuador, Greece, Vietnam and Hong Kong. By the time he arrived in Iraq, Negroponte already possessed an impressive resume as a diplomat, having served as ambassador to Mexico, the Philippines, Honduras and as the U.S. representative to the United Nations.

It was also during this same turbulent period, when General Casey was beginning to integrate into his newest command duties in Baghdad, that Ambassador Negroponte was given the monumental charge of standing up a traditional U.S. Embassy in an area still considered to be in a combat zone due to a strong insurgency movement. This represented an unprecedented historical moment for the State Department, Stratman explained, since most embassies were known to pack up and abruptly depart regions that were embroiled in such conflict.

For the first thirty days of this process, General Casey and Ambassador Negroponte conducted their work in offices established inside the palace complex of ousted Iraqi President Saddam Hussein. Possessing more of the characteristics of a military commander rather than political aficionado, General Casey soon decided that he needed to move his operations to the airfield in Baghdad to be "in the field" and within arm's reach of the headquarters for the units he commanded. Stratman, whose position title was changed to Deputy Chief of Staff (Political Military Economic), was tasked with serving as the general officer who would coordinate between the U.S. Embassy, military units and provisional Iraqi government authorities.

Following his return to Iraq in June 2004, Major General Stratman (far right) was assigned as the Deputy Chief of Staff [Political-Military-Economic] under the auspices of the Multi-National Force-Iraq. In this capacity, he regularly coordinated with Ambassador John Negroponte (seated, left), an experienced diplomat, who had been sent to Baghdad by President George W. Bush to reestablish a U.S. Embassy and craft the new Iraqi government structure.

Transfer of authority from the Coalition Provisional Authority and Ambassador Paul Bremer to the Iraqi Interim government had taken place on June 28, 2004, shortly after Stratman's return to the Middle East. In the process of nurturing and developing the restructured government, there were many diplomatic, military and economic factors in the works, all of which had to be integrated to ensure a smooth and beneficial operating environment between disparate organizations.

"Essentially, I was the guy situated 'in the middle' between the military divisional commanders, the Iraqi Reconstruction and Management Office and US AID—a humanitarian organization," he said. "The ambassador was calling all the shots in the region for the first six-to-eight months, until President Bush selected Negroponte as the first Director of National Intelligence."

The *Record-Journal*, on October 31, 2004, reported on the overall mission in Iraq, "The broader context, senior officers and embassy officials say, is for the United States to continue on course and be patient, with the aim of restoring local control to Iraqis and helping rebuild the security forces and economy." The newspaper went on to quote Major General Stratman as stressing the point, "We can't lose this one."[119]

One of the first arrivals in Baghdad to help set the stage for Ambassador Negroponte and the embassy was Robert "Bob" Earle. Serving as Ambassador Negroponte's "right-hand-man," Earle assisted in fulfilling the role of the intellectual, strategist and writer for the ambassador. For years, Earle maintained a senior position in the U.S. Foreign Service that included a lengthy stint as senior adviser and counselor to Negroponte. With his arrival in Iraq, Stratman soon began working closely with Earle to conduct a summary assessment of the situation they were facing in rebuilding the nation. During their collaboration, a Joint Mission Statement was developed to identify the roles of the agencies involved in addition to that of the coalition forces. The statement was structured to define who were the enemies in the process of rebuilding the government while also mulling the best means to mitigate the effects of the insurgency operations that continued to grow.

"Earle and I worked closely together and developed a Joint Mission Statement that was only two pages long," Stratman said. "During the first thirty days of being in Iraq, my entire focus was working with him. It was an important and high-profile task especially since there was $18 billion in reconstruction money that had been committed to the process of rebuilding Iraq," he added.

The Joint Mission Statement, he affirmed, formalized and established the assurance that embassy and coalition forces shared the same vision and goals in the reconstruction process. Both Ambassador Negroponte and General Casey went on to sign the statement, shift-

---

[119] October 31, 2004 edition of *the Record Journal* (Meriden, Connecticut).

ing much of Stratman's and Earle's work associated to executing the vision that had been formed by educating the military commanders on the statement's goals and objectives while ensuring the smoothest integration achievable between the efforts of both embassy and coalition forces.

In his daily coordination with the ambassador and his designated representatives such as Earle, Stratman recalls attending daily country team meetings that consisted of senior embassy staff, military leaders, CIA representatives, Department of Commerce staff and Department of Justice experts. One of the moments Stratman clearly recalls from this exciting timeframe was being extended the opportunity to write the talking points used by an interim Iraqi prime minister who shared it with his cabinet members as a means to convince them of the importance of the first battle of Fallujah. It was not simply a speech designed to garner their support for the pending military operation, but was penned in a fashion to inspire them to maintain support even after the U.S. military activity was concluded.

"There were times when we were planning a major military operation to counter the insurgencies in certain locations and we had to make sure that the interim government didn't get cold feet on us," he explained. "We might have the situation where the interim Iraqi leadership is Sunni (a major denomination of Islam) and we needed to conduct an operation in a Sunni-controlled area. It was critical to ensure they wouldn't retract their support of the operation or else it might prove unsuccessful and deadly for our forces." He added, "This official needed talking points in briefing his cabinet, who were nascent and inexperienced. It was a way to ensure that we were there to support building their government and that they had our full cooperation in the process, but that we needed theirs as well."

To assist in his developing duties and responsibilities, Stratman soon began to receive a staff consisting of colonels, majors and captains, who he trained to attend to the many embassy and Iraq Reconstruction Management Office (IRMO) and Multi-National Force—Iraq meetings, ensuring synchronization of activities. For approximately two months, Stratman and Earle continued their collaborative efforts to identify means to mitigate the worsening insurgency situation, especially in light of approaching parliamentary elections scheduled for January 30, 2005, during which new National Assembly would be elected. The coordinated work of the pair continued at a rapid pace, until their team experienced a minor interruption when Earle nearly succumbed to an unexpected medical development and had to rapidly depart Baghdad.

"About two months into his assignment, Bob Earle developed a blood clot in one of his legs that nearly spread to other parts of his body and could have killed him," Stratman said. "He was medically evacuated from Baghdad and treated through the military medical system. He nearly died," he added.

In his absence, Stratman continued to educate the military leadership and staff on the details of the mission statement while also striving to synchronize the available resources in the region with those being provided by benevolent organizations. In his position, he had been appointed the principal allocator of Department of Defense

During his deployment to Iraq, Stratman was granted leave in November 2004 to return to the states for the wedding of his only son, Jon.

funds being used by division commanders in their sectors to fundamentally buy cooperation, totaling as much as $400-$500 million a year. These funds were intended not only to assist in the reconstruction efforts, but to demonstrate good will on behalf of the United States. Additionally, his daily outreach and coordination efforts strived to prevent unnecessary duplication of work being performed in the region, coordinating with agencies such as U.S. AID so that development dollars were spent wisely and effectively.

Stratman requested and received approval for mid-term deployment leave in November 2004 so he could attend the wedding of his only son, Jon. Prior to his departure, Bob Earle was called back to Iraq because of the worsening insurgency situation to develop an ambassador's report to President Bush with recommendations on the way forward. In his absence, Stratman assigned a seasoned colonel to work with Earle in developing the report, resulting in a thirty-page document that outlined a long-term strategy for building and maintaining the political process in Iraq. It was an unenviable moment for Earle, whose boss, Ambassador Negroponte, had to inform President Bush and the Washington, D.C., crowd what needed to be done to secure Iraq for the reconstruction to be successful. This occurred after President George W. Bush had declared "mission accomplished" in Iraq more than a year earlier, during his visit to the USS *Abraham Lincoln*.[120] Sadly, the situation in the embattled country would continue to worsen.

While home on two weeks of leave, Hank and Linda Stratman proudly watched as their son married his fiancée, the former Colleen Covey, in a ceremony held in Cincinnati, Ohio, on November 20, 2004.

Following his brief visit back in the U.S., Stratman returned to Baghdad and hastily immersed himself in his previous work of finding resolutions for the increasing insurgency issue. Shortly after Stratman's return to Iraq, Senator John F. Kerry of Massachusetts led a Congressional delegation comprised of several senators on a visit for a review of the efforts being made to rebuild the country. Their

---

[120] On May 1, 2003, President George W. Bush landed aboard the USS Abraham Lincoln in the co-pilot's seat of a Navy fighter aircraft. He spoke to a receptive crowd, noting that "Major combat operations in Iraq have ended," while a banner stating "Mission Accomplished" hung above him. Although the moment was intended to signal the end of major combat operations, "...the speech and the banner became a symbol of the unpopular war, which would last another eight brutal years." Cline, *The Other Symbol of George W. Bush's Legacy*, May 1, 2013.

trip occurred only a few weeks after Senator Kerry lost his bid for the presidency to the incumbent, George W. Bush. While participating in one of the country team meetings, Major General Stratman was the only senior military officer in attendance. Senator Kerry abruptly focused his attention on the general and began "drilling" him with detailed questions regarding the number of Iraqi military members who had been trained by U.S. forces thus far, how many trainees were currently in the pipeline, how many trained personnel there would be when the training regimen was completed and other associated questions.

"I politely responded to the senator that this had not been my specific area of focus and that's when he began to get ugly with me," Stratman recalled.

While deployed to Baghdad in 2005, Major General Stratman made the decision to retire from the U.S. Army and return to his home in Missouri after serving thirty-three years in uniform.

"Ambassador Negroponte interrupted him and defended me, stressing to the senator that he will be able to visit with Lieutenant General David Petraeus, who was responsible for training the Iraqi security forces."

The professional relationship Stratman developed with Ambassador Negroponte during the process of rebuilding Iraq was highlighted in an article researched and written by Stratman in 2006 for the military journal *Joint Force Quarterly*. In the article, Stratman explained, "Dialogue, cooperation and teamwork are necessary elements of the relationship between the U.S. Embassy Baghdad, Multi-National Force-Iraq, and the Interim Government in order to achieve the vision of a vibrant and democratic Iraq. That teamwork resolved many of the difficulties cited prior to the transfer of authority ... and established the foundation on which to ensure mission success." He added, "There was no doctrine outlining the steps to accomplish this team relationship. It was achieved through initiative and high-level commitment to teamwork ..."[121]

Taking a few moments to reflect on his broad range of unique experiences in support of the rebuilding of the Iraqi government, Stratman remarked, "It seems as though I have always been involved in non-standard missions—the two tours in Bosnia and working at the embassy in Baghdad. But then again," he said, "the more senior you get in the military, the more challenging your assignments tend to become."

As mid-spring 2005 passed by on the calendar, Stratman explained, discussions took place regarding his next duty assignment. He was advised by the Pentagon that he was slated to assume the position as ROTC commander for the U.S. Army. Having worked with the previous ROTC commander during his time at TRADOC, Stratman realized that this was not an assignment that possessed enough appeal or promise to inspire his desire to remain in the U.S. Army.

"It was not a career-enhancing assignment," he bluntly recalled. "For me, the writing was on the wall that I was not going to get a division command and that I had peaked out as a major general who wasn't going any further in the Army. In the past," he continued, "I had watched other two-stars hang on to their careers only to become absolutely miserable in what they were doing"

In lieu of his departure ceremony, Statman's retirement ceremony was held in Baghdad on June 20, 2005. In the presence of ambassadors and flag officers with whom he had worked during the

---

[121] *Joint Force Quarterly* (Issue 41, 2nd Quarter 2006), Orchestrating Instruments of Power for Nationbuilding, 32-37.

previous year, Stratman's remarks reflected upon his participation in the "historic undertaking to bring democracy to the Middle East."

Embracing his signature honest reflection, he continued, "I never intended to make a career of the Army, which wasn't held in very high esteem in the 1970s. I joined the Army based upon the results of the first national draft lottery, which ended the draft, during the troubling days of 'make love, not war' 1960s and '70s. I am proud to say I was a small part of fixing the Army failings of the Vietnam era—and the all-volunteer force that evolved into the best, most capable and respected Army ever fielded. It took us about ten years to grow and train this Army we are so proud of today; we shouldn't expect the Iraqi army to do it in a couple of years."

In addition to his own experiences during the Persian Gulf War and the Global War on Terrorism, Stratman has enjoyed reading a number of biographies and military historical reviews that "fill in some of the gaps."

Soon, he was aboard a flight back to the states to complete the process of mustering out of the Army at the Pentagon. He returned home to Missouri on July 2, 2005, with his official discharge date being January 1, 2006, representing thirty-three years of honorable service to his country. Any joys that should have been associated with entering retirement and embarking upon new adventures with his wife were tempered by the unfortunate news he received upon his arrival home.

"Linda and my son picked me up at the airport in St. Louis and that's when they told me my mother-in-law, Phyllis, had passed away the previous day," he glumly explained. "It certainly was bittersweet to be coming home from ending my career to attend a family funeral. Phyllis and I had shared a special relationship throughout the years. At first, she wasn't happy that I married her daughter because they were Protestant and I was Catholic, but I would tease her that I was her favorite son-in-law … her only son-in-law," he chuckled. He further noted, "She learned to love me and I had many great discussions with her. She was very proud to see me make general officer and was supportive of my career."[122]

His military legacy of more than three decades resulted in the issuance of several prestigious awards including the Distinguished Service Medal, Defense Superior Service Medal, multiple Legion of Merit presentations and a Bronze Star. The time had come where his service was now a period to be viewed in reflection, serving as a reminder that although most professional soldiers never want their careers to end, their comes a time to store away one's combat boots and move on to other missions in life.

"Old soldiers don't die, they just fade away," he mirthfully remarked. "As a commander, one of the primary admonishments I had always given my troops was that if they were not willing to give one-hundred percent in every assignment they were given, then it was time for them to move on. That was something I always believed

---

[122] Phyllis Ruth Deakins was eighty-one years old when she passed away on July 1, 2005. She was laid to rest next to her husband, John, in Dripping Spring Christian Church Cemetery in Columbia.

in." Pausing, he humbly added, "Now, it had become my turn to abide by that same advice."

With a new adventure on the horizon, Stratman explained that despite all the difficulties he encountered and overcame during his varied experiences, he could not exit the service without acknowledging the essential support of an individual whom he viewed as most responsible for the successes of this military career.

"I married well above my paygrade," Stratman mirthfully remarked in his retirement speech. "Linda has had the more difficult role to play throughout our career—managing frequent moves to strange places, numerous separations and the frustrations associated with caring for family members during deployments. Being an Army spouse is certainly the hardest job in the Army."

He concluded, "Thank you Linda for being my most reliable critic, my staunchest supporter, lover and friend—and to paraphrase Tammy Wynette's country song, thank you Linda for standing by your man, through the good times and bad. I love you, be home soon."

CHAPTER 15

Hanging up the Uniform

"It's a visible recognition of the need for good quality service members," Stratman said. "My advice to all youth, whether they serve in the military or not, is focus on 'ask not what the country can do for you, but what you can do for your country.' Don't look for entitlements or a free ride — that's not a sustainable America." –Hank Stratman in a 2017 interview discussing the "Freedom Corner" memorial.

For a few days during the summer of 2005, Stratman returned to the Pentagon to attend a transition course designed to assist general officers who were returning to the private sector. After returning home and attending the funeral of his mother-in-law, he and his wife chose to focus their efforts throughout the next several months by overseeing the local contractor they had hired to build their retirement home in Callaway County, Missouri. Upon moving into the house in April 2006, the couple became actively involved in completing the array of small tasks that would make it a more hospitable location to spend their retirement. In addition to all of the finishing touches that would provide them with greater comforts in the coming years, they also began to explore several elements of a business prospect that might help them become engaged in the local communities.

"That pretty well consumed my entire year of 2006: establishing our new home, attending various welcome home parties and reconnecting with friends and family," Stratman said. "At the time, one of my early goals was to develop eighteen acres of the property adjacent to our home, but then the housing bubble burst in 2007 and 2008." He added, "With the uncertainty of the housing market along with the fact I was not known as a developer in the area, Linda and I thought it best to place that goal on hold."

For only a brief period, Stratman disconnected from the military machine but was soon recruited by Military Professionals Resources, Inc. (MPRI), a Department of Defense contractor that provided a variety of military training and operations support to the U.S. and foreign militaries. As a general officer, MPRI sought to leverage the knowledge and skills possessed by Stratman and have him serve as a senior advisor on a team that conducted force protection visits to U.S. Army installations worldwide.

He explained, "We would travel to these installations and assist the staff in running force protection exercises. This was post 9-11 and one of the focal points in national security was integration of military, fire, media and law enforcement at the local, state and federal level. The primary purpose of the combined exercises and training that we coordinated was designed to help the installation staff effectively work alongside other agencies in a situation where they might be responding to active shooter and terrorist events or natural and man-made disasters."

The team's work to improve the local installation's techniques and procedures within the paradigm of force protection lasted approximately three years, Stratman noted. When the new administration of President Barrack Obama took over, many defense budgets were cut significantly and the training was eliminated.

The contracting work was a light load, Stratman explained, which had only consumed about one week of his time each month. During the three years of his part-time work with MPRI, he and Linda had made the decision to sell a duplex in Jefferson City at a profit. Cognizant of the tax liabilities that would abruptly come in the new tax year following the recent sale of the property, he and his wife chose to reinvest their profits by purchasing another property.

"Not only was it a matter of taxes, but we realized that we needed to do something to become known as developers in the local community," Stratman maintained. "Also, we had always possessed an interest in historic preservation based upon our travels to different sites in the world, so when we learned that Warwick Village was available for purchase as a bank foreclosure property, everything just seemed to come together."

Established in 1935 and erected on a triangular slice of property less than an acre in size, Warwick Village was originally flanked by U.S. Highway 50 (now McCarty Street) and U.S. 63 East (now High Street). The facade of the buildings of Warwick Village were designed to possess the appeal of Tudor-style cabins hearkening to the bygone days of Medieval architecture that might be found in England and Wales. The cluster of quaint cottages became a welcome sight for many a weary traveler who sought a place to rest for the night. In addition to the accommodations provided, the cluster of cottages was accentuated by a restaurant that served a variety of comfort foods that could satisfy the hunger pangs of travelers and make a long journey more enjoyable.

Warwick Village, pictured in its early days of operation, was a quaint travel destination established in the east end of Jefferson City in 1935. After years of catering to travelers, it fell into a state of disrepair. Hank and Linda Stratman purchased the business in 2007 and have since revitalized the property.

The well-known roadside attraction suffered the decline of many such businesses, a large part of it caused by the relocation of the major highways that once caressed its perimeter. Falling into a regrettable state of disrepair and suffering from depleted profit margins, the property was eyed for development by a couple of interested investors, but ended up back under the ownership of a local bank due to foreclosure. In 2007, after other investors had become discouraged after realizing the potential challenge they faced in the redevelopment of Warwick Village, Hank and Linda Stratman set their sights on a successful revitalization of the area in the east side of Jefferson City.

"We saw the value of the property from not only a historical context, but also realized we would need to make it economically viable as well," he said. "And though we were able to purchase it for a reasonable price, we realized it would require a significant investment of capital and sweat equity from both of us," he added. "But just like my service in the Army, failure was never an option and that included this development," he affirmed.

The progress of their vision of achieving revitalization of the property met with some early opposition by local government. City staff advised the couple they would need to provide engineer designed drawings for every step of the reconstruction process, representing a significant amount of cost being added to their budget. Soon, Stratman began to challenge the requirement after he discovered there was an exception in the city code for historical places, and he was being held to standards that had been established for those embarking upon new construction.

"Linda and I took on city hall and most of the time we won," he said. "When we began, we realized it would be a five-year process and we worked many long hours. I believe we poured about 600 cubic yards of concrete together, and that's not anything easy," he added.

Naming their new business Cottage Industries of Jefferson City, the Stratmans envisioned the process of renovation occurring in three phases. The first phase of their grand vision included "gutting" the hotel section of the property and converting it into loft studio apartments, which had become popular in the area and would begin to provide an income stream once completed. The second phase focused on the restaurant, a timely achievement that was rented and initially became a coffee shop. Finally, in the third phase, the couple invested hundreds of hours in the renovation of the European-style cottages situated around the perimeter of the property. As they completed each of these cottages, they were listed for rental and many have transitioned to the retail outlets and salons for a variety of local small businesses.

The east side of Jefferson City, Stratman explained, had essentially been neglected by local government for many years and he recognized there were several potential risks associated with the purchase of the property and its subsequent renovation. However, there was a proposal for federal-level funding of a new federal courthouse on the east side along with plans for updated Lafayette Street interchanges and multiple road improvements. The nearby Missouri State Penitentiary campus, which had been sitting vacant since October 2004, became a highlight of spirited discussions amongst the city council and a host of other local organizations, all whom believed it had the potential for a renovation that would accommodate historical tours and help establish it as a tourist destination. Additionally, a short distance to the east, along the U.S. 50 corridor, plans were being finalized for the installation of a new interchange with roundabouts to support access for the construction of a new Wal-Mart Supercenter.

Stratman said, "So, there were several dynamics at play and we recognized both the area and our property had all of this potential and there was nowhere to go but up. We were able to maximize every square inch of the property and promote a small-town, European village environment ... and there was nothing like it in the region," he added.

The apartments were easily rented followed by us finding an interested and responsible tenant that opened the restaurant area as a coffee shop. Another challenge soon emerged when the coffee shop owner explained to the Stratmans that they would like to open a drive-through lane for their fledgling business.

"I did my due diligence and went to the city about putting in a drive-through and they were very supportive. When I went to the city planner, I was told it would never happen. I told him to tell me the specs and was able to meet every requirement except for one that pertained to an offset from the road. That's when I informed him that the city council and mayor were supportive of what I was trying to do. We were able to get the drive-thru approved, much of which was due to the large amount of support I got from local councilmen and women who wanted to see the area grow and improve."

The name of the property was then changed from Warwick Village to the Village Square. In addition to the rental of the apartments and restaurant areas, the couple completed the cottages, one at a time, and then began renting them to prospective small business owners. On the fourth year of their five-year plan, Stratman was approached by a city public works official who advised him that the Boy Scouts had agreed to maintain for two years the nearby intersection that contained a memorial, but they were no longer going to be able to do so.

Although located on city right-of-way, Stratman took a lead role in developing the intersection adjacent to the Village Square into "Freedom Corner," paying homage to all who have served in the nation's Armed Forces.

The area of the intersection that contained the memorial, though situated on city right-of-way, was adjacent to the property that housed the Village Square. In 1976, a civic organization of local businesses known as the East Side Betterment Association, steered a beautification and improvement project to the intersection by installing a flagpole, monument and plaque as a tribute to those who had served in the Armed Forces during the previous two hundred years.[123] Flowers and other plants were placed around the area to make it look

---

[123] The East Side Betterment Association was established in 1971 by forty-three business and property owners. Upon its founding, the association cited its goals as the promotion of the economic, civic and general welfare of Jefferson City with a particular focus on the East Side. They developed the slogan "better living through community cooperation" and hosted a number of social activities such as a St. Patrick's Day Dinner and an annual barbecue.

more attractive to passersby. Although the request from the city official for Stratman to accept the responsibility for maintenance of the area was not a daunting task, when combined with his many responsibilities in developing the property, it was a major obligation. But recognizing the need to help maintain the area for community pride and to be involved in the area where he now operated a business, he agreed to take on yet another new challenge.

The East Side Betterment Association later became the Jefferson City East Side Business Association. As a business owner in the area, Stratman joined the association

Stratman is pictured during a ceremony held at Freedom Corner on Veteran's Day 2015. Accompanying him, from left: Linda Stratman (wife); Georgena Hayes (his oldest sister); and, Marian Fleischman (his youngest sister).

to not only help promote his own business, the Village Square, but to improve the area for all who lived, worked and operated businesses on the east side of the city. He approached the association about assisting with the process of maintaining the memorial, suggesting an upgrade to make it a more appropriate veterans' tribute, honoring all who had served in the military.

"When I went to the East Side Business Association about adopting the spot, I had a plan and a vision," Stratman said. "Many in the association agreed right away. Architect Alliance provided a professional concept drawing that featured an eagle on a pedestal. Fortunately, I received donations to cover the cost of the eagle and we sold brick pavers to raise the rest of the money. My sister Marian told me about a bronze eagle for sale at an antique store in Centertown that would be perfect for the memorial, which we purchased."

Another early step in the process was seeking approval from the city for making the upgrades to the memorial, since it was located on the city's right-of-way. Embracing the years of experience developed and refined by briefing general officers and representatives of foreign governments, Stratman described what he intended to accomplish through the project along with the specific timeline for completion.

Major General (retired) Stratman spoke at a school assembly held at Helias Catholic High School in October 2019, honoring the late Major General Don D. Pittman. Pictured, from left: Father Stephen Jones, Stratman, Col. (retired) John Clark, and Lt. Gov. Mike Kehoe.

"When I briefed the city council for approval on September 1, 2013, I told them to mark their calendars for Veterans Day 2013 because that's when we were going to hold the dedication ceremony." Smiling, he added, "The city council approved it but they all just kind of rolled their eyes, not believing that we would be able to get it done within only a couple of months."

The project was funded primarily through the sale of commemorative bricks and supplemented by a fundraising drive. Many local companies graciously donated labor and materials for the cause while the old monument was removed and the flagpole restored. As part of the tribute, a bronze eagle in flight was fitted atop a fourteen-foot-tall granite pedestal. The day prior to the dedication ceremony, the last brick paver was laid at the site. The intersection was designated "Freedom Corner," and an inaugural ceremony held on Veterans Day 2013, becoming the location where a patriotic ceremony is held annually and involves not only members of the community, but students from the local schools and cadets from the Lincoln University ROTC program—Stratman's alma mater.

During the dedication, he remarked of the new monument, "It's a visible recognition of the need for good quality service members," Stratman said. "My advice to all youth, whether they serve in the military or not, is focus on 'ask not what the country can do for you, but what you can do for your country.' Don't look for entitlements or a free ride — that's not a sustainable America."[124]

He went on to describe his experiences with

Hank Stratman, right, attends a Jefferson City Council meeting in February 2019 to discuss the patriotic roundabout initiative. Also pictured are Mayor Carrie Tergin and DeeDee Mehmert-Cryderman, who represented American Legion Post 5. City Council members are pictured in the background.

---

[124] November 12, 2017 edition of the *Fulton Sun*.

Freedom Corner: "That's how I do business—I make things happen and find a way to get things done. As a veteran, I was committed to making the monument a reality while, as a business person, I had an interest in the intersection having a professional appearance," he added.

Maintaining active membership in the Jefferson City East Side Business Association, Stratman paralleled his early career in the U.S. Army by "moving up in the ranks." In 2018, he became the association's president during a period when discussions were being held on what should be done to improve membership. Stratman suggested a visible project with East Side Business Association signage. The East McCarty Street roundabouts had been installed to accommodate the traffic flow for the new WalMart Supercenter but were not being maintained. After seeing a stunning piece of roundabout artwork that had been funded and maintained by a local hospital at the center of a Stadium Boulevard roundabout across town, Stratman saw the

This is one of two stunning monuments installed in the roundabouts along East McCarty Street in Jefferson City. It was part of a cooperative project between the East Side Business Association and the American Legion Post 5. Photo by Kathleen Stratman, Hank and Linda's granddaughter.

opportunity to hang the East Side Business Association's "shingle" in a highly visible location.

"We partnered with the American Legion Post 5 and launched an initiative to adopt the roundabouts and install patriotic displays," Stratman said. "The property was owned by MODOT (Missouri Department of Transportation) and it took six months for us to gain approval for the displays. MODOT regional leadership was concerned with the patriotic themes because one of the proposals included a monument featuring the Pledge of Allegiance with the words 'under God.' I informed them that those words in the pledge had been approved by Congress decades ago and that I could not change the words." He added, "They also began to express an issue with the battlefield cross on one of the 'freedom is not free' monuments because they said we could not have a religious symbol. I tried to explain that the battlefield cross was a symbol recognizing fallen comrades and featured a helmet, rifle, boots and dog tags.

Stratman and members of the local American Legion briefed Lieutenant Governor Mike Kehoe on the initiative, which he liked. Learning of the pushback Stratman and the Legion were encountering from MODOT, Kehoe scheduled a meeting with MODOT leadership and then said to give him a couple of weeks to discuss the issue with state transportation commissioners. Permission for installation of the monuments along with the initially-proposed wording and symbols was soon granted.

Much like the development of Freedom Corner a few years earlier, many individuals, businesses and organizations donated work and the funds to complete the two roundabouts. Additionally, the East Side Business Association partnered with Roscoe Enloe American Legion Post 5 to help raise funds and generate support and awareness for the project. The patriotic roundabouts were officially dedicated in a ceremony held in April 2019. An agreement was established whereby the roundabout with the flagpole is maintained by the American Legion Post 5 while the East Side Business Association maintains the roundabout with the eagle statue.

Another special opportunity to honor local veterans came in June 2019, when a special ceremony was held at the Veterans of

Foreign Wars Post 1003 in nearby St. Martins, Missouri. Wearing his crisp U.S. Army dress blues, Major General (retired) Stratman spoke at an event, along with local dignitaries such as Lieutenant Governor Mike Kehoe and State Representative Rudy Veit, paying tribute to the ninety-six-year-old James Shipley of Tipton, Missouri. During World War II, Shipley had made the decision to enlist in the U.S. Army Air Forces and trained to become a crew chief and mechanic for the famed Tuskegee Airmen before deploying to Italy. Shipley was never able to finish his high school education and, under a special program administered by the Missouri Department of Elementary and Secondary Education titled *Operation Recognition*, was awarded his high school diploma more than eighty years after leaving school.

Ever the proponent of promoting the spirit of patriotism and the benefits of military service to the younger generation, Stratman has, for the last several years, maintained active involvement with *Operation Bugle Boy (OBB)*. Established in 2001, OBB "is a community response to the September 11, 2001, terrorist attack on our nation," explained the organization's website. "The mission of Operation Bugle Boy is to initiate and carry out activities and programs that honor and support our troops, veterans, and first responders, and help make us more appreciative of their sacrifices." Among the host of events sponsored by OBB, perhaps the most recognizable activity of the all-volunteer organization is *Veterans Appreciation Night,* a USO-style dinner held in November of every year to pay tribute to local veterans. Additionally, the organization holds an annual seminar to help educate the public—with a focus on area youth—about the sacrifices made by our nation's armed forces and to inspire a sense of duty and service to the country.[125]

His participation in a number of patriotic events has become his means of honoring those with whom he has served while also inculcating in younger generations an inspiration to become a part of something much bigger than themselves.

---

[125] Operation Bugle Boy, *About Us*, https://www.operationbugleboy.com.

Stratman smiles in the background while Missouri Lt. Gov. Mike Kehoe presents James Shipley with his high school diploma in 2019. Shipley was unable to finish high school because of his service with the Tuskegee Airmen in World War II, and was awarded his diploma under a special state program known as Operation Recognition.

"I'm most interested in encouraging the young kids to serve in our all-volunteer armed forces," he said. "It's not so much about the older veterans—they have served and already possess that deeply embedded sense of pride in our country. But the younger generations, they are very important to the survival of our nation, because they will be responsible for defending our country and our constitutional rights."

Reflecting on the last several decades and the incalculable interesting moments he has been blessed to experience in his career, Stratman maintains that he and his wife now enjoy a much lighter pace of activity. When not engaged in attending local events or expanding their entrepreneurial endeavors, they welcome opportunities to witness the many accomplishments of their seven grandchildren.

"It has been an exciting transition for Linda and I to leave the U.S. Army lifestyle and learn along the way how to become entrepreneurs and develop various properties," he explained. "Throughout my entire military career, no matter the missions that was assigned, failure has never been an option in anything that I pursued."

Pausing, he sharply folded his hands, leaned forward slowly in his chair and remarked, "I will always find a way to make it happen, which is the same way that I was in the military."

Epilogue

The term "Golden Years" has come to be associated with the point in one's life where they have earned the privilege to bask in the reflection of past accomplishments, concurrently finding enjoyment in the comforts that come with the quiet life of retirement. Hank and Linda Stratman, however, are not the types to glide silently into the background of their communities and let the world pass them by during their retirement years, but have instead found ways to remain active and continue to make contributions on the local level.

They concede that they have begun to develop much of the land surrounding their home that will be sold off, as a way to downsize their farm while also providing some additional income and establishing a nice community adjacent to their home. Their own home, where both he and Linda intend to spend their remaining years, has stunning views of the rural landscape and local wildlife. It is "living the dream!" he maintains.

Remaining actively involved in activities that support and honor the nation's veterans, Stratman volunteered with a committee that helped raise the funds to install a stunning memorial to Gold Star Families on the grounds of the Missouri State Capitol.

The retired general enjoys working on his small farm, spending time focused on assorted tasks outside the home but is regularly contacted to speak at a host of events, lending his experiences as a soldier and leader. Not only did he serve on the planning committee that helped bring a stunning Gold Star Families monument to the grounds of the Missouri State Capitol, he rarely turns down an opportunity to share lessons learned during his time in uniform before audiences of students and youth groups.[126] His time in command of soldiers may have long since passed, but he recognizes the importance of remembering those who died while in the service and acknowledges the future of the country and the state of the Armed Forces lies with young individuals who will help shape the future. In this spirit, he not only seeks to inspire the younger generations to consider careers in public service, but calls upon his fellow veterans and adults to strive to inculcate a sense of patriotism and duty in their own children.

One of the many joys of retirement for Hank and Linda Stratman is spending time with their grandchildren. Pictured are the children of their son, Jon, and his wife, Colleen. From left: Margaret, Brian and Kathleen.

"President Lincoln ... said, 'A Nation that does not honor its heroes will not long endure,'" Stratman remarked during a ceremony held in Russellville, Missouri, in October 2020, during the dedica-

---

[126] Gold Star Families represent those who have lost a loved one as the result of their military service.

tion of a Gold Star memorial in the city's park. "That includes honoring the Gold Star Families of this great nation. Now, it is our call to duty to honor those who made the ultimate sacrifice, by doing everything we can to protect freedom for future generations, whenever and wherever, it is threatened at home or abroad."

Slowly raising the tone of his voice, he firmly stated, "Parents and grandparents, it's *your duty* to instill a passion for patriotism in your children and grandchildren, and encourage our public schools to do the same! We must always remain the 'Beacon of Hope' for oppressed people around the world. America, however imperfect, is the *best* place in the world to live, work and raise a family – and to Be All that You Can Be!"

Luck may have played a role in certain aspects of his career, Stratman admits, but it was hard work, dedication and focus, combined with the support of his loving wife, Linda, that led to a rewarding experience with the U.S. Army. Rising from the obscurity of a hardscrabble farm family in the rural community of Vienna, Missouri, to earning his degree and commission as a military officer through the historically-black education institution of Lincoln University, Stratman's is a story of a young man able to rise above his meager circumstances to great heights within the military community. The journey, he affirms, is not one absent of opportunity for others aspiring to reach for the stars, but a simple narrative within the grand story that highlights the many prospects available to anyone resolved to applying themselves to succeed in life.

*Pictured are Hank and Linda's grandchildren by their
daughter, Jodie, and her husband, Richard. From
left: Andrew, Eucolona, Russell and Richard.*

Patriotism and love of country are characteristics forever embedded in Stratman's composite. His journeys throughout the world
have revealed to him that the United States, although possessing its
own imperfections, remains the greatest nation in the world and has
a noble leadership legacy that is still being written. It is the country
he has always looked forward to returning to following an absence
and home to a democracy and freedoms forever worth preserving.

"I'm going to wrap up my remarks with lyrics from my favorite country singer, Lee Greenwood," Stratman said during the aforementioned Gold Star dedication.[127]

"I'm Proud to be an American where at least I know I'm free.
And I won't forget the men—and women—who died who gave that

---

[127] *God Bless the U.S.A.* is a patriotic son written by country singer Lee Greenwood
and was released by MCA Nashville in 1984. The song is frequently played at
patriotic events and found newfound popularity during the Persian Gulf War
and following the September 11 attacks.

right to me. And I'd gladly stand up next to you and defend her still today – cause there ain't no doubt I love this land – *God Bless the USA!*"

-End-

Major General Henry "Hank" Stratman
U.S. Army – December 20, 1972 to January 1, 2006

This photograph was taken during the playing of the National Anthem at a Memorial Day ceremony held at Camp Doha, Kuwait in 2003. Maj. Gen. Stratman was the keynote speaker and spoke in tribute to the many soldiers recently killed during intense combat operations in Afghanistan and Iraq. Emotions and resolve, he recalled, were at an all-time high. He noted it was a very emotional event and that he received a standing ovation for his remarks.

Appendix A

Military Promotion dates for Henry "Hank" Stratman

Second Lieutenant	December 20, 1972
First Lieutenant	December 20, 1974
Captain	December 20, 1976
Major	March 1, 1984
Lieutenant Colonel	March 1, 1990
Colonel	September 1, 1994
Brigadier General	November 1, 1998
Major General	December 8, 2001

Appendix B

Below is a copy of the invitation Hank Stratman and other graduating cadets of the Lincoln University ROTC program sent to friends and family for their commissioning ceremony in December 1972.

The Department of Military Science
Lincoln University

requests the honor of your presence

at

The R.O.T.C. Mid-year
Commissioning Ceremony

Wednesday, the twentieth of December
Nineteen hundred and seventy-two
at eleven o'clock in the morning

Scruggs University Center
Jefferson City, Missouri

Appendix C

Below is the cover of the program Captain Stratman received when grad-
uating from U.S. Army Command and General Staff College at Fort
Leavenworth, Kansas, on June 3, 1983.

1983
Graduation Program

U.S. Army Command and General Staff College
Fort Leavenworth, Kansas

Appendix D

During Stratman's deployment to Saudi Arabia, Kuwait and Iraq during the Persian Gulf War in early 1991, he recalls the Air Force dropping tens of thousands of leaflets written in Arabic to encourage Iraqi soldiers and sympathizers to think about their families and surrender.

Appendix E

ARMY OF THE REPUBLIC OF SRPSKA
  MAIN HEADQUARTERS

No. 06/17-15
21 Jan 1996

To: ARRC Headquarters
      General Michael Walker

Dear Sir,

Three chairmen of our Corps level military commissions informed me that they have received a document from Colonel Henry W Stratman - JMC of the Multinational Division North East, demanding from them to submit the most detailed information concerning their respective areas and in connection to D+30 deadline of the Peace Agreement.

At the meeting of Joint Military Commission on 20 Jan 1996 our side submitted appropriate documents concerning the above deadline. I was informed by the head of our delegation that the above documents would be analyzed by you and possible amendments would be required in the following 2 or 3 days.

I believe that Colonel Stratman does not have the authority to give new tasks concerning this issue, especially due to the fact that such obligations of lower military commissions were not discussed at the last JMC meeting chaired by you.

It would be desirable to define tasks of lower military commissions at future meetings of JMC, especially concerning reporting, in order to avoid any possible misunderstanding and to have the work on implementation of the Peace Agreement more efficient.

Sincerely,

COMMANDER
General
Ratko Mladic

Appendix F

This flyer is an advertisement that was distributed in the search for information leading to the apprehension of former Yugoslavian President Slobodan Milosevic in addition to Bosnian Serb leaders Radovan Karadzic and Ratko Mladic.

Appendix G

During his deployment with the Multi-National Force-Iraq as part of the Global War on Terrorism in 2004-2005, this sign hung the door of the office of Major General Hank Stratman, which was located inside the former palace complex of Saddam Hussein.

Appendix H

As part of a project to improve roundabouts on the East Side of Jefferson City, two stunning monuments were installed along East McCarty Street. This became part of a cooperative project between the East Side Business Association and the American Legion Post 5. (Photograph courtesy of Julie Smith.)

Works Cited

NEWSPAPERS

Bangor Daily News, (Bangor, Maine)
Champion Times (Baumholder, Germany)
Daily Capital News (Jefferson City, Missouri)
Daily Press (Newport News, Virginia)
Des Moines Register (Des Moines, Iowa)
Fort Worth Star-Telegram (Fort Worth, Texas)
Fulton Sun (Fulton, Missouri)
Los Angeles Times
Miami Herald (Miami, Florida)
New York Times
Record Journal (Meriden, Connecticut)
Sacramento Bee (Sacramento, California)
Washington Times (Washington, D.C.)
Wisconsin State Journal (Madison, Wisconsin)

BOOKS AND ARTICLES

Andrews, Patricia L. *Methods for Predicting Fire Behavior—You Do Have a Choice*. Fire Management Notes, 47, No. 2 (1986): 6-10.
Bacevich, Andrew J. Fault Lines: *Inside Rumsfeld's Pentagon*. Boston Review, July 1, 2008. http://bostonreview.net/andrew-bacevich-inside-rumsfelds-pentagon·
Bolger, Lt. Gen. (Ret.) *Daniel. America Takes on Difficult Mission in Balkans*. ARMY magazine, December 2020.

Brokaw, Tom. *The Greatest Generation*. New York, NY: Random House, 1998.

Cline, Seth. *The Other Symbol of George W. Bush's Legacy*. U.S. News & World Report, May 1, 2013.

The Desert Jayhawk. *VII Corps in Action*. VII Corps Public Affairs Office, Undated.

Field Artillery. *Field Artillery Equipment and Munitions Update*, December 1989.

Fontenot, Col. Gregory, Lt. Col. E.J. Degen & Lt. Col. David Tohn. On Point: The United States Army in Operation Iraqi Freedom. Fort Leavenworth, Kansas: Combat Institute Press, 2004.

Frank, Gen. Fred & Col. Gregory Fontenot. "The First Gulf War: Decisive U.S. Response was Both End of an Era, Birth of a New One." *Army Magazine 65, No. 7 (July 2015):40-43*.

Franks, General Tommy. *American Soldier*. New York, NY: HarperCollins, 2004.

Johns, Dave. *The Crimes of Saddam Hussein*. Frontline World. December 12, 2020. https://www.pbs.org/frontlineworld/stories/iraq501/events_kuwait.html

Kamphoefner, Walter D. *The Westfalians: From Germany to Missouri*. Princeton, NJ: Princeton University Press, 2014.

Kriner, Douglas L. and Francis X. Shen. *The Casualty Gap: The Causes and Consequences of American Wartime Inequalities*. Oxford, United Kingdom: Oxford University Press, 2010.

Mitzman, Dany. "It's 200 Years Old, But What is Italy's Carabinieri?" *BBC News (July 13, 2014)*.

Raugh Jr., Dr. Harold E. *Operation Joint Endeavor: V Corps in Bosnia-Herzegovina, An Oral History*. Fort Leavenworth, KS: Combat Studies Institute Press, 2010. https://www.armyupress.army.mil/Portals/7/combat-studies-institute/csi-books/OperationJointEndeavor.pdf. (accessed February 10, 2021).

Salisbury, LTC Alan B. *The Making of a Weapons System: TACFIRE, 1959-1978*. Washington, D.C.: National Defense University Research Directorate, August 1978.

Stratman, Henry. "Orchestrating Instruments of Power for Nationbuilding." *Joint Force Quarterly*, Issue 41, Quarter 2006.

Taylor, Frederick. *The Berlin Wall: A World Divided, 1961-1989*. New York: HarperCollins Publishers, 2004.

Roache, Specialist George. "Joint Military Commission Enhances Peace Efforts." *The Talon*, Vol. 2, No. 2 (January 26, 1996):5.

ONLINE RESOURCES

Army War College. *Historic Carlisle Barracks*. Accessed January 22, 2021. https://www.armywarcollege.edu/history.cfm

Army Transformation War Game 2001. *Vigilant Warriors*. Accessed April 12, 2021. https://apps.dtic.mil/dtic/tr/fulltext/u2/a393451.pdf

Barron's. Grandson Reveals Late 'Regret' of Yugoslavia's Tito. Accessed February 8, 2021. https://www.barrons.com/news/grandson-reveals-late-regret-of-yugoslavia-s-tito-01588211409

Burke, Peter. *The King of Battle Gets Stronger*. Accessed December 30, 2020. https://www.army.mil/article/195413/the_king_of_battle_gets_stronger.

Correll, John. "The Strategy of Desert Storm." *Air Force Magazine*, January 1, 2006. Accessed January 2, 2021. https://www.air-forcemag.com/article/0106storm/.

Defense Technical Information Center. *The ATT/TPI (Army Training Test/Technical Proficiency Inspection*. Accessed December 1, 2020. https://apps.dtic.mil/docs/citations/AD0778876. Department of State: Office of the Historian. *The Breakup of Yugoslavia, 1990-1992*. Accessed January 31, 2021. https://history.state.gov/milestones/1989-1992/breakup-yugoslavia.

Department of State: Office of the Historian. *The Collapse of the Soviet Union*. Accessed November 25, 2020. https://history.state.gov/milestones/1989-1992/collapse-soviet-union#:~:text=On%20December%2025%2C%201991%2C%20the,the%20newly%20independe nt%20Russian%20state.

Federal Bureau of Investigation. Oklahoma City Bombing. Accessed March 21, 2021. https://www.fbi.gov/history/famous-cases/oklahoma-city-bombing

Federation of American Scientists. United States European Command: Overview and Key Issues. Accessed January 28, 2021. https://fas.org/sgp/crs/natsec/IF11130.pdf.

Government of Canada. *Operation Desert Thunder I and II.* Accessed March 10, 2021. https://www.canada.ca/en/department-national-defence/services/military-history/history-heritage/past-operations/middle-east/desert-thunder-i-ii.html.

Historic Valley Forge. Molly Pitcher. Accessed January 25, 2021. https://www.ushistory.org/valleyforge/youasked/070.htm

History of Computing Information. *Electronic Computers Within the Ordnance Corps.* Accessed October 10, 2020. https://ftp.arl.army.mil/~mike/comphist/61ordnance/chap6.html.

Lincoln University. *ROTC Hall of Fame Induction Ceremony.* Accessed March 1, 2021. https://www.lincolnu.edu/web/homecoming/homecoming/hall-of-fame-induction

Lockheed Martin. *Army Tactical Missile System Block IA Unitary.* Accessed October 31, 2020. https://www.lockheedmartin.com/en-us/products/army-tactical-missile-system-block-ia-unitary-atacms.html.

Lockheed Martin. *ATACMS: Long-Range Precision Tactical Missile System.* Accessed November 21, 2020. https://www.lockheedmartin.com/content/dam/lockheed-martin/mfc/pc/army-tacticle-missile-system-block-ia-unitary-atacms/mfc-atacms-block-1a-unitary-pc.pdf.

Military Analysis Network. *AN/TPQ-36 Firefinder Radar.* Accessed November 4, 2020. https://fas.org/man/dod-101/sys/land/an-tpq-36.htm.

Military Bases.com. *USAG Baumholder Army Base in Baumholder, Germany.* Accessed November 22, 2020. https://militarybases.com/overseas/germany/baumholder/

NATO. *SFOR Troops Play Supporting Role in Balkans Summit.* Accessed March 12, 2021. https://www.nato.int/sfor/advisory/1999/p990727a.htm

Office of the Secretary of Defense. *National Military Strategy.* Accessed March 18, 2021. https://history.defense.gov/Historical-Sources/National-Military-Strategy/

Operation Bugle Boy. *About Us.* Accessed August 29, 2021. https://www.operationbugleboy.com/about/·

Organization for Security and Co-operation in Europe. *Dayton Peace Agreement.* Accessed February 8, 2021. https://www.osce.org/bih/126173.

7ᵗʰ Army Training Command. *100 Years of History.* Accessed December 5, 2020. https://www.7atc.army.mil/History/·

Smithsonian. *The Blue Force Tracker System.* Accessed May 2, 2021. https://timeandnavigation.si.edu/multimedia-asset/the-blue-force-tracker-system·

Suits, Devon L. *Changes to Promotion Process Provide Officers More Career Flexibility.* Army News Service. Accessed November 10, 2020. https://www.army.mil/article/232809/changes_to_promotion_process_provide_officers_more_career_flexibility

The White House. *Proclamation on World Freedom Day, 2020.* Accessed November 23, 2020. https://www.whitehouse.gov/briefings-statements/proclamation-world-freedom-day-2020/·

The White House. *President Clinton: Promoting Stability for Southeast Europe.* Accessed March 11, 2021. https://clintonwhitehouse4.archives.gov/WH/Work/073099.html.

United Nations. *United Nations Special Commission.* Accessed March 10, 2021. https://www.un.org/Depts/unscom/unscom.htm#ESTABLISH.

United States Army. *Airborne School.* Accessed October 12, 2020. https://www.goarmy.com/soldier-life/being-a-soldier/ongoing-training/specialized-schools/airborne-school.html

U.S Army Aviation and Missile Life Cycle Management Command, *LANCE.* Accessed October 12, 2020. https://history.redstone.army.mil/miss-lance.html.

United States Army Command & General Staff College. *CGSC Circular 350-1.* Accessed November 10, 2020. https://usacac.army.mil/sites/default/files/documents/cace/350-1_cgsccatalog.pdf.

United States Army Europe and Africa. *Gen. David M. Maddox.* Accessed December 20, 2020. https://www.europeafrica.army.mil/Imagery/igphoto/2001884532/.

United States Army Training and Doctrine Command. *About TRADOC.* Accessed November 20, 2020. https://www.tradoc.army.mil/About-Us/.

United States Central Command. *Area of Responsibility.* Accessed January 28, 2021. https://www.centcom.mil/AREA-OF-RESPONSIBILITY/

United States Department of State, Office of the Historian. *The Reagan Administration and Lebanon, 1981-1984.* Accessed November 10, 2020. https://history.state.gov/milestones/1981-1988/lebanon.

Woodrow Wilson International Center for Scholars. *Military planning of the USA and NATO for the operation of the V. Army Corps/USA in times of tension and in war.* Accessed October 31, 2020. https://digitalarchive.wilsoncenter.org/document/112680.

Index

CPSIA information can be obtained
at www.ICGtesting.com
Printed in the USA
LVHW051732080322
712939LV00012B/1312